MW01062945

THE POETS' BOOK *of* PSALMS

THE POETS' BOOK *of* PSALMS

The Complete Psalter
as Rendered by Twenty-Five Poets
from the Sixteenth to the Twentieth Centuries

Compiled, Edited, and Introduced by

LAURANCE WIEDER

HarperSanFrancisco
A Division of HarperCollins*Publishers*

Grateful acknowledgment is made to the following for permission to reprint material: Psalms 30, 36, 58, 82, 101, and 133 from *A Poet's Bible: Rediscovering the Voices of the Original Text* by David Rosenberg. Reprinted by permission of Hyperion, a division of Disney Book Publishing Group, Inc.

FIRST EDITION

Book design by Claudia Smelser

Library of Congress Cataloging-in-Publication Data

The poets' book of Psalms : the complete psalter as rendered by twenty-five poets from the sixteenth to the twentieth centuries / compiled, edited, and introduced by Laurance Wieder.

p. cm.

Includes index.

ISBN 0-06-069284-7 (cloth : alk. paper)

1. Bible. O.T. Psalms—Paraphrases, English. I. Wieder, Laurance.

BS1440.P36 1995

223'.205209—dc20 94-43244

CIP

---

95 96 97 98 99 HAD 10 9 8 7 6 5 4 3 2 1

This edition is printed on acid-free paper that meets the American National Standards Institute Z39.48 Standard.

To Jehovah now
We do vow
Hymns of praise, psalms of thanksgiving;
By whose only grace and power,
At this hour,
I do breathe among the living!

Hymns, which in the Hebrew tongue,
First were sung,
By Israel's sweet and royal singer;
Whose rich harp the heavenly choir
Did desire
To hear touched with his sweet finger:

To which the orbs celestial,
Joining all,
Made all parts so fully sounding,
As no thought, 'til earth we leave,
Can conceive
Aught with pleasure so abounding.

Francis Davis

CONTENTS

INTRODUCTION *Laurance Wieder* **xiii**

UPON THE TRANSLATION OF THE PSALMS *John Donne* 3

BOOK ONE

The First Psalm ROBERT BURNS 7

The Second Psalm JOHN MILTON 7

The Third Psalm JOSEPH HALL 8

The Fourth Psalm PHILIP SIDNEY 9

The Fifth Psalm JOHN DAVIES 10

The Sixth Psalm THOMAS WYATT 10

The Seventh Psalm JOHN MILTON 13

The Eighth Psalm HENRY HOWARD OF SURREY 15

The Ninth Psalm LAURANCE WIEDER 16

The Tenth Psalm PHILIP SIDNEY 17

The Eleventh Psalm GEORGE WITHER 19

The Twelfth Psalm FRANCIS BACON 20

The Thirteenth Psalm PHILIP SIDNEY 21

The Fourteenth Psalm MILES COVERDALE 21

The Fifteenth Psalm P. HATELY WADDELL 23

The Sixteenth Psalm FRANCIS QUARLES 23

The Seventeenth Psalm CHRISTOPHER SMART 24

The Eighteenth Psalm PHILIP SIDNEY 25

The Nineteenth Psalm THOMAS CAMPION 28

The Twentieth Psalm JOHN DAVIES 29

The Twenty-first Psalm LAURANCE WIEDER 29

The Twenty-second Psalm PHILIP SIDNEY 30

The Twenty-third Psalm GEORGE HERBERT 32

The Twenty-fourth Psalm PHILIP SIDNEY 33

The Twenty-fifth Psalm JOHN HALL 33

The Twenty-sixth Psalm PHILIP SIDNEY 36

The Twenty-seventh Psalm GEORGE WITHER 37

The Twenty-eighth Psalm JOHN DAVIES 38

The Twenty-ninth Psalm CHRISTOPHER SMART 38

The Thirtieth Psalm DAVID ROSENBERG 40

The Thirty-first Psalm PHILIP SIDNEY 41

The Thirty-second Psalm THOMAS WYATT 43

The Thirty-third Psalm LAURANCE WIEDER 45

The Thirty-fourth Psalm JOHN HALL 45

The Thirty-fifth Psalm CHRISTOPHER SMART 48

The Thirty-sixth Psalm DAVID ROSENBERG 51

The Thirty-seventh Psalm PHILIP SIDNEY 52

The Thirty-eighth Psalm THOMAS WYATT 55

The Thirty-ninth Psalm LAURANCE WIEDER 56

The Fortieth Psalm PHILIP SIDNEY 57

The Forty-first Psalm PHILIP SIDNEY 59

BOOK TWO

The Forty-second Psalm CHRISTOPHER SMART 63

The Forty-third Psalm JOHN DAVIES 64

The Forty-fourth Psalm MARY SIDNEY HERBERT 65

The Forty-fifth Psalm MARY SIDNEY HERBERT 67

The Forty-sixth Psalm SAMUEL TAYLOR COLERIDGE 69

The Forty-seventh Psalm JOHN DAVIES 69

The Forty-eighth Psalm GEORGE WITHER 70

The Forty-ninth Psalm CHRISTOPHER SMART 71

The Fiftieth Psalm MARY SIDNEY HERBERT 73

The Fifty-first Psalm THOMAS CAREW 75
The Fifty-second Psalm MARY SIDNEY HERBERT 76
The Fifty-third Psalm LAURANCE WIEDER 77
The Fifty-fourth Psalm JOHN HALL 78
The Fifty-fifth Psalm HENRY HOWARD OF SURREY 79
The Fifty-sixth Psalm MARY SIDNEY HERBERT 80
The Fifty-seventh Psalm P. HATELY WADDELL 82
The Fifty-eighth Psalm DAVID ROSENBERG 83
The Fifty-ninth Psalm MARY SIDNEY HERBERT 84
The Sixtieth Psalm LAURANCE WIEDER 86
The Sixty-first Psalm CHRISTOPHER SMART 87
The Sixty-second Psalm MARY SIDNEY HERBERT 88
The Sixty-third Psalm P. HATELY WADDELL 89
The Sixty-fourth Psalm CHRISTOPHER SMART 90
The Sixty-fifth Psalm HENRY VAUGHAN 92
The Sixty-sixth Psalm MARY SIDNEY HERBERT 93
The Sixty-seventh Psalm JOHN DAVIES 95
The Sixty-eighth Psalm CHRISTOPHER SMART 95
The Sixty-ninth Psalm MARY SIDNEY HERBERT 100
The Seventieth Psalm P. HATELY WADDELL 103
The Seventy-first Psalm MARY SIDNEY HERBERT 104
The Seventy-second Psalm LAURANCE WIEDER 106

BOOK THREE

The Seventy-third Psalm HENRY HOWARD OF SURREY 109
The Seventy-fourth Psalm LAURANCE WIEDER 110
The Seventy-fifth Psalm MARY SIDNEY HERBERT 111
The Seventy-sixth Psalm MARY SIDNEY HERBERT 112
The Seventy-seventh Psalm GEORGE SANDYS 113
The Seventy-eighth Psalm LAURANCE WIEDER 114
The Seventy-ninth Psalm CHRISTOPHER SMART 116
The Eightieth Psalm JOHN MILTON 117

The Eighty-first Psalm GEORGE WITHER 119

The Eighty-second Psalm DAVID ROSENBERG 120

The Eighty-third Psalm P. HATELY WADDELL 122

The Eighty-fourth Psalm MARY SIDNEY HERBERT 123

The Eighty-fifth Psalm JOHN MILTON 124

The Eighty-sixth Psalm CHRISTOPHER SMART 125

The Eighty-seventh Psalm JOHN MILTON 127

The Eighty-eighth Psalm HENRY HOWARD OF SURREY 128

The Eighty-ninth Psalm CHRISTOPHER SMART 129

BOOK FOUR

The Ninetieth Psalm FRANCIS BACON 137

The Ninety-first Psalm THOMAS CAREW 138

The Ninety-second Psalm MARY SIDNEY HERBERT 139

The Ninety-third Psalm MARY SIDNEY HERBERT 140

The Ninety-fourth Psalm GEORGE SANDYS 141

The Ninety-fifth Psalm JOHN DAVIES 142

The Ninety-sixth Psalm MARY SIDNEY HERBERT 143

The Ninety-seventh Psalm LAURANCE WIEDER 144

The Ninety-eighth Psalm MARY SIDNEY HERBERT 145

The Ninety-ninth Psalm MARY SIDNEY HERBERT 146

The Hundredth Psalm LAURANCE WIEDER 147

The Hundred-first Psalm DAVID ROSENBERG 147

The Hundred-second Psalm THOMAS WYATT 148

The Hundred-third Psalm JOHN DAVIES 150

The Hundred-fourth Psalm HENRY VAUGHAN 152

The Hundred-fifth Psalm CHRISTOPHER SMART 154

The Hundred-sixth Psalm GEORGE SANDYS 159

BOOK FIVE

The Hundred-seventh Psalm LAURANCE WIEDER 165

The Hundred-eighth Psalm MARY SIDNEY HERBERT 166

The Hundred-ninth Psalm LAURANCE WIEDER 167
The Hundred-tenth Psalm P. HATELY WADDELL 168
The Hundred-eleventh Psalm MARY SIDNEY HERBERT 169
The Hundred-twelfth Psalm GEORGE WITHER 169
The Hundred-thirteenth Psalm THOMAS CAREW 170
The Hundred-fourteenth Psalm THOMAS CAREW 170
The Hundred-fifteenth Psalm CHRISTOPHER SMART 171
The Hundred-sixteenth Psalm GEORGE WITHER 173
The Hundred-seventeenth Psalm MARY SIDNEY HERBERT 174
The Hundred-eighteenth Psalm LAURANCE WIEDER 174
The Hundred-nineteenth Psalm MARY SIDNEY HERBERT 175
The Hundred-twentieth Psalm LAURANCE WIEDER 189
The Hundred-twenty-first Psalm HENRY VAUGHAN 190
The Hundred-twenty-second Psalm MARY SIDNEY HERBERT 190
The Hundred-twenty-third Psalm CHRISTOPHER SMART 191
The Hundred-twenty-fourth Psalm MILES COVERDALE 191
The Hundred-twenty-fifth Psalm GEORGE WITHER 192
The Hundred-twenty-sixth Psalm FRANCIS BACON 192
The Hundred-twenty-seventh Psalm CHRISTOPHER SMART 193
The Hundred-twenty-eighth Psalm MILES COVERDALE 194
The Hundred-twenty-ninth Psalm MARY SIDNEY HERBERT 194
The Hundred-thirtieth Psalm THOMAS WYATT 195
The Hundred-thirty-first Psalm P. HATELY WADDELL 196
The Hundred-thirty-second Psalm GEORGE WITHER 196
The Hundred-thirty-third Psalm DAVID ROSENBERG 197
The Hundred-thirty-fourth Psalm MARY SIDNEY HERBERT 197
The Hundred-thirty-fifth Psalm CHRISTOPHER SMART 198
The Hundred-thirty-sixth Psalm JOHN MILTON 200
The Hundred-thirty-seventh Psalm THOMAS CAREW 202
The Hundred-thirty-eighth Psalm MARY SIDNEY HERBERT 204
The Hundred-thirty-ninth Psalm MARY SIDNEY HERBERT 204
The Hundred-fortieth Psalm JOHN HALL 207

The Hundred-forty-first Psalm CHRISTOPHER SMART **208**

The Hundred-forty-second Psalm GEORGE WITHER **210**

The Hundred-forty-third Psalm THOMAS WYATT **210**

The Hundred-forty-fourth Psalm MARY SIDNEY HERBERT **212**

The Hundred-forty-fifth Psalm CHRISTOPHER SMART **214**

The Hundred-forty-sixth Psalm ANNE FINCH **216**

The Hundred-forty-seventh Psalm MARY SIDNEY HERBERT **217**

The Hundred-forty-eighth Psalm THOMAS STANLEY **219**

The Hundred-forty-ninth Psalm LAURANCE WIEDER **225**

The Hundred-fiftieth Psalm JOHN DAVIES **226**

THE BOOK OF PSALMS *King James Version* **229**

INDEX OF FIRST LINES **307**

INDEX OF POETS **311**

INTRODUCTION

In Babel, where the tower fell, strangers
Do not speak our language. We were taken
There in chains and captive by the rivers
Told to sing them songs of Zion. Crushed,
Could we sing Hebrew praises in translation?

Most readers know the Book of Psalms in one of the many translations that have appeared since the beginning of the Common Era: Aramaic, Greek, Latin, the demotic Bibles of Martin Luther's European Reformation. English versions include the Wycliffe Bible, the Great Bible, the Geneva, the First Douay, the King James Version and its several revisions, the Jerusalem Bible, The Jewish Publication Society bibles, the Anchor Bible, and others. The Hebrew original stands before these versions like a model before an art class. Even, or especially, if the artists are all masters, no two depictions look the same. Still, the casual visitor to the studio can judge how closely, if at all, the artwork resembles the model. If unrecognizable, then the picture may be something else, but it is not a picture of "the book." This representational standard separates literary or classical from scriptural poetry.

But the original is elusive. The Hebrew text was received without vowels, is unpronounceable like the name of God. So the Masoretes, those scholars who committed the tradition to paper, made two columns: the text as received (what is read), and the same text with vowel points inserted (what is said). To speak the words is to translate, to interpret. The unpointed text poses for the rabbis, as a model, a question, a picture of the unseen and unimaginable. All agree that the it is there, but no two mouths can say the same or show the all of it.

Save for Psalm 23 and the opening verses of Psalm 137, I always found it difficult to think of the Bible's Book of Psalms as poetry in English. The King James Version has authority but not a living person's voice. Yet David's Psalms have been celebrated too long, and are too beloved by those many competing faiths and sects that otherwise insist on their abysmal differences, for its voices not to live in fact, if not in translation. While researching another book, I found that modern English poetry (the sonnets of Wyatt and Surrey) bloomed at the same time that the first translation of the Bible from the original tongues (the *Five Books of Moses and the New Testament* by William Tyndale) was made into English. I also learned that from that time to the present, on a high place commanding plains of Bible prose and overgrown with hymns, poets have made their own versions of the Psalms.

For Jews and other readers of Hebrew, there is no difference between the words bound in their Bible and the words sung on such occasions as the Passover service. But for those whose Old Testament is done in Latin, or in Greek, or in some modern language, the Psalm that's read is not necessarily the Psalm that's sung. If an English language religious service requires a demotic scripture, it also needs singable psalms.

From the outset, metrical psalters—written to conform to the notes and measures of established hymn tunes (often borrowed from the German, French, or Dutch)—took the place of prose scripture in worship. Aside from having been written to be sung, and so bending sense and usage to established strains, the first accepted metrical version of the Psalms in English (by Thomas Sternhold and John Hopkins, published in 1562) was a stuffed owl. Final judgment on that collection was passed by John Wilmot, Earl of Rochester (1647–1680):

> Sternhold and Hopkins had great qualms
> When they translated David's psalms
>   To make the heart full glad;
> But had it been poor David's fate
> To hear thee sing, and them translate,
>   By God! 'twould have made him mad.

In succeeding generations, poets have attempted to right the failures of Sternhold and Hopkins. The editors of *The Bay Psalm Book* (1640), an anthology compiled for the Pilgrim settlers of Massachusetts, hoped to answer the difficulty of the Puritan "Ainsworth's tunes, and the corruptions in our common psalm books" with "a plain and familiar translation of the psalms and words of David into English meter." In 1698, poet laureate Nahum Tate and Nicholas Brady collaborated on *A New Version of the Psalms of David* which inherited both the place and the reputation held by Sternhold and Hopkins.

In 1719, Reverend Isaac Watts, an Englishman, published *The Psalms of David Imitated in the Language of the New Testament,* meaning he read the Hebrew through the Christian theological lens that sees David as a type of Jesus. New England's pillar Cotton Mather responded to the deliberate departures from the Hebrew by contemporary psalmists, including his correspondent and "very dear friend" Watts, with the strictly literal *Psalterium Americanum* (1718), which Mather described as a "Gospel according to David." In contrast, *A Translation of the Psalms of David* (1765), by Christopher Smart, is an explosion of religious enthusiasm rather than an expression of doctrine. *The Psalter: or Psalms of David: in English Verse* (1839) by John Keble, catered to the needs of a sentimental generation. With the exception of Smart, none of these pious versifiers appears here. The work of Dr. Watts, like the hymns of John and Charles Wesley, belongs to church history, not in an anthology of poetry.

The Poets' Book of Psalms is a complete Psalter, written by twenty-five different poets from the early 16th to the late 20th century. To assemble it, I gathered together all the poets' versions of Psalms in English—by close to fifty different hands, none anonymous—and sorted them by number. I then reread through every version of each Psalm, and chose the strongest poem. In some cases, such as Psalms 1 through 10, 23, 65, 80–88, and 137, there were many alternatives. In other cases, the only available sources were the Philip Sidney/Mary Sidney Herbert Psalter, the whole Psalm books of George Sandys (the Cavalier supporter of Charles I and the Church of England) and George Wither (the Puritan), Christopher Smart (who often conflates David with Jesus), and P. Hately Waddell, who wrote in Scots. I undertook my own Psalms in part to make dialogue with Mary Herbert, who sometimes otherwise and grandly held the stage alone.

From the available material, I tried to choose works that could stand as poetry, without begging off as translations. I preferred poems without anachronisms, Christological or otherwise, that honored the prose sense without doing violence to the English language. Where possible, I chose versions that imitated the form (such as acrostic), as well as the content, of the original. I preferred the plain to the fancy, meaning Wither to Sandys, and Mary Herbert or Philip Sidney or Sir John Davies (who translated more than a third of the Psalms) to either of those Georges. I have modernized the spelling of all the poems, to remove extrinsic obstacles to reading the text and to make of the many voices, one book. Rather than try to guess which words require glosses, I made certain that every word in the *Poets' Book of Psalms* can be found in the dictionary. Anonymous works, and those written to be sung, were excluded. The complete King James Version of the Psalms is appended, so that a reader can consult the prose sense of what may sound far away, or hard, or unfamiliar.

When forced to decide between poetry and fidelity, I opted for diction over doctrine and palpable belief over ritual profession. In the case of Psalm 68, this meant setting aside my discomfort with Christopher Smart's praise of Jesus in a Psalm of David, because by any other measure, his version was the best poem. Smart grows upon acquaintance. Strong and direct, his language and thought don't get thumped or swamped by his surging meters. Smart's poem about the Bible, "Taste," even settles for a moment the strife between literature and scripture, the esthetic and the earnest. It ends:

The Psalmist and proverbial Seer,
   And all the prophets' sons of song,
Make all things precious, all things dear,
   And bear the brilliant word along.

O take the book from off the shelf,
   And con it meekly on thy knees;
Best panegyric on itself,
   And self-avouched to teach and please.

Respect, adore it heart and mind.
   How greatly sweet, how sweetly grand,
Who reads the most, is most refined,
   And polished by the Master's hand.

The Book of Psalms is an anthology with no obvious organization. Yet reading the Psalms straight through is not a chaotic experience. The book's esthetic integrity resists analysis as stubbornly as it insists on its reality. In *The Midrash on Psalms,* the rabbis teach that Moses has five books, and David has five. I divided the *Poets' Book of Psalms* into five parts in accordance with this tradition.

Both literary and religious traditions identify other books-within-the-book. Sir Thomas Wyatt's versions of Petrarch's love sonnets are balanced and answered in his translation of the seven Penitential Psalms (numbers 6, 32, 38, 51, 102, 130, and 143), so-called because they refer to David's sin with Bathsheba in the matter of Uriah the Hittite. The Songs of Ascent, or Pilgrim Psalms (numbers 120–134), were supposedly known to and chanted by the patriarch Jacob. There are two sets of Hallelujah Psalms: the Hallel recited at the Passover Seder (numbers 111–117, with the Great Hallel, 136) and the praises of God (numbers 105, 106, 135, 146–150).

The Psalms organize themselves in other ways. The *Midrash* states that just as the Psalms are attributed to ten authors, so there are also ten kinds of song: glory, melody, Psalm, song, praise, prayer, blessing, thanksgiving, Hallelujah, and exultation. Furthermore, the same source records that "all the Psalms which David composed apply either to himself, or to all Israel. Each Psalm that speaks in the singular applies to David's own person, and each Psalm that speaks in the plural applies to all Israel. Wherever 'For the leader; with string music' is used, the Psalm deals with the age-to-come. 'A Psalm of David' means that David played [upon his harp], and that then the Holy Spirit rested upon him. But where it is said 'Unto David, a Psalm,' the Holy Spirit rested upon David, and then he played. . . . The phrase 'Maschil of David' indicates that the Psalm has to be explained by a skillful commentator. . . . The phrase 'A Song; A Psalm' indicates that the Psalm has to be rendered by singers."

The life of David is recounted in the first and second Books of Samuel, and in the Chronicles. As the authors of the *Bay Psalm Book* note in their preface, "The translators of the psalms into meter usually annexed to our Bibles . . . have rather presented a paraphrase than the words of David translated according to the rule 2 Chronicles 29:30, and . . . their addition to the words, detractions from the words are not seldom and rare, but very frequent and many times needless (which we suppose would not be approved of if the psalms were so translated into prose). . . . Set against poet-paraphrasers, or at least against the golden style, the Puritan divines have prestated Ezra Pound's dictum in *The ABC of Reading,* that "poetry should be at least as well written as prose."

The Sages agree on the names of the ten contributors to the Book of Psalms: Adam, Melchizedek, Abraham, Moses, David, Solomon, Asaph, and the three sons of Korah. The names of David's court musicians, who probably composed some of the Psalms, are not recorded outside the incidental appearances of their names in scripture. The contributors to the *Poets' Book of Psalms,* however, have left at least traces of biography. In some cases, what remains of the life is which Psalm the poet chose to sing. Each singer's version illuminates some aspect of the original David who, unlike the rest of us, was perfect in God's sight.

In his life and person, Sir Philip Sidney (1554–1586) comprehends the sacred and profane, the courtly and the common, the contemplative and active. Poet and warrior, courtier and protestant if not shepherd and king, Sidney transcribed the sonnet cycle *Astrophel and Stella* ("Fool," said my muse to me, "look in your heart, and write") and translated the first forty-three psalms. In *An Apology for Poetry,* Sidney wrote that ". . . the holy David's Psalms are a divine poem. . . . Even the name 'Psalms' will speak for me, which being interpreted, is nothing but songs; then, that it is fully written in meter, as all learned Hebricians agree, although the rules be not fully found; lastly and principally, his handling his prophecy, which is merely poetical. For what else is the awaking his musical instruments? The often and free changing of persons? His notable *prosopopoeias,* when he maketh you, as it were, see God coming in his majesty? His telling of the beasts' joyfulness and hills leaping, but a heavenly poesy, wherein (almost) he showeth himself a passionate lover of that unspeakable and everlasting beauty to be seen by the eyes of the mind, only cleared by faith."

Sidney accomplished most of his literary work (most famously, *Arcadia*) at his sister's home. Mary Sidney Herbert, Countess of Pembroke (1561–1621), devoted much of her life and considerable resources to other people's poetry. Edmund Spenser and Samuel Daniel benefitted from her patronage; John Donne and Ben Jonson celebrated her in verse. Except for some occasional lyrics, Mary Herbert's poetic work consists of her Psalms. She finished the project begun by her brother and circulated it privately in 1592. A monument of English poetry, the Sidney Psalter was not published until 1823 (in an edition of 250) and only again in 1963.

Two complete psalters—one Puritan, one Cavalier—appeared in the 1630s. The Roundheads' Book of Psalms issued from the pen of George Wither (1588–1667), Hampshire poet and pamphleteer. After his *The Songs of the Old Testament Translated into English Measures: preserving the Natural Phrase and genuine sense of the Holy Text: and with as little circumlocution as in most prose translations* (1620) won universal applause, in 1623 Wither obtained a royal patent compelling printers to include his *Canonical Hymns and Spiritual Songs* as part of every copy of the authorized *Psalm Book in Meter* published for the next fifty-one years. Booksellers and poets alike resented Wither's attempt to corner the publishing market for holy songs. Not only did the printers not bind Wither's hymns into the authorized psalter, they even warned their customers against the quality of his performance. Wither spent some years abroad, and had his *The Psalms of David* (1632) printed in Netherlands. During the siege of Farnham Castle in 1642, Wither was captured by the Royalists. Sir John Denham pleaded the poet's cause before King Charles "and desired his Majesty not to hang him, for that whilest George Wither lived, he [Denham] should not be the worst poet in England." The Royalists had their own psalmist: George Sandys (1578–1644), the poet son of the Archbishop of York. A serious traveler, Sandys made a pilgrimage to the Near East, including Egypt and Jerusalem, while a youth. His active interest in the King's colonies carried him to the New World in 1620, where he served as treasurer of the Virginia Company. During the decade he spent in America, Sandys translated most of Ovid's *Metamorphoses.* He returned to England and in 1636 published *A Paraphrase upon the Psalms of David,* which occupied Charles I while he awaited execution.

Christopher Smart (1722–1771) wrote *Psalms of David,* "Song to David," and "Jubilate Agno," over a three-year period that saw him in and out of the madhouse. Samuel Johnson subscribed to the 1765 edition of Smart's Psalms and defended the poet in conversation. In *The Life of Samuel Johnson,* by James Boswell, Doctor Johnson is said to have observed that "Madness frequently discovers itself merely by unnecessary deviation from the usual modes of the world. My poor friend Smart showed the disturbance of his mind, by falling on his knees, and saying his prayers in the street, or in any other unusual place. Now although, rationally speaking, it is greater madness not to pray at all, than to pray as Smart did, I am afraid there are so many who do not pray, that their understanding is not called into question. . . ." Johnson continues, "I did not think he ought to be shut up. His infirmities were not noxious to society. He insisted on people praying with him; and I'd as lief pray with Kit Smart as anyone else."

If the Psalms are indeed songs of David, then the Scots ballads of Robert Burns (1759–1796) must be one equivalent of the Hebrew shepherd's songs. Born into a farm family and self-educated, Burns attained great fame during his lifetime, and his reputation never waned. As P. Hately Waddell (1817–1891), Burns's editor and poetic disciple, explains it, Burns's Scots is a literary invention (like Edmund Spenser's English) rather than a heightened form of common speech as espoused by the Romantic poets. Burns rendered scripture into Scots verse in the superscriptions to his poems "Scotch Drink" and the "Address to the Unco Guid, or the Rigidly Righteous." His only translations of the Psalms, the First and a part of the Ninetieth, were into conventional English. Those scriptural snatches and the Highland ballads, inspired Waddell to translate not only the entire *Book of Psalms Frae Hebrew intill Scottis,* but also *Isaiah.*

The elder of the two moderns in this Psalter, David Rosenberg (b. 1943) published the initial installment of his translations of poetry from the Hebrew Bible, *Blues of the Sky* (Psalms), in the early 1970s. Over the next twenty years, including a term as editor-in-chief of the Jewish Publication Society, he pursued his project of "rediscovering in English the voices of the original Hebrew text." Rosenberg's *A Poet's Bible* collects those poems and probes the lives of the early Hebrew writers. His version of the J text in the Pentateuch appeared in *The Book of J,* followed by *The Lost Book of Paradise,* the Bible's poetical source for the story of Adam and Eve.

Born in 1946, I am the other modern represented in this collaborative psalter. My *One Hundred Fifty Psalms* is the first complete psalter by a poet since Christopher Smart's.

Puritan preacher Miles Coverdale (1488–1568) did not put his name to an entire Book of Psalms, but his edition of the *Great Bible* "out of the Latin and the Dutch" (1535) was the first complete English version of the holy writ. *Goostly Psalms and Spiritual Songs,* by Coverdale, contains selected metrical and verse Psalms and a rousing Puritan anthem "Let Go the Whore of Babylon." Plain-spun John Hall (1529–1566), Coverdale's literary and lay counterpart, wrote verse paraphrases of *Proverbs, Ecclesiastes and Psalms; A Poesy in Form of a Vision . . . Against Necromancy, Witchcraft, Sorcery, Incantations, and Divers Other Detestable and Devilish Practices;* and the *Court of Virtue,* a sacred alternative to a then-popular miscellany called *The Court of Venus.* Hall's censure of the Venus anthology included an attack on Sir Thomas Wyatt (1503–1542), whose Penitential Psalms had appeared with some of Hall's Psalms and Proverbs in a 1550 edition of *The Psalms of David.* Common gossip at the court of Henry VIII accepted that Thomas Wyatt had been the future queen Anne Boleyn's lover from his seventeenth year, until she was officially noticed by the King. The Penitential Psalms are sometimes associated with the end of that affair but are more commonly traced to Wyatt's fall from favor after Anne lost her head and Catherine was Queen. Wyatt's son, also named Thomas (executed after the Lady Jane Grey rebellion), caroused with his father's poetic disciple, Henry Howard, Earl of Surrey (1516–1547). Another swimmer in the treacherous waters of Henry's court, Surrey managed to survive being cousin to Queen Catherine Howard, only to be accused later of treason and beheaded. Courtier, favorite, and poet, Surrey was an avatar of Sir Philip Sidney. This smoother and polisher of the English sonnet also paraphrased the book of Ecclesiastes in verse. His Psalms done into meter cross the English ballad with a verse form that resembles *Piers Ploughman.*

Joseph Hall, Bishop of Norwich (1574–1656) published his translations of David's Psalms 1–10 in 1607. A disappointed satirist and staunch supporter of the Church of England, Hall defended the Bishops and Church when Parliament attacked them in 1640–41. That defense and its answer, written by five Puritan divines whose initials made up the word Smectymnuus, involved Hall in a controversy with another psalmist, the pamphleteer John Milton. In this book, Hall's version of Psalm 3 ("Ah Lord! How many be my foes!") follows Milton's "Why do the Gentiles tumult?"

Like David, Thomas Campion (1567–1619) was a notable musician. He wrote against the use of rhyme in English poetry in his *Observations on the Art of English Poetry* (1602), a work that John Milton's musician father must have known well. Milton himself wrote against rhyme and, in *Samson Agonistes,* employed what the theorist Campion termed quantitative verse. Thomas Campion's *Four Books of Airs,* published between 1601 and 1617, contained his paraphrases of some psalms, among numerous lyrics and musical settings.

Francis Bacon, Lord Verulam (1561–1626) son of Queen Elizabeth's Lord Keeper, rose to be Lord Chancellor (1618), only to be accused and convicted of corruption and censured by the House of Lords (1621). Bacon's *Novum Organum* propounds a method for the natural sciences to replace Aristotle's empiricism; his *Essays* are still in print and still read. Bacon dedicated *A Translation of Certain Psalms into English Verse,* which he wrote during a sickness in 1624, to George Herbert. Sir John Davies (1569–1626), another man of affairs, published two verse satires of considerable length—*Orchestra* and *Nosce Teipsum*—that brought him to the attention of King James I. The King (himself a translator of psalms) sent the poet to Ireland as attorney general for the Crown. There, Davies banished Catholic priests and tried to establish the Protestant religion. Davies, a very fat man whose death from apoplexy provided food for wags, translated more than fifty psalms.

Of the spirit rather than of the world, George Herbert (1593–1633) belonged to a distinguished literary family. He was brother to the poet Lord Herbert of Cherbury, a trained musician and a classical scholar. Herbert sought and won the post of public (Latin) orator at Cambridge University, a position he held most of his short life. Three years before his death, the poet took orders and assumed a living awarded him by Charles I. Of the eight psalms attached to his name, only Psalm 23, which appears in his book *The Temple,* is unquestionably Herbert's. *The Temple,* like George Sandys' Psalms, was read by King Charles while confined in Carisbrooke. Herbert's volume inspired Henry Vaughan to cease writing love poetry and to take up sacred verse.

Francis Quarles (1592–1644) was perhaps the most famous writer of his day. The J. S. Bach of pious paraphrase, Quarles wrote almost entirely verse variations on scriptural themes. And, he fathered 18 children. The poet's popular *Divine Poems, Alphabet of Elegies,* and *Emblems* along with its sequel *Hieroglyphics of the Life of Man* were all overshadowed by the enormous success of his posthumous works, beginning with *Solomon's Recantation.* Although a Puritan by disposition and profession, Quarles was an ardent Royalist. His version of Psalm 16 (along with five others) was carried to John Winthrop and John Cotton in Boston, who printed all six in the *Bay Psalm Book.* It is hard to imagine, but, as Horace Walpole remarked, "Milton was forced to wait till the world had done admiring Quarles."

Thomas Carew (ca. 1598–ca. 1639) was a favorite of Charles I. Little is known of his life, save that an early preferment went sour when Carew spoke ill of his benefactors. The reputed scapegrace and idler was an elegant lyric poet, whose 19th century editor rejected

Carew's "wretched attempts at versifying a few of the Psalms." Thomas Stanley (1625–1678), acclaimed as Carew's poetic heir, spent part of his youth in France with the court of Charles II. A cousin of George Sandys, tutored by William Fairfax (whose father translated *Jerusalem Delivered*), the cultivated Stanley translated Anacreon and wrote love lyrics. In 1657, Stanley published the *Psalterium Carolinum,* which recounted the last days of Charles I in terms of David's exile during Absalom's rebellion. Stanley's paraphrases of psalms, possibly translated from French, are echoed in William Blake's *Songs of Innocence and Experience.*

Blake made John Milton (1608–1674) the subject of a prophetic book. The most learned Englishman of his age, Milton served as Latin Secretary to Oliver Cromwell from 1649 through the end of the Protectorate—even after 1653, when his blindness became total. Milton gave early signs of his intention to unite pagan and Hebrew learning, sacred and profane poetry, and so, through a great victory in language, to undo the Fall and justify God's ways to man. At age fifteen, he translated Psalms 114 and 136. Milton's versions of Psalms 80–88 were composed following Fairfax's 1648 victory over the Royalist armies. His versions of Psalms 1–8 belong to 1653, when his sight eclipsed. That marriage of the spiritual with the earthly which Milton attempted in blank verse epic, Henry Vaughan (1622–1695) undertook in lyric poetry. For almost his entire life, Vaughan practiced medicine (and poetry) in his native Silures, the countryside of Brecknockshire and Herefordshire. George Herbert's role in Vaughan's conversion from satire to religious poetry has been mentioned above. But where Herbert wrote of religion as a church, and Milton deployed his talents to imagine the unattempted unimaginable, Vaughan infused his rural landscape with a passion identical to that of religion, and translated psalms that let him speak of nature.

William Wordsworth admired the poems of Anne Finch, Countess of Winchilsea (1661–1720) for their use of images from external nature. She published one volume of poetry. Both Finch and her ally Alexander Pope went out of literary fashion after Samuel Taylor Coleridge (1772–1834) and Wordsworth issued *Lyrical Ballads* in 1798, launching the Romantic movement. It is said that on the two poets' foot excursions through the Lake District, Wordsworth walked straight on, while Coleridge weaved and circled about him, talking and gesturing the while. Ruined by laudanum addiction, Coleridge nonetheless managed to forge a permanent place for himself in poetry, literary criticism, and esthetic philosophy. His version of Psalm 46 grew out of a conversation with his brother, George Coleridge, about hexameters. In a letter to George dated September 29, 1799, Coleridge proposed to "fill up the paper with a translation of one of my favorite Psalms into that meter which allowing trochees for spondees, as the nature of our language demands, you will find pretty accurate a scansion."

Coleridge's consciousness of the need for accuracy, and Wordsworth's contention that poetry should be written in the language of everyday get a retrospective second from the compilers of the *Bay Psalm Book.* The Pilgrim Fathers assumed that "the Psalms are penned in such verses as are suitable to the poetry of the Hebrew language, and not in the common style of such other books of the Old Testament as are not poetical; . . . hence the psalms are to be translated into our English tongue . . . in such verses as are familiar to an English ear. . . . Neither let any think, that for the meter sake we have taken liberty or poetical licence to depart from the true and proper sense of David's words in the Hebrew verses, no; but it hath been one part of our religious care and faithful endeavor, to keep close to the original text."

Coleridge never became a Divine, and the Boston Puritans would have shuddered at the suggestion that they practise poetry. Alongside the religious rule, that paraphrase be true to the original, stands Coleridge's observation, that poetry has its own logic with a reason assignable for every word. And, as Mitchell Dahood cited in the Anchor Bible *Book of Psalms,* Coleridge believed: "Poetry gives most pleasure when only generally and not perfectly understood."

A midrash records that Rabbi Huna said in the name of Rabbi Assi: Though certain psalms bear the name of one of the ten authors, the book as a whole bears the name of David, king of Israel. As a parable tells us, there was a company of musicians who sought to sing a hymn to the king. The king said to them: To be sure, all of you are skilled musicians, all of you are devout, all of you are worthy of taking part in the singing of a hymn before me, yet let the hymn be sung by So-and-so only, on behalf of all of you. Why? Because his voice is sweetest.

Laurance Wieder

THE POETS' BOOK *of* PSALMS

UPON THE TRANSLATION OF THE PSALMS

by Sir Philip Sidney and the Countess of Pembroke his Sister.

~ *John Donne*

Eternal God, (for whom who ever dare
Seek new expressions, do the circle square,
And thrust into strait corners of poor wit
Thee, who art cornerless and infinite)
I would but bless thy Name, not name thee now;
(And thy gifts are as infinite as thou:)
Fix we our praises therefore on this one,
That, as thy blessed spirit fell upon
These psalms first author in a cloven tongue;
(For 'twas a double power by which he sung
The highest matter in the noblest form;)
So thou hast cleft that spirit, to perform
That work again, and shed it, here, upon
Two, by their bloods, and by thy spirit one;
A brother and a sister, made by thee
The organ, where thou art the harmony.
Two that make one John Baptist's holy voice,
And who that psalm, now let the isles rejoice,
Have both translated, and applied it too,
Both told us what, and taught us how to do.
They show us islanders our joy, our king,
They tell us why, and teach us how to sing;
Make all this All, three choirs, heaven, earth, and spheres:
The first, heaven, hath a song, but no man hears;
The spheres have music, but they have no tongue,
Their harmony is rather danced than sung;
But our third choir, to which the first gives ear,
(For, angels learn by what the church does here)
This choir hath all. The organist is he
Who hath tuned God and Man, the organ we:
The songs are these, which heaven's high holy muse
Whispered to David, David to the Jews:
And David's successors, in holy zeal,
In forms of joy and art do re-reveal
To us so sweetly and sincerely too,
That I must not rejoice as I would do
When I behold that these psalms are become
So well attired abroad, so ill at home,

So well in chambers, in thy church so ill,
As I can scarce call that reformed until
This be reformed; Would a whole state present
A lesser gift than some one man hath sent?
And shall our church, unto our spouse and king
More hoarse, more harsh than any other, sing?
For that we pray, we praise thy name for this,
Which, by this Moses and this Miriam, is
Already done; and as those psalms we call
(Though some have other authors) David's all:
So though some have, some may some psalms translate,
We thy Sidnean Psalms shall celebrate,
And, till we come the extemporal song to sing,
(Learned the first hour, that we see the king,
Who hath translated those translators) may
These their sweet learned labors, all the way
Be as our tuning; that, when hence we part,
We may fall in with them, and sing our part.

BOOK ONE

In Life Wherever Placed

THE FIRST PSALM

Robert Burns

The man, in life wherever placed,
Hath happiness in store,
Who walks not in the wicked's way,
Nor learns their guilty lore!

Nor from the seat of scornful pride
Casts forth his eyes abroad,
But with humility and awe
Still walks before his God.

That man shall flourish like the trees
Which by the streamlets grow;
The fruitful top is spread on high,
And firm the root below.

But he whose blossom buds in guilt
Shall to the ground be cast,
And like the rootless stubble tossed,
Before the sweeping blast.

For why? that God the good adore
Hath given them peace and rest,
But hath decreed that wicked men
Shall ne'er be truly blessed.

THE SECOND PSALM

John Milton

Why do the Gentiles tumult, and the nations
Muse a vain thing, the kings of the earth upstand
With power, and princes in their congregations
Lay deep their plots together through each land,
Against the Lord and his messiah dear?
Let us break off, say they, by strength of hand
Their bonds, and cast from us, no more to wear,
Their twisted cords: he who in Heaven doth dwell
Shall laugh, the Lord shall scoff them, then severe
Speak to them in his wrath, and in his fell
And fierce ire trouble them; but I, saith he,
Anointed have my king (though ye rebel)
On Sion my holy hill. A firm decree
I will declare; the Lord to me hath said,

Thou art my son, I have begotten thee
This day; ask of me, and the grant is made;
As thy possession I on thee bestow
The heathen, and as thy conquest to be swayed
Earth's utmost bounds: them shalt thou bring full low
With iron scepter bruised, and them disperse
Like to a potter's vessel shivered so.
And now be wise at length, ye kings averse,
Be taught, ye judges of the earth; with fear
Jehovah serve, and let your joy converse
With trembling; kiss the son lest he appear
In anger and ye perish in the way,
If once his wrath take fire like fuel sere.
Happy all those who have in him their stay.

THE THIRD PSALM

A Psalm of David, when he fled from Absalom his son.

Joseph Hall

Ah Lord! how many be my foes!
How many are against me rose,
That to my grieved soul have said,
Tush: God shall him no succor yield;
While thou Lord art my praise, my shield
And dost advance my careful head.

Loud with my voice to God I cried:
His grace unto my suit replied,
From out his Sion's holy hill.
I laid me down, slept, rose again.
For thou O Lord dost me sustain,
And savest my soul from feared ill.

Not if ten thousand armed foes
My naked side should round enclose,
Would I be thereof ought adread.
Up Lord and shield me from disgrace:
For thou hast broke my foe-men's face,
And all the wickeds' teeth hast shed.

From thee O God is safe defence;
Do thou thy free beneficence
Upon thy people largely spread.

THE FOURTH PSALM

To the chief Musician on Neginoth, A Psalm of David.

~ Philip Sidney

Hear me, O hear me, when I call,
O God, God of my equity:
Thou settst me free when I was thrall,
Have mercy therefore still on me,
And harken how I pray to thee.

O men, whose fathers were but men,
'Til when will ye my honor high
Stain with your blasphemies? 'til when
Such pleasure take in vanity,
And only hunt where lies do lie?

Yet know this too, that God did take
When he chose me, a godly one:
Such one, I say, that when I make
My crying plaints to him alone,
He will give good ear to my moan.

O tremble then with awful will:
Sin from all rule in you depose,
Talk with your hearts and yet be still:
And when your chamber you do close,
Yourselves, yet to your selves disclose.

The sacrifices sacrifice
Of just desires, on justice stayed
Trust in that Lord that cannot lie.
Indeed full many folks have said,
From whence shall come to us such aid?

But, Lord, lift thou upon our sight
The shining clearness of thy face,
Where I have found more heart's delight
Than they whose store in harvests space
Of grain and wine fills storing place.

So I in peace and peaceful bliss
Will lay me down and take my rest:
For it is thou, Lord, thou it is,
By power of whose own only breast
I dwell, laid up in safest nest.

THE FIFTH PSALM

To the chief Musician upon Nehiloth, A Psalm of David.

John Davies

Lord weigh my words, and take consideration
Of my sad thoughts, and silent meditation:
My God, my King, bow down thine ear to me,
While I send up mine humble prayer to thee.
Early before the morn doth bring the day
I will, O Lord, look up to thee and pray;
For thou with sin art never pleased well,
Nor any ill may with thy goodness dwell:
The fool may not before thy wisdom stand,
Nor shall the impious scape thy wrathful hand;
Thou wilt destroy all such as utter lies;
Blood and deceit are odious in thine eyes;
But trusting in thy many mercies dear,
I will approach thy house with holy fear.
Teach me thy plain and righteous way to go,
That I may never fall before my foe,
Whose flattering tongue is false, and heart impure,
And throat an open place of sepulture:
Destroy them Lord, and frustrate their devices,
Cast out those rebels for their many vices,
But all that trust in thee, and love thy name,
Make them rejoice, and rescue them from shame.
Thou wilt thy blessing to the righteous yield,
And guard them with thy grace as with a shield.

THE SIXTH PSALM

To the chief Musician on Neginoth upon Sheminith, A Psalm of David.

Thomas Wyatt

O Lord, since in my mouth thy mighty name
Suffers itself my Lord to name and call,
Here hath my heart hope taken by the same,
That the repentance which I have and shall
May at thy hand seek mercy as the thing,
Only comfort of wretched sinners all.
Whereby I dare with humble bemoaning
By thy goodness of thee this thing require:
Chastise me not for my deserving
According to thy just conceived ire!

O Lord, I dread, and that I did not dread
I me repent, and evermore desire
Thee, thee to dread! I open here and spread
My fault to thee, but thou for thy goodness
Measure it not in largeness nor in bread,
Punish it not as asketh the greatness
Of thy furor, provoked by my offence.
Temper, O Lord, the harm of my excess
With mending will that I for recompense
Prepare again, and rather pity me,
For I am weak, and clean without defence:
More is the need I have of remedy,
For of the whole the leech taketh no cure.
The sheep that strays the shepherd seeks to see:
I, Lord, am strayed; I, sick without recure,
Feel all my limbs, that have rebelled, for fear
Shake in despair unless thou me assure.
My flesh is troubled, my heart doth fear the spear
That dread of death, of death that ever lasts,
Threateth of right and draweth near and near.
Much more my soul is troubled by the blasts
Of these assaults, that come as thick as hail,
Of worldly vanity, that temptation casts
Against the weak bulwark of the flesh frail,
Wherein the soul in great perplexity
Feeleth the senses with them that assail
Conspire, corrupt by use and vanity,
Whereby the wretch doth to the shade resort
Of hope in thee, in this extremity.
But thou, O Lord, how long after this sort
Forbearest thou to see my misery?
Suffer me yet, in hope of some comfort,
Fear and not feel that thou forgettest me.
Return, O Lord, O Lord, I thee beseech,
Unto thy old, wonted benignity!
Reduce, revive my soul: be thou the leech,
And reconcile the great hatred and strife
That it hath taken against the flesh, the wretch
That stirred hath stirred thy wrath by filthy life.
See how my soul doth fret it to the bones:
Inward remorse so sharps it like a knife
That but thou help the caitiff that bemoans
His great offence, it turns anon to dust.
Here hath thy mercy matter for the nonce,

For if thy righteous hand that is so just
  Suffer no sin or strike with damnation,
  Thy infinite mercy want needs it must
Subject matter for his operation:
  For that in death there is no memory
  Among the damned, nor yet no mention
Of thy great name, ground of all glory.
  Then if I die and go whereas I fear
  To think thereon, how shall thy great mercy
Sound in my mouth unto the world's ear?
  For there is none that can thee laud and love,
  For that thou nilt no love among them there.
Suffer my cries thy mercy for to move,
  That wonted is a hundred years' offence
  In moment of repentance to remove.
How oft have I called up with diligence
  This slothful flesh long afore the day
  For to confess his fault and negligence,
That to the down for ought that I could say
  Hath still returned to shroud itself from cold,
  Whereby it suffers now for such delay.
By nightly plaints, instead of pleasures old,
  I wash my bed with tears continual,
  To dull my sight that it be never bold
To stir my heart again to such a fall.
  Thus dry I up among my foes in woe,
  That with my fall do rise and grow withal
And me beset even now where I am, so
  With secret traps to trouble my penance.
  Some do present to my weeping eyes, lo,
The cheer, the manner, beauty and countenance
  Of her whose look alas did make me blind;
  Some other offer to my remembrance
Those pleasant words, now bitter to my mind;
  And some show me the power of my armor,
  Triumph and conquest, and to my head assigned
Double diadem; some show the favor
  Of people frail, palace, pomp, and riches.
  To these mermaids and their baits of error
I stop mine ears with help of thy goodness,
  And for I feel it cometh alone of thee
  That to my heart these foes have none access
I dare them bid: "Avoid, wretches, and flee!
  The Lord hath heard the voice of my complaint;

Your engines take no more effect in me.
The Lord hath heard I say, and seen me faint
Under your hand, and pities my distress.
He shall do make my senses by constraint
Obey the rule that reason shall express,
Where the deceit of your glozing bait
Made them usurp a power in all excess."
Shamed be they all that so lie in wait
To compass me, by missing of their prey!
Shame and rebuke redound to such deceit!
Sudden confusion's stroke without delay
Shall so deface their crafty suggestion
That they to hurt my health no more essay,
Since I, O Lord, remain in thy protection.

THE SEVENTH PSALM

Shiggaon of David, which he sang unto the Lord, concerning the words of Cush the Benjamite.

~ *John Milton*

Lord my God to thee I fly,
Save me and secure me under
Thy protection while I cry;
Lest as a lion (and no wonder)
He haste to tear my soul asunder,
Tearing and no rescue nigh.
Lord my God, if I have thought
Or done this, if wickedness
Be in my hands, if I have wrought
Ill to him that meant me peace,
Or to him have rendered less,
And not freed my foe for naught;
Let the enemy pursue my soul
And overtake it, let him tread
My life down to the earth and roll
In the dust my glory dead,
In the dust and there outspread
Lodge it with dishonor foul.
Rise Jehovah in thine ire
Rouse thyself amidst the rage
Of my foes that urge like fire;
And wake for me, their fury assuage;
Judgment here thou didst engage

And command which I desire.
So the assemblies of each nation
Will surround thee, seeking right,
Thence to thy glorious habitation
Return on high and in their sight.
Jehovah judgeth most upright
All people from the world's foundation.
Judge me Lord, be judge in this
According to my righteousness
And the innocence which is
Upon me: cause at length to cease
Of evil men the wickedness,
And their power that do amiss.
But the just establish fast,
Since thou art the just God that tries
Hearts and reins. On God is cast
My defence, and in him lies,
In him who both just and wise
Saves the upright of heart at last.
God is a just judge and severe,
And God is every day offended;
If the unjust will not forbear,
His sword he whets, his bow hath bended
Already, and for him intended
The tools of death, that waits him near.
(His arrows purposely made he
For them that persecute.) Behold
He travails big with vanity,
Trouble he hath conceived of old
As in a womb, and from that mold
Hath at length brought forth a lie.
He digged a pit, and delved it deep,
And fell into the pit he made;
His mischief that due course doth keep,
Turns on his head, and his ill trade
Of violence will undelayed
Fall on his crown with ruin steep.
Then will I Jehovah's praise
According to his justice raise
And sing the Name and Deity
Of Jehovah the most high.

THE EIGHTH PSALM

To the chief Musician upon Gittith, A Psalm of David.

~ *Henry Howard of Surrey*

Thy name, O Lord, how great is found before our sight!
It fills the earth, and spreads the air: the great works of thy might!
For even unto the heavens thy power hath given a place,
And closed it above their heads, a mighty, large, compass.
Thy praise what cloud can hide? but it will shine again,
Since young and tender sucking babes, have power to show it plain.
Which in despite of those that would thy glory hide,
Thou hast put into such infants' mouths for to confound their pride.
Wherefore I shall behold thy figured heaven so high,
Which shows such prints of diverse forms within the cloudy sky
As hills, and shapes of men eke beasts of sundry kind,
Monstrous to our outward sight, and fancies of our mind.
And eke the wanish moon, which sheens by night also;
And each one of the wandering stars, which after her do go.
And how these keep their course; and which are those that stand,
Because they be thy wondrous works, and labors of thy hand.
But yet among all these I ask, "What thing is man?"
Whose turn to serve in his poor need this work thou first began?
Or what is Adam's son that bears his father's mark?
For whose delight and comfort eke thou hast wrought all this work.
I see thou mindest him much, that dost reward him so:
Being but earth, to rule the earth, whereon himself doth go.
From angel's substance eke thou madest him differ small;
Save one doth change his life awhile; the other, not at all.
The sun and moon also thou madest to give him light;
And each one of the wandering stars to twinkle sparkles bright.
The air to give him breath; the water for his health;
The earth to bring forth grain and fruit, for to increase his wealth.
And many metals too, for pleasure of the eye;
Which in the hollow sounded ground in privy veins do lie.
The sheep to give his wool, to wrap his body in;
And for such other needful things, the ox to spare his skin.
The horse even at his will to bear him to and fro;
And as him list each other beast to serve his turn also.
The fishes of the sea likewise to feed him oft;
And eke the birds, whose feathers serve to make his sides lie soft.
On whose head thou hast set a crown of glory too,
To whom also thou didst appoint, that honor should be do.
And thus thou madest him lord of all this work of thine;
Of man that goes, of beast that creeps, whose look doth down decline;

Of fish that swim below, of fowls that fly on high,
Of sea that finds the air his rain, and of the land so dry.
And underneath his feet, Thou hast set all this same;
To make him know, and plain confess, that marvellous is thy name.
And Lord, which art our Lord, how marvellous it is found
The heavens do show, the earth doth tell, and eke the world so round.
Glory, therefore, be given, to thee first, which art three;
And yet but one almighty God, in substance and degree:
As first it was when thou the dark confused heap
Clotted in one, didst part in four; which elements we clepe:
And as the same as now, even here within our time;
So ever shall hereafter be, when we be filth and slime.

THE NINTH PSALM

To the chief Musician upon Muthlabben, A Psalm of David.

~ Laurance Wieder

If I could tell it all,
I would say thank you
For the toppled statues,
For the dusk of gods sung
Only in dead languages,
For wild grape vines tangled
In the timbers of a century
That frame our little picture
Of eternity. And I remember
There was justice, maybe, since
I hope the dead might be
Remembered, though their names,
Outnumbered by the stones
Once used to mark the exit spot,
Are worn down, in an alphabet
That can't be read aloud.

Not always and not ever, maybe
Masters will stick in the mud
Of what they most admired,
Boasting how their acts
Engraved in stone erased
Accounts of people sacrificed
To feed the maw, the pointless
Grim machinery of nations:
If there is something other

Than our selves, they will not win
Forever, will some time remember
They are human, and may even
Know themselves, and feel afraid.

THE TENTH PSALM

Philip Sidney

Why standest thou so far,
O God, our only star,
In time most fit for thee
To help who vexed be!
For lo, with pride the wicked man
Still plagues the poor the most he can:
O, let proud him be thoroughly caught
In craft of his own crafty thought.

For he himself doth praise
When he his lust doth ease:
Extolling ravenous gain,
But doth God's self disdain.
Nay so proud is his puffed thought,
That after God he never sought;
But rather much he fancies this,
That name of God a fable is.

For while his ways do prove,
On them he sets his love;
Thy judgments are too high,
He can them not espy.
Therefore he doth defy all those
That dare themselves to him oppose;
And sayeth, in his bragging heart,
This gotten bliss shall never part.

Nor he removed be,
Nor danger ever see:
Yet from his mouth doth spring
Cursing and cozening;
Under his tongue do harbored lie
Both mischief and iniquity.
For proof, oft lain in wait he is,
In secret by-way villages.

In such a place unknown
To slay the hurtless one;
With winking eyes aye bent
Against the innocent,
Like lurking lion in his den,
He waits to spoil the simple men:
Whom to their loss he still doth get,
When once he draweth his wily net.

O, with how simple look
He oft layeth out his hook!
And with how humble shows
To trap poor souls he goes!
Thus freely sayeth he in his sprite:
God sleeps, or hath forgotten quite;
His far-off sight now hoodwinked is,
He leisure wants to mark all this.

Then rise, and come abroad,
O Lord, our only God:
Lift up thy heavenly hand
And by the silly stand.
Why should the evil, so evil, despise
The power of thy through-seeing eyes?
And why should he in heart so hard
Say, thou dost not thine own regard?

But naked, before thine eyes
All wrong and mischief lies:
For of them in thy hands
The balance evenly stands:
But who aright poor-minded be
Commit their cause, themselves, to thee,
The succor of the succorless,
The father of the fatherless.

Break thou the wicked arm,
Whose fury bends to harm:
Search them, and wicked he
Will straight way nothing be.
O Lord, we shall thy title sing,
Ever and ever, to be king
Who hast the heatheny folk destroyed
From out thy land by them annoyed.

Thou openest heavenly door
To prayers of the poor:
Thou first prepared their mind,
Then ear to them inclined.
O, be thou still the orphans' aid,
That poor from ruin may be stayed:
Lest we should ever fear the lust
Of earthly man, a lord of dust.

THE ELEVENTH PSALM

To the chief Musician, A Psalm of David.

George Wither

In God, my trust is placed still;
Then, wherefore do you say
That, as a bird unto the hill,
My soul should fly away?
For, lo, their bow the wicked bend,
And arrows they prepare,
That they, unseen, their shafts may send,
At such as needy are.
If overthrown the groundworks lie,
What can the best men do?
God's holy seat is heaven on high,
And he must look thereto.
Mankind, with closed and open eyes,
(Even righteous men) God proves;
And him he doth, in soul, despise
That wicked courses loves.
For wicked men, the Lord prepares
(And rains into their cup)
A storm of brimstone, fire, and snares,
Which they must swallow up.
But, being in himself upright,
He justice doth affect;
And godly men have, in his sight,
A look of good respect.

THE TWELFTH PSALM

To the chief Musician upon Sheminith, A Psalm of David.

~ *Francis Bacon*

Help, Lord, for godly men have took their flight,
And left the earth to be the wicked's den:
Not one that standeth fast to truth and right,
But fears, or seeks to please, the eyes of men.
When one with other falls in talk apart,
Their meaning goeth not with their words, in proof;
But fair they flatter, with a cloven heart,
By pleasing words, to work their own behoof.

But God cut off the lips, that are all set
To trap the harmless soul, that peace hath vowed;
And pierce the tongues, that seek to counterfeit
The confidence of truth, by lying loud:
Yet so they think to reign, and work their will
By subtle speech, which enters everywhere;
And say, Our tongues are ours, to help us still;
What need we any higher power to fear?

Now for the bitter sighing of the poor,
The Lord hath said, I will no more forbear
The wicked's kingdom to invade and scour,
And set at large the men restrained in fear.
And sure the word of God is pure and fine,
And in the trial never loseth weight;
Like noble gold, which, since it left the mine,
Hath seven times passed through the fiery strait.

And now thou wilt not first thy word forsake,
Nor yet the righteous man that leans thereto;
But wilt his safe protection undertake,
In spite of all their force and wiles can do.
And time it is, O Lord, thou didst draw nigh;
The wicked daily do enlarge their bands;
And that which makes them follow ill advise,
Rule is betaken to unworthy hands.

THE THIRTEENTH PSALM

To the chief Musician, A Psalm of David.

~ *Philip Sidney*

How long (O Lord) shall I forgotten be?
What? ever?
How long wilt thou thy hidden face from me
Dissever?
How long shall I consult with careful sprite
In anguish?
How long shall I with foes' triumphant might
Thus languish?
Behold me Lord, let to thy hearing creep
My crying.
Nay, give me eyes, and light, lest that I sleep
In dying:
Lest my foe brag, that in my ruin he
Prevailed;
And at my fall they joy that, troublous, me
Assailed.
No, no, I trust on thee, and joy in thy
Great pity:
Still therefore of thy graces shall be my
Song's ditty.

THE FOURTEENTH PSALM

To the chief Musician, A Psalm of David.

~ *Miles Coverdale*

The foolish wicked men can say,
They hold of God right perfectly;
Yet are they far out of the way;
For in their hearts they him deny:
Corrupt and abominable are they also
In all the things that they do;
There will not one do good truly.

The Lord did look here down from heaven,
Men to consider and their doing;
To see if any men were given,
To God's knowledge above all thing;
If there were any, that perfectly

Regarded God so earnestly,
To follow his word in his living.

Then said God these words moreover:
Is every man gone so far by,
Swerved so far now all together
From the right way so parlously;
So unprofitable and perished,
That no man will do good in deed,
No not so much as one truly?

Are they out of their minds so far,
All these workers of wickedness?
Behold now, for they nothing care
My people to devour for greediness,
As one should eat a piece of bread:
The Lord's fear is out of their head,
They do not regard it much doubtless.

Wherefore they shall be feared truly
With fear incomparable and endless.
O righteous man, thou mayst be merry;
For they that besieged the guiltless,
Their bones hath God shaken altogether.
How shalt thou despise them forever!
For God hath left them comfortless.

God is in just men's company,
And in the righteous nation.
But wicked men mock them daily,
For none other cause nor reason,
But for because they follow the mind
Of the poor afflict, which was God's friend,
To trust in the Lord's redemption.

O would God that the saving health
Would come from the hill of Sion;
That Israel might have his wealth,
And God to loose him from prison!
Then should Jacob be full of joy,
And Israel should make full merry,
Because of his redemption.

THE FIFTEENTH PSALM

A Psalm of David.

~ P. Hately Waddell

Lord, wha sal bide i' that howff o' thine?
Or wha be lown on yer halie height?
Wha gangs ay straught;
An' wha does ay right;
An' wha speaks frae his heart sikkerlie:
Wha double-deals nane wi' his tongue;
Wha warks nae ill till his frien';
Nor tholes nae skaithe on his niebor:
In whase een the little worth are lightlied eneugh,
Bot whasae fear the Lord he likes fu' weel;
Wha swears till his frien', an' steers-na:
His siller wha sets-na till gather gear;
Nor nae fee will he tak on the saikless loon:
Wha siclike does sal ne'er be steer'd,
Frae the height o' the Lord, for evir.

THE SIXTEENTH PSALM

Michtam of David.

~ Francis Quarles

O mighty God, preserve thou me, for on thee do I rest.
Thou art my God, unto the Lord my soul thou hast professed:
My goodness reacheth not to thee, but to the saints upon
The earth and to the excellent, whom all my joy is on.
They who give gifts to a strange god, their sorrows multiply:
Their drink oblations of blood offer up will not I.
Neither will I into my lips the names of them take up.
Jehovah is the portion of my part, and my cup:
Thou art maintainer of my lot, to me the lines fallen be
In pleasant places: yea, fair is the heritage for me.
I will Jehovah humbly bless, who hath me counselled:
Yea in the nights my reins have me chastising nurtured.
Jehovah I have always set as present before me:
Because he is at my right hand I shall not moved be.
Wherefore my heart rejoiced hath, and glad is my glory:
Moreover also my flesh shall in hope lodge securely.
Because thou wilt not leave my soul within the grave to be,
Nor wilt thou give thine holy one, corruption for to see.
Thou wilt show me the path of life, of joys abundant store,
Before thy face, at thy right hand are pleasures evermore.

THE SEVENTEENTH PSALM

A Prayer of David.

~ Christopher Smart

In this my cause, O Lord, preside,
 Weigh my complaint and take my part;
Attend my prayer, untaught to glide
 From lips of practised art.

Let me from thee my sentence learn,
 Do thou mine innocence declare;
And let thine equal eyes discern
 The bounds of false and fair.

I stand acquitted in the night
 When my still heart thy spirit proves;
For I am bound with all my might
 To speak as best behooves.

Warned by the works that men commit,
 Against the word Jehovah spake,
By grace I kept me from the pit
 Which sin and misery make.

O bear me up as I proceed
 In this my pilgrimage of pain;
And lest I fail in strength or speed
 My heart and feet sustain.

To God my suit I have referred,
 And he shall his attention lend;
O grant an audience to the word
 Of meekness which I send.

O thy stupendous goodness show,
 And all thy copious mildness shower;
Thou saviour of the faithful few,
 From such as thwart thy power.

Choice as the lustre of an eye,
 Preserve me with thy precious things,
And let me to the covering fly
 Of thy paternal wings,

To guard me from my foes professed,
 That torture me with endless strife;
My enemies my bounds invest
 To take away my life.

They're swollen with fatness, as their days
To sumptuous banquets they devote;
Their mouths are filled with pompous phrase,
As on their wealth they gloat.

On every side our way they block,
And turn their eyes on every place,
Our steadfast purposes to shock,
And to prevent our race.

Like as a greedy lion works,
His prey from safety to decoy;
Or as his whelp in secret lurks
The traveler to destroy.

Up, Lord, the godless disconcert,
And to humility control;
That bitter sword of thine avert
From David's faithful soul.

The worldly men, who're better sped,
Who have their portion here below;
Who from thy treasuries are fed
The prosperous carnal foe.

A numerous offspring they conceive
According to their gross desires;
And their ill-gotten wealth they leave
To children like their fires.

Meanwhile to these my joyful eyes
Thou shalt thyself in truth present;
And when I in thy semblance rise,
My heart shall rest content.

THE EIGHTEENTH PSALM

To the chief Musician, A Psalm of David, the servant of the Lord, who spake unto the Lord the words of this song in the day that the Lord delivered him from the hand of all his enemies, and from the hand of Saul.

Philip Sidney

And he said,

Thee will I love, O Lord, with all my heart's delight,
My strength, my strongest rock, which my defence hast born:

My God, and helping God, my might, and trustful might,
My never-pierced shield, my ever-saving horn,
My refuge; refuge then when most I am forlorn:
Whom then shall I invoke, but thee, most worthy praise,
On whom (against my foes) my only safety stays?

On me the pains of death already gan to prey:
The floods of wickedness on me did horrors throw:
Like in a winding sheet, wretch, I already lay,
All-ready, ready to my snaring grave to go.
This my distress to God, with wailful cries I show:
My cries climbed up; and he bent down, from sacred throne,
His eyes unto my case, his ears unto my moan.

And so the earth did fall to tremble and to quake,
The mountains proudly high, and their foundations bent
With motion of his rage, did to the bottom shake.
He came, but came with smoke, from out his nostrils sent:
Flames issued from his mouth, and burning coals outwent;
He bowed the heavens, and from the bowed heavens did descend
With hugy darkness, which about his feet did wend.

The Cherubims their backs, the winds did yield their wings
To bear his sacred flight, in secret place then closed;
About which he dim clouds like a pavilion brings,
Clouds, even of waters dark, and thickest air composed.
But straight his shining eyes this misty mass disclosed,
Then hail, then fiery coals, then thundered, heavenly sire,
Then spake he his loud voice, then hailstones, coals, and fire.

Then out his arrows fly; and straight they scattered been:
Lightning on lightning he did for their wrack augment:
The gulfs of waters then were through their channels seen:
The world's foundations then lay bare; because he shent
With blasting breath, O Lord, that in thy chiding went.
Then sent he from above, and took me from below,
Even from the waters depth, my God preserved me so.

So did he save me, from my mighty furious foe,
So did he save me, from their then prevailing hate:
For they had caught me up when I was weak in woe:
But he, staff of my age, he stayed my stumbling state:
This much: yet more, when I by him this freedom gat,

By him, because I did find in his eye-sight grace,
He lifted me unto a largely noble place.

My justice, my just hands thus did the Lord reward,
Because I walked his ways, nor gainst him evilly went:
Still to his judgments looked, still for his statutes cared
Sound and upright with him, to wickedness not bent.
Therefore, I say again, this goodness he me sent,
As he before his eyes did see my justice stand,
According as he saw the pureness of my hand.

Meek to the meek thou art, the good thy goodness taste:
Pure, to the pure, thou dealest with crooked crookedly:
Up then, thou lifts the poor, and down the proud wilt cast;
Up, thou dost light my light, and clear my darkened eye.
I hosts by thee o'ercome; by thee o'er walls I fly:
Thy way is soundly sure, thy word is purely tried:
To them that trust in thee, a shield thou dost abide.

For who is God besides this great Jehovah ours?
And so besides our God, who is endued with might?
This God then girded me in his almighty powers,
He made my cumbrous way, to me most plainly right:
To match with lightfoot stags, he made my foot so light,
That I climbed highest hill; he me war-points did show,
Strengthening mine arms, that they could break an iron bow.

Thou gavest me saving shield; thy right hand was my stay;
Me in increasing still, thy kindness did maintain:
Unto my strengthened steps, thou didst enlarge the way,
My heels, and plants, thou didst from stumbling slip sustain:
What foes I did pursue, my force did them attain
That I, ere I returned, destroyed them utterly,
With such brave wounds, that they under my feet did lie.

For why my fighting strength, by thy strength, strengthened was:
Not I, but thou, throwst down those, who gainst me do rise,
Thou gavest me their necks, on them thou madest me pass:
Behold they cry, but who to them his help applies?
Nay, unto thee they cried, but thou heardst not their cries:
I beat those folks as small as dust which wind doth raise,
I beat them as the clay is beat in beaten ways.

Thus freed from mutine men, thou makest me to reign;
Yea, thou dost make me served by folks I never knew:
My name their ears, their ears their hearts, to me enchain:
Even fear makes strangers show much love, though much untrue.
But they do fail, and in their mazed corners rue:
Then live Jehovah still, my rock still blessed be:
Let him be lifted up, that hath preserved me.

He that is my revenge, in whom I realms subdue;
Who freed me from my foes, from rebels guarded me:
And rid me from the wrongs which cruel wits did brew.
Among the Gentiles then I (Lord) yield thanks to thee,
I to thy name will sing, and this my song shall be:
He nobly saves his king, and kindness keeps in store,
For David his anoint, and his seed, evermore.

THE NINETEENTH PSALM

To the chief Musician, A Psalm of David.

~ Thomas Campion

Come, let us sound with melody the praises
Of the kings' king, the omnipotent creator,
Author of number, that hath all the world in
Harmony framed.

Heaven is his throne perpetually shining,
His divine power and glory thence he thunders,
One in all, and all still in one abiding,
Both father, and son.

O sacred sprite, invisible, eternal,
Every where, yet unlimited, that all things
Canst in one moment penetrate, revive me,
O holy spirit.

Rescue, O rescue me from earthly darkness,
Banish hence all these elemental objects,
Guide my soul that thirsts to the lively fountain
Of thy divineness.

Cleanse my soul, O God, thy bespotted image,
Altered with sin so that heavenly pureness
Cannot acknowledge me but in thy mercies,
O father of grace.

But when once thy beams do remove my darkness,
O then I'll shine forth as an angel of light,
And record, with more than an earthly voice, thy
Infinite honors.

THE TWENTIETH PSALM

To the chief Musician, A Psalm of David.

~ John Davies

The Lord give ear to thee in thy distress,
And be thy shield when troubles thee oppress,
And let his help come down from heaven for thee,
And strength from Sion hill imparted be;
Let him remember and accept withal
Thine offerings, and thy sacrifices all,
And of his bounty evermore fulfill
Thy heart's desire, and satisfy thy will.
But we will glory in our great God's name,
And joy in our salvation through the same,
And pray unto the Lord our God that he
The effect of all thy prayers will grant to thee.
He now I know will hear, and help will bring,
With his strong hand to his anointed king;
On chariots some, on horses some rely,
But we invoke the name of God most high.
Those others are bowed down, and fall full low,
When we are risen and upright do go;
Save us O Lord of heaven, and hear us thence,
When we invoke thy name for our defence.

THE TWENTY-FIRST PSALM

To the chief Musician, A Psalm of David.

~ Laurance Wieder

The haves shall have and have more
Than they ask, will live a long time,
Winter in palm sunshine,
Watch herons fish the squall line
And be neither fish, nor fowl, but eye,
A cup to taste immensity.

The others drink December polar murk.
They listen for the furnace switch, the pilot
Light, hot water pump: the damned could stick
No closer to their fires. Outside, the wind
Drives a person back into himself, where
All he knows is what he has imagined.

THE TWENTY-SECOND PSALM

To the chief Musician upon Aijeleth Shahar, A Psalm of David.

~ *Philip Sidney*

My God, my God, why hast thou me forsaken?
Woe me, from me, why is thy presence taken?
So far from seeing, mine unhealthful eyes,
So far from hearing to my roaring cries.

O God, my God, I cry while day appeareth:
But, God, thy ear my crying never heareth.
O God, the night is privy to my plaint
Yet to my plaint thou hast no audience lent.

But thou art holy, and dost hold thy dwelling
Where Israel thy lauds is ever telling.
Our fathers still to thee their trust did bear;
They trusted, and, by thee, delivered were.

They were set free, when they upon thee called,
They hoped on thee, and they were not appalled.
But I, a worm not I of mankind am,
Nay shame of men, the people's scorning game.

The lookers now at me, poor wretch, be mocking;
With moues, and nods, they stand about me flocking.
Let God help him (say they) whom he did trust:
Let God save him in whom was all his lust.

And yet even from the womb thy self didst take me:
At mother's breasts, thou didst good hope betake me.
No sooner my child eyes could look abroad,
Then I was given to thee, thou wert my God.

O be not far, since pain so nearly presseth,
And since there is not one who it redresseth.
I am enclosed with young bulls madded rout;
Nay Bashan mighty bulls close me about.

With gaping mouths, these folks on me have charged
Like lions fierce, with roaring jaws enlarged:
On me all this, who do like water slide,
Whose loosed bones quite out of joint be wried;

Whose heart, with these huge flames, like wax o'erheated
Doth melt away, though it be inmost seated:
My moistening strength is like a potsherd dried,
My cleaving tongue, close to my roof doth bide.

And now am brought, alas, brought by thy power
Unto the dust of my death's running hour:
For bawling dogs have compassed me about,
Yea, worse than dogs, a naughty, wicked, rout.

My humble hands, my fainting feet they pierced:
They look, they gaze, my bones might be rehearsed;
Of my poor weeds they do partition make,
And do cast lots who should my vesture take.

But be not far, O Lord, my strength, my comfort,
Hasten to help me, in this deep discomfort.
Ah, from the sword, yet save my vital sprite,
My desolated life from dogged might.

From lion's mouth (O help) and show to hear me,
By aiding, when fierce unicorns come near me:
To brethren, then, I will declare thy fame,
And with these words, when they meet, praise thy name.

Who fear the Lord, all praise and glory bear him:
You Israel's seed, you come of Jacob, fear him.
For He hath not abhorred, nor yet disdained
The silly wretch, with foul affliction stained,

Nor hid from him his face's fair appearing;
But, when he called, this Lord did give him hearing:
In congregation great, I will praise thee:
Who fear thee shall my vows performed see.

The afflicted then shall eat, and be well pleased,
And God shall be, by those his seekers, praised.
Indeed, O you, you that be such of mind,
You shall the life that ever-liveth find.

But what? I say, from earth's remotest border
Unto due thoughts, mankind his thoughts shall order
And turn to God, and all the nations be
Made worshippers, before almighty thee.

And reason, since the crown to God pertaineth,
And that by right upon all realms he reigneth,
They that be made, even fat, with earth's fat good,
Shall feed, and laud the giver of their food.

To him shall kneel even who to dust be stricken,
Even he whose life no help of man can quicken;
His service shall from child to child descend,
His dooms one age shall to another send.

THE TWENTY-THIRD PSALM

A Psalm of David.

George Herbert

The God of love my shepherd is,
And he that doth me feed:
While he is mine, and I am his,
What can I want or need?

He leads me to the tender grass,
Where I both feed and rest;
Then to the streams that gently pass:
In both I have the best.

Or if I stray, he doth convert
And bring my mind in frame:
And all this not for my desert,
But for his holy name.

Yea, in death's shady black abode
Well may I walk, not fear:
For thou art with me; and thy rod
To guide, thy staff to bear.

Nay, thou dost make me sit and dine,
Even in my enemies' sight:
My head with oil, my cup with wine
Runs over day and night.

Surely thy sweet and wondrous love
Shall measure all my days;
And as it never shall remove,
So neither shall my praise.

THE TWENTY-FOURTH PSALM

A Psalm of David.

Philip Sidney

The earth is God's, and what the globe of earth containeth,
And all who in that globe do dwell;
For by his power, the land upon the ocean reigneth,
Through him the floods to their beds fell.

Who shall climb the hill, which God's own hill is named?
Who shall stand in his holy place?
He that hath hurtless hand, whose inward heart is framed
All pureness ever to embrace;

Who shunning vanity and works of vainness leaving
Vainly doth not puff up his mind,
Who never doth deceive, and much less his deceiving
With perjury doth falsely bind.

A blessing from the Lord, from God of his salvation
Sweet righteousness shall he receive,
Jacob this is thy seed, God seeking generation,
Who search of God's face never leave.

Lift up your heads you gates; and you doors ever biding;
In comes the king of glory bright.
Who is this glorious king? in might and power riding?
The Lord, whose strength makes battles fight.

Lift up your heads you gates; and you doors ever biding;
In comes the king of glory bright.
Who is this glorious king? the lord of armies guiding?
Even he the king of glory hight.

THE TWENTY-FIFTH PSALM

A Psalm of David.

John Hall

To thee, O Lord, I lift my soul,
My God, I trust in thee:
O suffer not mine enemies
To triumph over me.

Nor yet let such as in thee trust
Rebuke or shame sustain:
But rather confound scornful men,
That spitefully disdain.

To thee I pray, my king and God,
O show to me thy ways:
And teach thy paths, O Lord, to me,
Thy name, that I may praise.

O Lord, lead me to speak thy truth,
And learn me to be just:
Mine only God and saving health,
All day in thee I trust.

Forget not Lord, but call to mind
Thy tender mercy pure,
Let not thy loving kindness slack
That ever hath been sure.

Forget my sins, remember not
The frailness of my youth:
For thy goodness and mercy, Lord,
Think upon me with ruth.

O righteous Lord, with friendliness,
Vouchsafe to show thy might:
Whereby thou shalt the sinners teach
To walk thy way aright.

The simple thou dost teach and guide
Thy perfect ways to know,
And thou dost such instruct aright
As humble be and low.

Thy ways, O Lord, are merciful,
Thy faithfulness is bent,
To all that keep thy covenant,
And faithful testament.

For thy name's sake therefore, O Lord
Be merciful to me,
And to my sins that are so great
And mine iniquity.

Who so therefore doth fear the Lord,
He will him show, I say:
His high and his divine precepts,
His pure and chosen way.

His soul shall ever be at ease,
His ways shall prosper well:
His seed also shall still possess
The land, therein to dwell.

The Lord his secrets doth show forth
To such as fear him still,
Declaring them his testament,
His covenant and will.

O Lord my God, to thee therefore
I will mine eyes direct,
And pray to thee till thou hast loosed
My feet out of the net.

O turn thee unto me therefore
Now for thy mercy's sake,
Consider, Lord, my misery,
How I am desolate.

The sorrows of my heart are great,
Right sore they do me grieve:
O rid me from these troubles all,
For in thee I believe.

O look on mine adversity,
And my great misery:
Forgive me all my sins also
Where I offended thee.

Consider how mine enemies
Are many and pervert,
That towards me maliciously
Are bent with hateful heart.

O preserve thou my soul therefore
Within thy keeping just:
And let me not confounded be,
For in thee do I trust.

Let just dealing and innocent,
O God, still with me dwell:
And from all vile adversity
Deliver Israel.

THE TWENTY-SIXTH PSALM

A Psalm of David.

~ Philip Sidney

Lord, judge me and my case,
  For I have made my race
Within the bounds of innocence to bide:
  And setting thee for scope
  Of all my trustful hope,
I held for sure that I should never slide.

Prove me, O Lord most high,
  Me with thy touchstone try:
Yea, sound my reins, and inmost of my heart.
  For so thy loving hand
  Before my eyes did stand,
That from thy truth I would not once depart.

I did not them frequent,
  Who be to vainness bent,
Nor kept with base dissemblers company.
  Nay, I did even detest
  Of wicked wights the nest,
And from the haunts of such bad folks did fly.

In the innocence of me
  My hands shall washed be;
And with those hands, about thy altar wait;
  That I may still express
  With voice of thankfulness
The works performed by thee, most wondrous great.

Lord, I have loved well
  The house where thou dost dwell,
Even where thou makest thy honors' biding place.
  Sweet Lord, write not my soul
  Within the sinners' role:
Nor my life's cause match with blood-seekers' case,

With hands of wicked shifts,
  With right hands stained with gifts.
But while I walk in my unspotted ways,
  Redeem and show me grace,
  So I in public place,
Set on plain ground, will thee, Jehovah praise.

THE TWENTY-SEVENTH PSALM

A Psalm of David.

George Wither

God is my light, my health, mine aid,
My life's defence: whom should I fear?
When wicked foes my death assayed,
They tripped, and fell, and ruined were.
Although an host besiegeth me,
If God will not this boon deny,
For which I'll now a suitor be:
Even that he grace to me afford,
My lifetime in his house to spend;
To view the beauty of the Lord,
And in his temple to attend.
For, in his tent, when dangers threat,
In secret, he should me enclose;
Upon a rock my footing set
And raise my head above my foes.
Then in God's house a sacrifice
Of praises I would also give:
Hear, therefore, Lord; and let my cries
A gracious answer now receive.
When thou dost bid me seek thy face,
Thy face I'll seek, my heart replies:
Reject not therefore, nor disgrace
Thy servant who on thee relies.
O Lord, who didst my soul preserve
When me my parents did forsake,
(Because of them who me observe)
Now plain to me thy path-ways make.
Yea, from the pleasure of my foes,
Protect me Lord: for, lo, with lies
False witnesses do me oppose,
And cruel words they do devise.
That, had I not belief to see
God's grace (within that land of bliss
Where endless life shall granted be),
My soul had fainted long ere this.
Attend thou still upon the Lord,
And faint thou not (whoe'er thou art.)
Attend, I say, upon the Lord
And he shall fortify thy heart.

THE TWENTY-EIGHTH PSALM

A Psalm of David.

~ John Davies

Hear (Lord my strength) the cries I make to thee;
I am but dead if thou seem deaf to me.
Hear when with humble prayer I thee entreat,
With lifted hand before thy mercy seat;
But rank me not with those which wicked are,
Whose lips speak peace, whose hearts are full of war;
According to their actions let them speed,
And as their merit is, so make their meed.
For that they see thy works, and yet neglect them,
Thou shalt destroy and never more erect them;
The Lord be praised, who hath vouchsafed to hear,
And lend unto my prayer a gracious ear.
His shield protects, his strength doth me advance;
My tongue shall sing his praise, my heart shall dance:
He to his servants force and virtue gives,
Through him in safety his anointed lives.
Save thy peculiar people Lord, and bless them,
And lift their heads above them that oppress them.

THE TWENTY-NINTH PSALM

A Psalm of David.

~ Christopher Smart

Ye men of birth and high renown,
Who, zealous for the heavenly crown,
    Have gallant deeds achieved,
The Lord with thankfulness adore,
The strength, the praise to him restore,
    From whom ye both received.

Give to the Lord's most holy name
The honor which his merits claim,
    In meekness as ye kneel;
With reverence pay your daily vow;
In seemliness and order bow
    With lively faith and zeal.

The word of infinite command,
August, adorable and grand,
    The water-flood controls;

And in terrific glory breaks
Upon the billows, and he speaks
The thunder as it rolls.

The voice of God and power are one,
The mandate which he gives is done
In all the dread profound;
Vast operative strength and skill,
The proclamation of his will
Is of majestic sound!

The voice of God in anger drives
The tempest to the mark, and rives
The cedar trees in twain,
Yea Lebanon, with all his growth,
Was rifted when the Lord was wroth
And strewn along the plain.

The lofty mountains huge and steep
At voice of his commandment leap
Like calves upon the sod,
And Libanus and Sirion too
Bound like young unicorns to do
Obeisance to their God.

The voice of God divides the flakes
Of torrent fire, his mandate shakes
The wilderness with fear;
Yea Kadesh with his voice he shocks,
And caverns, mountains, woods and rocks
With dreadful trembling hear.

The voice of God upon the lawn
Descends and causes hinds to fawn,
The thicket disarrays;
With terror strikes the human race
Who that tremendous time embrace
For public prayer and praise.

The Lord in highest heaven ascends,
The while his steadfast course he bends
All ocean's depth to ford;
From eastern to the western beam,
The Lord is evermore supreme,
Is evermore adored.

The Lord shall make his people strong,
With corn and wine our lives prolong

And clothe us with his fleece;
He shall the bonds of sin unloose,
And on our consciences diffuse
The blessing of his peace.

THE THIRTIETH PSALM

A Psalm and Song at the dedication of the house of David.

David Rosenberg

High praises
to you who raised me
up

so my critics fall silent
from their death wishes
over me

Lord Most High
I called you
and I was made new

you pulled me back
from the cold lip of the grave
and I am alive

to sing to you
friends, play in his honor
band of steady hearts

his anger like death
passes in a moment
his love lasts forever

cry yourself to sleep
but when you awake
light is all around you

I thought I was experienced
nothing was going to shake me
I was serious as a mountain

Lord, you were with me and then
you were gone
I looked for your face in terror

my body was made of clay
My Lord, it is now
I call you

what good is my blood my tears
sinking in the mud
is mere dust singing

can it speak
these words on my tongue, Lord
help me

turn my heavy sighing into dance
loosen my shirt and pants
and wrap me in your glow

so my heart can find its voice
through my lips to you
warm and alive

rising
above all bitterness
high praises.

THE THIRTY-FIRST PSALM

To the chief Musician, A Psalm of David.

~ *Philip Sidney*

All, all my trust, Lord, I have put in thee.
Never, therefore, let me confounded be,
But save me, save me in my righteousness.
Bow down thine ear to hear how much I need;
Deliver me, deliver me in speed:
Be my strong rock, be thou my fortress.

In deed thou art my rock, my fortress:
Then since my tongue delights that name to bless,
Direct me how to go, and guide me right.
Preserve me from the wily wrapping net,
Which they for me, with privy craft, have set:
For still I say, thou art my only might.

Into thy hands I do commend my sprite:
For it is thou, that hast restored my light:
O Lord, that art the God of verity.
I hated have those men, whose thoughts do cleave
To vanities: which most trust, most deceive:
For all my hope fixed upon God doth lie.

Thy mercy shall fill me with jollity,
For my annoys have come before thine eye:
Thou well hast known what plunge my soul was in.
And thou hast not for aye enclosed me
Within the hand of hateful enmity:
But hast enlarged my feet from mortal gin.

O Lord, of thee, let me still mercy win;
For troubles, of all sides, have me within:
My eye, my guts, yea my soul, grief doth waste.
My life with heaviness, my years with moan
Do pine: my strength with pain is wholly gone:
And even my bones consume, where they be placed.

All my fierce foes reproach on me did cast:
Yea neighbors, more, my mates, were so aghast,
That in the streets from sight of me they fled:
Now I, now I myself forgotten find,
Even like a dead man, dreamed out of mind,
Or like a broken pot, in mire tread.

I understand what railing great men spread:
Fear was each where, while they their councils led
All to this point, how my poor life to take;
But I did trust in thee Lord, I did say,
Thou art my God, my time on thee doth stay:
Save me from foes, who seek my bane to bake.

Thy face to shine upon thy servant make,
And save me in, and for, thy mercy's sake;
Let me not taste of shame, O Lord most high.
For I have called on thee; let wicked folk
Confounded be; and pass away like smoke;
Let them in bed of endless silence die.

Let those lips be made dumb which love to lie:
Which full of spite, of pride, and cruelty
Do throw their words against the most upright.
O, of thy grace what endless pleasure flows
To whom fear thee! what thou hast done for those
That trust in thee, even in most open sight!

And when need were, from pride in privy plight
Thou hast hid them; yet leaving them thy light,
From strife of tongues, in thy pavilions placed.
Then praise, then praise I do the Lord of us

Who was to me more than most gracious:
Far far more sure, than walls most firmly fast.

Yet I confess in that tempestuous haste,
I said, that I from out thy sight was cast:
But thou didst hear when I to thee did moan.
Then love the Lord all ye that feel his grace;
Who pares the proud, preserves the faithful race:
Be strong in hope, his strength shall you supply.

THE THIRTY-SECOND PSALM

A Psalm of David, Maschil.

~ *Thomas Wyatt*

O happy are they that have forgiveness got
Of their offence—not by their penitence
As by merit which recompenseth not,
Although that yet pardon hath none offence
Without the same—but by the goodness
Of Him that hath perfect intelligence
Of heart contrite, and covers the greatness
Of sin within a merciful discharge.
And happy are they that have the willfulness
Of lust restrained afore it went at large,
Provoked by the dread of God's furor,
Whereby they have not on their backs the charge
Of other's fault to suffer the dolor,
For that their fault was never execute
In open sight, example of error.
And happy is he to whom God doth impute
No more his fault, by knowledging his sin,
But cleansed now the Lord doth him repute,
As adder fresh, new, stripped from his skin,
Nor in his sprite is ought undiscovered.
I for because I hid it still within,
Thinking by state in fault to be preferred,
Do find by hiding of my fault my harm,
As he that feels his health to be hindered
By secret wound concealed from the charm
Of leech's cure, that else had had redress,
And feel my bones consume and wax unfirm
By daily rage, roaring in excess.
Thy heavy hand on me was so increased

Both day and night, and held my heart in press
With pricking thoughts bereaving me my rest,
That withered is my lustiness away
As summer heats that hath the green oppressed;
Wherefore I did another way essay,
And sought forthwith to open in thy sight
My fault, my fear, my filthiness I say,
And not to hide from thee my great unright.
"I shall," quoth I, "against myself confess
Unto the Lord all my sinful plight."
And thou forthwith didst wash the wickedness
Of mine offence, of truth right thus it is,
Wherefore they that have tasted thy goodness
At me shall take example as of this,
And pray and seek in time for time of grace:
Then shall the storms and floods of harm him miss,
And him to reach shall never have the space.
Thou art my refuge and only safeguard
From the troubles that compass me the place.
Such joy as he that scapes his enemies' ward
With loosed bonds hath in his liberty,
Such joy, my joy, thou hast to me prepared;
That as the seaman in his jeopardy
By sudden light perceived hath the port,
So by thy great merciful property
Within thy look thus read I my comfort:
"I shall thee teach and give understanding,
And point to thee what way thou shalt resort
For thy address, to keep thee from wandering;
Mine eye shall take the charge to be thy guide.
I ask thereto of thee alone this thing:
Be not like horse or mule that man doth ride,
That not alone doth not his master know,
But for the good thou dost him must be tied
And bridled lest his guide he bite or throw."
O divers are the chastisings of sin,
In meat, in drink, in breath that man doth blow,
In sleep, in watch, in fretting still within,
That never suffer rest unto the mind
Filled with offence, that new and new begin
With thousand fears the heart to strain and bind!
But for all this he that in God doth trust
With mercy shall himself defended find.
Joy and rejoice I say, ye that be just,

In Him that maketh and holdeth you so still;
In Him your glory alway set you must,
All ye that be of upright heart and will.

THE THIRTY-THIRD PSALM

~ Laurance Wieder

There is no new thing in God's sight.
(The day, the moon, are new to us.)
Play a new song to the Lord,
Glass full enough to pass along
Without a spill.
Such ink made sky black,
Kissed stars through pinholes, caught
Their night tears in a jar, each drop an ocean.

"Let be there was"—the deep mind stamped
A pattern on the nothing of before
What was to be stood forth:
When time, one chord, struck there
To now. Whatever
One possesses
Is a gift from elsewhere.
Inspiration comes unbidden.
One guessed
At what's inside our nature.
Truth stays hidden, feeds upon
The question.
Some try to steal
A march on death, drown fear in senses.
Some chosen can believe the soul is real.

THE THIRTY-FOURTH PSALM

A Psalm of David, when he changed his behaviour before Abimelech; who drove him away, and he departed.

~ John Hall

I will unto the Lord
Be giving thanks always,
My mouth and tongue shall ever be
A speaking of his praise.

My soul shall make her boast
In God, the Lord of might,
That poor oppressed men may hear
The same, them to delight.

Together let us now
In honor do our parts,
His name to praise and magnify,
With meek and humble hearts.

For when I him besought,
He heard my prayer so,
That he did straight deliver me
From all my care and woe.

Receive therefore the light
And to him draw you near:
And so without all shamefacedness
Your faces shall appear.

For I poor man made once
To him my plaint and moan:
He heard me cry, and did me rid,
From troubles every one.

His angel pitched hath
His tent about his sheep,
I mean all such as fear the Lord,
In safety them to keep.

His friendship prove and see,
And take thereof a taste:
For they that trust in him are sure
Most happy at the last.

O fear the Lord all ye
His saints of him elect:
For such as fear him lack nothing,
He doth them well protect.

The lions oft do chase
And hunger for their food:
But they which seek the Lord shall want
Nothing the which is good.

Ye children all, I say,
Come harken to my voice:
I will you teach to fear the Lord,
And in him to rejoice.

If thou to live in joy
And see good days be fain,
Thy lips and tongue from guile and wrong
See that thou do refrain.

So that thou do none ill,
In goodness never cease:
But see thou seek and follow fast
On quietness and peace.

The Lord doth fix his eyes
On just men lovingly,
And to their prayers openly
He doth his ears apply.

Contrariwise the Lord
Doth bend his countenance,
Off from the earth ill men to move
And their remembrance.

But to the just the Lord
Doth so incline his ear,
That when they pray he will them rid
From all trouble and fear.

The Lord is nigh to such
As are in heart contrite,
And he will save such as be meek,
And of an humble sprite.

Though just men's troubles be
Both manifold and great,
The Lord from care will make them free,
When they do him entreat.

Their bones he will defend,
And keep so free from crime:
That not so much as one of them
Shall break at any time.

Misfortune or ill hap,
The wicked men shall kill,
And such as do the just men hate,
Shall perish in their ill.

The Lord will save the souls
Of all that do him serve,
And all that put their trust in him
Shall not in peril swerve.

THE THIRTY-FIFTH PSALM

A Psalm of David.

~ Christopher Smart

O my God, my cause espousing,
From mine enemies protect;
On my side thy might arousing,
Let their insolence be checked.

Take the weapon of the spirit
Faith's invulnerable shield,
Rear the standard of thy merit,
And assist me in the field.

Couch thy spear, and stand to parry
Every lance opposers send;
Say thy suit shall not miscarry,
I thy saviour am thy friend.

Let their efforts be diverted,
Hunting souls and finding shame,
And their schemes be disconcerted,
Which at me direct their aim.

To the wind the dust condenses,
Settles when the skies are clear;
Thus let them and their offences
At thy bidding disappear.

To the thorny way, that narrows
Into final comfort, lead;
And let vengeance sheathe its arrows,
As they on their travel speed;

That no more, by dark combining,
They their secret nets may lay;
Nor by falsehood undermining,
Me without a cause betray.

Let no violent perdition
Come upon them unaware;
Let them scape by true contrition
Every terror, every snare.

And my soul with exultation,
Shall the Lord in truth profess;
And rejoice in his salvation,
Who delights to bear and bless.

All my frame shall sing in rapture,
  Who, like God, shall things adjust,
When the poor is made the capture
  Of the man of lawless lust?

By false witnesses convicted
  That against me were suborned,
I was punished and afflicted
  For the very things I scorned.

For good offices, ungrateful,
  They could evil things return,
In despite of kindness hateful
  To my sorrowing soul's concern.

Yet when they were sick and ailing,
  I was clad in weeds of woe;
But my service unavailing,
  Shall into my bosom flow.

I behaved as for a brother,
  Or a dear familiar friend,
As one mourning for his mother
  Just approaching to her end.

But in my distress they jested,
  Yea the very abjects met,
Making mouths, my peace infested
  Without ceasing or regret.

Fawning gluttons, in conjunction
  With the mimicking buffoon,
Gnash their teeth without compunction,
  And my miseries importune.

How long will my saviour leave me
  To the mercy of such men;
O from lions fierce reprieve me,
  And my darling from the den.

So with thanks thy Godhead greeting,
  In thy church I will adore;
And frequent the general meeting,
  There my praises to restore.

O! let not my foes exulting,
  In defiance of thy laws,
And with nods and winks insulting,
  Bear me down without a cause.

For the scope of their communing
Is not insolence to curb;
But their tongue with treachery tuning,
They the public peace disturb.

With distended mows censorious,
Every rank offender cries,
Fie upon thy crimes notorious,
We have seen them with our eyes.

All their impudent behavior,
Thou, O God, from heaven hast viewed;
Be not silent, O my saviour,
Nor my just complaint exclude.

Rise, O Lord my God, attending
To the drift of this dispute,
And my righteous cause defending,
All mine enemies refute.

Judge me, O my God, to spare me,
As thy mercy is for all;
Let not clamor overbear me,
Nor exult upon my fall.

'All that we surmise has followed,'
Let them not with triumph boast,
'His remains the gulf has swallowed,
He has given up the ghost.'

Make them blush with shame ingenuous,
Which at my distress rejoice;
Who against the truth are strenuous,
Give them grace to hear her voice.

Let them say, which like the measure,
That in charity I deal;
Blessed be the Lord, whose pleasure
Is his servant's bliss to seal.

As for me in heavenly phrases
I will harmonize my tongue,
Day by day Jehovah's praises
Shall in sweeter notes be sung.

THE THIRTY-SIXTH PSALM

To the chief Musician, A Psalm of David the servant of the Lord.

David Rosenberg

Inside my heart I hear
how arrogance talks
to himself without fear

hidden from eyes
he flatters himself
but we see him on the faces

of false faces and words
thinking—even asleep—
how to squeeze love out

from feelings from words
how to put wisdom on her back
then hold his miniature knowledge back

your love fills a man, Lord
with a kind of air
making him lighter

he rises in measure of your judgment
above the mountains of thought
above the clouds of feeling

the strength of his measure stays
in the eyes returning to mountains
from the surface of the sea

he falls like any animal
standing up only by your mercy
his children grow in the shadow of your wings

feast on gourmet fare in your house
with water that sparkles from wells
beyond the reach of a mind

the fountain of life
is lit
by your light

you extend your embrace
to those who feel you are there
keep holding the loving

keep us from being crushed
by arrogant feet
by the hand of pride

the powerful are falling over themselves
their minds have pulled them down
there they will lie, flung down.

THE THIRTY-SEVENTH PSALM

A Psalm of David.

~ Philip Sidney

Fret not thyself, if thou do see
That wicked men do seem to flourish:
Nor envy in thy bosom nourish
Though ill deeds well succeeding be.

They soon shall be cut down like grass
And wither like green herb or flower;
Do well, and trust on heavenly power,
Thou shalt have both good food and place.

Delight in God, and he shall breed
The fullness of thy own heart's lusting:
Guide thee by him, lay all thy trusting
On him, and he will make it speed.

For like the light he shall display
Thy justice, in most shining lustre:
And of thy judgment make a muster
Like to the glory of noon day.

Wait on the Lord with patient hope;
Chafe not at some man's great good fortune
Though all his plots, without misfortune,
Attain unto their wished scope.

Fume not, rage not, fret not, I say,
Lest such things sin in thyself cherish;
For those bad folks, at last, shall perish:
Who stay for God, in bliss shall stay.

Watch but a while, and thou shalt see
The wicked, by his own pride, banished:
Look after him, he shall be vanished,
And never found again shall be.

But meek men shall the earth possess;
In quiet home they shall be planted:
And this delight to them is granted,
They shall have peace in plenteousness.

Evil men work ill to utmost right,
Gnashing their teeth full of disdaining:
But God shall scorn their moody meaning,
For their short time is in his sight.

The evil bent bows, and swords they drew,
To have their hate on good souls wroken:
But lo, their bows they shall be broken,
Their swords shall their own hearts embrew.

Small goods in good men better is
Than of bad folks the wealthy wonder:
For wicked arms shall break asunder;
But God upholds the just in bliss.

God keeps account of good men's days,
Their heritage shall last for ever:
In peril they shall perish never,
Nor want in dearth, their want to ease.

Bad folks shall fall, and fall for aye:
Who to make war with God presumed
Like fat of lambs shall be consumed,
Even with the smoke shall waste away.

The naughty borrows, paying not;
The good is kind, and freely giveth.
Lo, whom God blessed, he blessed liveth:
Whom he doth curse, to naught shall rot.

The man whom God directs doth stand
Firm on his way, his way God loveth;
Though he doth fall, no wrack he proveth:
He is upheld by heavenly hand.

I have been young: now old I am,
Yet I the man that was betaken
To justice, never saw forsaken;
Nor that his seed to begging came.

He lends, he gives, more he doth spend,
The more his seed in blessing flourish:
Then fly all ill, and goodness nourish,
And thy good state shall never end.

God, loving right, doth not forsake
His holy ones: they are preserved
From time to time; but who be swerved
To ill, both they and theirs shall wrack.

I say, I say the righteous minds
Shall have the land in their possessing,
Shall dwell thereon, and this their blessing
No time within his limits binds.

The good mouth will in wisdom bide,
His tongue of heavenly judgments telleth;
For God's high law in his heart dwelleth:
What comes thereof? he shall not slide.

The wicked watch the righteous much,
And seek of life for to bereave him:
But, in their hand, God will not leave him
Nor let him be condemned by such.

Wait thou on God, and keep his way,
He will exalt thee unto honor
And of the earth make thee an owner;
Yea thou shalt see the evil decay.

I have the wicked seen full sound,
Like laurel fresh, himself outspreading:
Lo, he was gone, print of his treading,
Though I did seek, I never found.

Mark the upright, the just, attend:
His end shall be in peace enjoyed:
But strayers vile, shall be destroyed,
And quite cut off with helpless end.

Still, still, the godly shall be stayed
By God's most sure, and sweet salvation:
In time of greatest tribulation
He shall be their true strength and aid.

He shall be their true strength and aid,
He shall save them from all the fetches
Against them used by wicked wretches:
Because on him their trust is laid.

THE THIRTY-EIGHTH PSALM

A Psalm of David, to bring to remembrance.

~ *Thomas Wyatt*

O Lord, as I thee have both prayed and pray
(Although in thee be no alteration
But that we men like as ourselves we say,
Measuring thy justice by our mutation)
Chastise me not, O Lord, in thy furor,
Nor me correct in wrathful castigation,
For that thy arrows of fear, of terror,
Of sword, of sickness, of famine and fire
Stick deep in me. I, lo, from mine error
Am plunged up as horse out of the mire
With stroke of spur. Such is thy hand on me
That in my flesh for terror of thy ire
Is not one point of firm stability,
Nor in my bones there is no steadfastness,
Such is my dread of mutability,
For that I know frailful wickedness:
For why my sins above my head are bound
Like heavy weight that doth my force oppress,
Under the which I stoop and bow to ground
As willow plant, haled by violence;
And of my flesh each not well cured wound,
That festered is by folly and negligence,
By secret lust hath rankled under skin,
Not duly cured by my penitence.
Perceiving thus the tyranny of sin
That with his weight hath humbled and depressed
My pride by grudging of the worm within
That never dieth, I live withouten rest.
So are mine entrails infect with fervent sore,
Feeding the harm that hath my wealth oppressed,
That in my flesh is left no health therefore.
So wondrous great hath been my vexation
That it hath forced my heart to cry and roar.
O Lord, thou knowst the inward contemplation
Of my desire, thou knowst my sighs and plaints,
Thou knowst the tears of my lamentation
Cannot express my heart's inward restraints.
My heart panteth, my force I feel it quail,
My sight, mine eyes, my look decays and faints.
And when mine enemies did me most assail,

My friends most sure, wherein I set most trust,
Mine own virtues, soonest then did fail,
And stood apart: reason and wit unjust
As kin unkind were farthest gone at need.
So had they place their venom out to thrust
That sought my death by naughty word and deed:
Their tongues reproach, their wits did fraud apply,
And I like deaf and dumb forth my way yede,
Like one that hears not, nor hath to reply
One word again, knowing that from thy hand
These things proceed and thou, O Lord, shalt supply
My trust in thee, wherein I stick and stand.
Yet have I had great cause to dread and fear
That thou wouldst give my foes the over hand,
For in my fall they showed such pleasant cheer;
And therewithal I always in the lash
Abide the stroke, and with me everywhere
I bear my fault, that greatly doth abash
My doleful cheer, for I my fault confess,
And my desert doth all my comfort dash.
In the meanwhile mine enemies safe increase
And my provokers hereby do augment,
That without cause to hurt me do not cease.
In evil for good against me they be bent,
And hinder shall my good pursuit of grace.
Lo now, my God, that seest my whole intent,
My Lord, I am thou knowst well in what case:
Forsake me not, be not far from me gone,
Haste to my help, haste, Lord, and haste apace,
O Lord, the Lord of all my health alone!

THE THIRTY-NINTH PSALM

To the chief Musician, even to Jeduthun, A Psalm of David.

~ Laurance Wieder

I said, I will watch my mouth
And made no comment even
On the good, and I was sad.
My heart raced, something hot
Inside me made me cry out loud:

Lord, let me know when I've begun
A thing, and when it will be done;

Let me know how my days will run
From hot and fat to dim, to fail
And fall without a flutter by your hand.

What's there to wait for? money? power?
What's there to hope for? old age? honor?
The mock of dimwits? spoiled children?
Your finger pressed across my mouth.
My lovely self was flannel, time a moth.

Hear me. Don't be put off by tears.
A stranger and a nomad like my father,
Give me strength enough to rise, to speak,
To spill a glass of water on the tabletop before
I thirst, and sip, and am no more.

THE FORTIETH PSALM

To the chief Musician, A Psalm of David.

Philip Sidney

While, long, I did with patient constancy
The pleasure of my God attend,
He did, himself, to me-ward bend
And harkened how and why that I did cry.
And me from pit, bemired,
From dungeon he retired,
Where I, in horrors lay:
Setting my feet upon
A steadfast rocky stone;
And my weak steps did stay.

So in my mouth he did a song afford,
New song unto our God of praise:
Which many seeing hearts shall raise
To fear with trust, and trust with fear the Lord.
O, he indeed is blessed
Whose trust is so addressed;
Who bends not wandering eyes
To great men's peacock pride,
Nor ever turns aside
To follow after lies.

My God, thy wondrous works how manifold!
What man thy thoughts can count to thee?
I fain of them would speaking be

But they are more than can by me be told.
Thou, sacrifice nor offering,
Burnt offering, nor sin offering
Didst like, much less didst crave;
But thou didst pierce my ear,
Which should thy lessons bear,
And witness me thy slave.

Thus bound, I said: Lo, Lord, I am at hand
For in thy book's role, I am writ;
And sought with deeds thy will to hit.
Yea, Lord, thy law within my heart doth stand:
I, to great congregation,
Thou knowst, made declaration
Of this sweet righteousness:
My lips shall still reveal,
My heart shall not conceal
Thy truth, health, graciousness.

Then, Lord, from me, draw not thy tender grace:
Me, still, in truth and mercy save.
For endless woes me compassed have,
So pressed with sins, I cannot see my case.
But trial well doth teach me;
Foul faults sore pains do reach me,
More than my head hath hairs,
So that my surest part,
My life-maintaining heart,
Fails me, with ugly fears.

Vouchsafe me help, O Lord, and help with haste:
Let them have shame, yea, blush for shame
Who jointly sought my bale to frame:
Let them be cursed away that would me waste;
Let them with shame be cloyed,
Yea let them be destroyed,
For guerdon of their shame,
Who-so unpiteous be
As now to say to me:
A ha! this is good game.

But fill their hearts with joy who bend their ways
To seek thy beauty past conceit;
Let them that love thy saving seat
Still gladly say, unto our God be praise.

Though I in want be shrinking,
Yet God on me is thinking.
Thou art my help for aye,
Thou only, thou art he
That dost deliver me;
My God, O make no stay.

THE FORTY-FIRST PSALM

To the chief Musician, A Psalm of David.

Philip Sidney

He blessed is who with wise temper can
Judge of the afflicted man,
For God shall him deliver in the time
When most his troubles climb.
The Lord will keep his life yet safe and sound
With blessings of the ground;
And will not him unto the will expose,
Of them that be his foes.

When bed from rest becomes his seat of woe,
In God his strength shall grow,
And turn his couch, where sick he couched late,
To well recovered state;
Therefore I said in most infirmity,
Have mercy, Lord, on me:
O, heal my soul, let there thy cure begin,
Where gainst thee lay my sin.

My foes' evil words, their hate of me display,
While thus, alas, they say:
When, when will death o'ertake this wretched wight,
And his name perish quite?
Their courteous visitings, are courting lies:
They inward evils disguise
Even heaps of wicked thoughts, which straight they show
As soon as out they go.

For then their hateful heads close whispering be,
With hurtful thoughts to me.
Now he is wracked, say they, lo, there he lies,
Who never more must rise.
O, yea my friend, to whom I did impart
The secrets of my heart,

My friend, I say, who at my table sate,
Did kick against my state.

Therefore, O Lord, abandoned thus of all,
On me let mercy fall;
And raise me up, that I may once have might,
Their merits to requite:
But what? this doth already well appear
That I to thee am dear:
Since foes, nor have, nor shall have cause to be
Triumphing over me.

But triumph well may I, whom thou dost stay
In my sound rightful way:
Whom thou (O place of places all) dost place,
For aye, before thy face.
So then be blessed now, then, at home, abroad,
Of Israel the god:
World without end, let this his blessing flow,
O so; O be it so.

BOOK TWO

The Hart Desires the Brook

THE FORTY-SECOND PSALM

To the chief Musician, Maschil, for the sons of Korah.

Christopher Smart

Like as the hart desires the brook
   In summer heat's extreme degree,
With panting breast and wishful look,
   So longs my soul for Thee!

O God—my spirit is athirst
   For God in whom we live and move;
When in God's church shall I be first
   My piety to prove?

My tears have been my constant food,
   Which day and night my griefs supply,
While with malevolence renewed
   Where is thy God, they cry?

Now when I think thereon I shed
   By stealth the showers of inward care;
For I before was wont to head
   These multitudes to prayer.

All in one voice of that delight
   Which from the great thanksgiving flows,
As youths and maids, a goodly sight,
   The festive wreath compose.

Why do I drag this loathsome load,
   Whence, O my soul, art thou oppressed;
And what are these the stings, that goad
   And wound my tortured breast?

O trust in God his power to save
   The cup of thankfulness fulfill,
He keeps thy head above the wave,
   And is thy saviour still.

O God, internal griefs assail,
   I therefore will direct my thought
To Hermon's hill and Jordan's vale,
   Where thou such wonders wrought.

One sea unto another calls,
   As to the whistling winds they swell;
But at thy word the tempest falls,
   And I am safe and well.

The Lord is good and loving-kind
Through all the service of the day,
And him which made me man and mind
By night I sing and pray.

I will inquire of God my strength:
Why hast thou left me thus to go
With such a load and such a length
Of life in war and woe?

My bones are smitten to the quick
As with the falchion's keener blade,
While at my face the cowards kick,
And my distress upbraid.

To wit while reprobates intrude
My soul's deliverer to deny,
And with malevolence renewed
Where is thy God, they cry?

Why do I drag this loathsome load,
Whence, O my soul, art thou oppressed,
And what are these the stings, that goad
And wound my tortured breast?

O put thy trust in God again
The cup of thankfulness fulfill;
He shall thy countenance sustain,
And is thy saviour still.

THE FORTY-THIRD PSALM

~ John Davies

Judge thou my cause, and right me
Against ungodly and deceitful men.
O God my strength, why settst thou me aside,
And leavest me to my foes' oppressing pride?
Send forth thy light and truth, and guide me still
In the right way to thy most holy hill:
God of my joy, before thine altar high
My thankful heart my harp shall justify.
Then why art thou, my soul, dejected so?
Why art thou troubled and so full of woe?
O put thy trust in God, and thankful be,
For that sweet aid his presence gives to thee.

THE FORTY-FOURTH PSALM

To the chief Musician for the sons of Korah, Maschil.

~ Mary Sidney Herbert

Lord, our fathers' true relation
Often made, hath made us know
How thy power in each occasion,
Thou of old for them didst show;
How thy hand the pagan foe
Rooting hence, thy folk implanting,
Leafless made that branch to grow,
This to spring, no verdure wanting.

Never could their sword procure them
Conquest of the promised land:
Never could their force assure them
When they did in danger stand.
No, it was thy arm, thy hand,
No, it was thy favor's treasure
Spent upon thy loved band,
Loved, why? for thy wise pleasure.

Unto thee stand I subjected,
I that did of Jacob spring:
Bid then that I be protected,
Thou that art my God, my king:
By that succor thou didst bring,
We their pride that us assailed,
Down did tread, and back did fling,
In thy name confused and quailed.

For my trust was not reposed
In my own, though strongest, bow:
Nor my scabbard held enclosed
That, whence should my safety flow.
Thou, O God, from every foe
Didst us shield, our haters shaming:
Thence thy daily praise we show,
Still thy name with honor naming.

But aloof thou now dost hover,
Grieving us with all disgrace:
Hast resigned and given over
In our camp thy captain's place.
Back we turn, that turned face,
Flying them, that erst we foiled:

See our goods (O changed case,)
Spoiled by them, that late we spoiled.

Right as sheep to be devoured,
Helpless here we lie alone:
Scattering lie by thee out-powered,
Slaves to dwell with lords unknown,
Sold we are, but silver none
Told for us: by thee so prized,
As for nought to be forgone,
Graceless, worthless, vile, despised.

By them all that dwell about us,
Tossed we fly as balls of scorn;
All our neighbors laugh and flout us,
Men by thee in shame forlorn.
Proverb-like our name is worn,
O how fast in foreign places!
What head-shakings are forborne!
Wordless taunts and dumb disgraces!

So rebuke before me goeth,
As myself do daily go:
So confusion on me groweth,
That my face I blush to show.
By reviling slandering foe
Inly wounded thus I languish:
Wreakful spite with outward blow
Anguish adds to inward anguish,

All, this all on us hath lighted,
Yet to thee our love doth last:
As we were, we are delighted
Still to hold thy covenant fast.
Unto none our hearts have past:
Unto none our feet have slidden:
Though us down to dragons cast
Thou in deadly shade hast hidden.

If our God we had forsaken,
Or forgot what he assigned:
If ourselves we had betaken
Gods to serve of other kind
Should not he our doubling find
Though concealed, and closely lurking?
Since his eye of deepest mind
Deeper sinks than deepest working?

Surely Lord, this daily murder
For thy sake we thus sustain:
For thy sake esteemed no further
Than as sheep, that must be slain.
Up O Lord, up once again:
Sleep not ever, slack not ever:
Why dost thou forget our pain?
Why to hide thy face persever?

Heavy grief our soul abaseth,
Prostrate it on dust doth lie:
Earth our body fast embraceth,
Nothing can the clasp untie.
Rise, and us with help supply
Lord, in mercy so esteem us,
That we may thy mercy try,
Mercy may from thrall redeem us.

THE FORTY-FIFTH PSALM

To the chief Musician upon Shoshannim, for the sons of Korah, Maschil, A Song of loves.

~ Mary Sidney Herbert

My heart indites an argument of worth,
The praise of him that doth the scepter sway:
My tongue the pen to paint his praises forth,
Shall write as swift as swiftest writer may.
Then to the king these are the words I say:
Fairer art thou than sons of mortal race:
Because high God hath blessed thee for aye,
Thy lips, as springs, do flow with speaking grace.

Thy honor's sword gird to this mighty side,
O thou that dost all things in might excel:
With glory prosper, on with triumph ride
Since justice, truth, and meekness with thee dwell.
So that right hand of thine shall teaching tell
Such things to thee, as well may terror bring,
And terror such, as never erst befell
To mortal minds at sight of mortal king.

Sharp are thy shafts to cleave their hearts in twain
Whose heads do cast thy conquests to withstand
Good cause to make the meaner people fain

With willing hearts to undergo thy hand.
Thy throne O God, doth never-falling stand:
Thy scepter, ensign of thy kingly might,
To righteousness is linked with such a band,
That righteous hand still holds thy scepter right.

Justice in love, in hate thou holdest wrong,
This makes that God, who so doth hate and love:
Glad-making oil, that oil on thee hath flung,
Which thee exalts thine equals far above.
The fragrant riches of Sabean grove
Myrrh, aloes, cassia, all thy robes do smell:
When thou from ivory palace dost remove
Thy breathing odors all thy train excel.

Daughters of kings among thy courtly band,
By honoring thee of thee do honor hold:
On thy right side thy dearest queen doth stand
Richly arrayed in cloth of Ophir gold.
O daughter hear what now to thee is told:
Mark what thou hearest, and what thou markst, obey:
Forget to keep in memory enrolled
The house, and folk, where first thou sawst the day.

So in the king, thy king, a dear delight
Thy beauty shall both breed, and bred, maintain:
For only he on thee hath lordly right,
Him only thou with awe must entertain.
Then unto thee both Tyrus shall be fain
Presents present, and richest nations more,
With humble suit thy royal grace to gain,
To thee shall do such homage as they owe.

This queen that can a king her father call,
Doth only she in upper garment shine?
Nay under clothes, and what she weareth all,
Gold is the stuff, the fashion art divine;
Brought to the king in robe embroidered fine,
Her maids of honor shall on her attend
With such, to whom more favor shall assign
In nearer place their happy days to spend.

Brought shall they be with mirth and marriage joy
And enter so the palace of the king:
Then let no grief thy mind, O Queen, annoy,
Nor parents left thy sad remembrance sting.

Instead of parents, children thou shalt bring
Of partaged earth the kings and lords to be:
Myself thy name in lasting verse will sing.
The world shall make no end of thanks to thee.

THE FORTY-SIXTH PSALM

To the chief Musician for the sons of Korah, A Song upon Alamoth.

~ *Samuel Taylor Coleridge*

God is our strength and our refuge: therefore will we not tremble,
Though the earth be removed and though the perpetual mountains
Sink in the swell of the ocean! God is our strength and our refuge.
There is a river the flowing whereof shall gladden the city,
Hallelujah! the city of God! Jehovah shall help her.
The idolaters raged, the kingdoms were moving in fury;
But he uttered his voice: Earth melted away from beneath them.
Hallelujah! The eternal is with us, almighty Jehovah!
Fearful the works of the Lord, yea fearful his desolations;
But he maketh the battle to cease, he burneth the spear and the chariot.
Hallelujah! The eternal is with us, the God of our fathers!

THE FORTY-SEVENTH PSALM

To the chief Musician, A Psalm for the sons of Korah.

~ *John Davies*

Clap hands ye people, with applause rejoice;
Sing to the Lord with loud and cheerful voice:
His throne is high, his judgment breedeth fear,
On all the earth he doth the scepter bear.
He makes much people our command obey,
And many nations at our feet doth lay,
And hath for us an heritage in store,
Even Jacob's portion, whom he loved before.
In glorious triumph God is mounted high,
The Lord with trumpets sound ascends the sky,
Sing, sing unto our God, unto our king;
All praises due, even all due praises sing.

Kingdoms of the earth to him belong,
Sing wisely then, and understand your song.
In all the heathen he doth reign alone,
And sits in judgment in his holy throne.
The heathen princes which were severed far,
To Abraham's faithful seed now joined are;
And God, whose highness doth the heavens transcend,
As with a buckler doth the earth defend.

THE FORTY-EIGHTH PSALM

A Song and Psalm for the sons of Korah.

George Wither

The Lord is great, and great his fame
Should in his holy mountain be:
For Sion is a goodly frame;
The praise of all the world is she.
  She northward stands, and she doth hight
  The City of the King of might.

The Lord is known to be her guard;
For, when great kings against her came,
They much admired; admiring, feared;
And, fearing, fled away with shame:
  Even with such pangs, and suchlike fear,
  As women that in travail are.

For thou didst raise an eastern wind
Which all the ships of Tarsus brake:
And, Lord of hosts, now true we find
What others of thy city spake:
  Yea, we have heard, and now we see
  That God will still her keeper be. *Selah*

Within thy temple we, O God,
Upon thy loving-kindness thought;
Thy name is published abroad;
With justice, thy right hand is fraught:
  And in thy judgments Sion shall
  Rejoice, with Judah's daughters all.

Through Sion go; about her walk,
Her bulwarks mark, her turrets heed;
That of her beauties you may talk
And tell her glories to your seed:

For God in life will be our guide;
And, in our death, our God abide.

THE FORTY-NINTH PSALM

To the chief Musician, A Psalm for the sons of Korah.

~ *Christopher Smart*

O ye people, hear and ponder
In your ears and in your mind,
All that dwell in homes or wander
Through the world of human kind.

You of high or low gradation
To my words alike attend,
Men as well of wealth and station
As the poor without a friend.

I will speak of things essential
To the folk that would be wise,
And with words and thoughts prudential
Heart and mouth I will advise.

My harmonious ear inclining
To the great mysterious verse,
And with harp and hand divining,
I will oracles rehearse.

Wherefore in these times flagitious
Should I my good courage lose,
When with practices pernicious
Guile prepares my heel to bruise?

Some there are that have affiance
In the goods they get by stealth,
And grow proud by vain reliance
On the rust of worldly wealth.

But for brotherly affection,
That in pride and pomp is lost;
Could they buy the Lord's protection,
They would scruple of the cost.

Deeds of charity and kindness,
Which would tend their souls to save,
They through vice and carnal blindness
Must relinquish to the grave.

Yea and that though God has lengthened
  The duration of their years,
And their fleshly veil has strengthened
  From the dread sepulchral fears—

For they see the general sentence,
  Fools and wise together die,
And the rich in late repentance
  With their hoards an heir supply—

Yet they think that their succession
  Shall not be extinct at all;
And the places at discretion
  After their own names they call.

Yet is man from his beginning
  Weak, nor honor long retains,
And degrades himself by sinning
  To the brutes o'er which he reigns.

Thus it is with self-deceivers,
  Fools which heavenly hope defeat,
And a race of unbelievers
  Praise and practise the deceit.

Such like rotten sheep infected
  Worms their beauty shall devour,
And o'er them the saints elected
  In eternal peace shall tower.

But from out the dreary mansion
  God my spirit hath set free,
Height sublime and free expansion,
  Bliss celestial are for me.

Be not daunted at the lustre
  Of thy neighbor's countless store,
At his glory, and the cluster
  Of dependents at his door.

For his wealth and gaudy splendor
  Shall not wait upon his bier;
Pomp and all he must surrender
  When the train of death appear.

While he lived, in his adherence
  To the world, he thought him blessed:
Long as thou supportst appearance,
  Busy tongues will speak the best.

Soon his father he shall follow,
 In the greedy grave to rot,
And the gulf his soul shall swallow,
 If repentance save him not.

Men of honor and promotion,
 Which of carnal things have fared,
Modeled to the vulgar notion,
 With the beasts are well compared.

THE FIFTIETH PSALM

A Psalm of Asaph.

~ Mary Sidney Herbert

The mighty God, the ever living Lord,
 All nations from earth's uttermost confines
Summoneth by his pursuivant, his word,
 And out of beauties beauty, Sion shines.
God comes, he comes, with ear and tongue restored:
 His guard huge storms, hot flames his ushers go:
And called, their appearance to record,
 Heaven hasteth from above, earth from below.

He sits his people's judge, and thus commands:
 Gather me hither that beloved line,
Whom solemn sacrifices holy bands
 Did in eternal league with me combine
Then when the heavens subsigned with their hands,
 That God in justice eminently reigns:
Controlling so, as nothing countermands
 What once decreed his sacred doom contains.

You then, my folk, to me your God attend:
 Hark, Israel, and hear thy people's blame:
Not want of sacrifice doth me offend,
 Nor do I miss thy altars' daily flame.
To me thy stall no fatted bull shall send:
 Should I exact one he-goat from thy fold?
I, that as far as hills, woods, fields extend,
 All birds and beasts in known possession hold?

Suppose me hungry; yet to beg thy meat,
 I would not tell thee that I hungry were:
Myself may take, what needs me then entreat?
 Since earth is mine, and all that earth doth bear?

But do I long the brawny flesh to eat
    Of that dull beast that serves the plowman's need?
Or do I thirst, to quench my thirsty heat,
    In what the throats of bearded cattle bleed?

O no: bring God of praise a sacrifice;
    Thy vowed debts unto the highest pay:
Invoke my name, to me erect thy cries,
    Thy praying plaints, when sorrow stops thy way;
I will undo the knot that anguish ties,
    And thou at peace shalt glorify my name:
Mildly the good, God schooleth in this wise,
    But this sharp check doth to the godless frame:

How fits it thee my statutes to report?
    And of my covenant in thy talk to prate
Hating to live in right reformed sort,
    And leaving in neglect what I relate?
Seest thou a thief? thou growst of his consort:
    Dost with adulterers to adultery go:
Thy mouth is slander's ever-open port,
    And from thy tongue doth nought, but treason flow.

Nay even thy brother thy rebukes disgrace,
    And thou in spite defamest thy mother's son:
And for I wink a while, thy thoughts embrace:
    God is like me, and doth as I have done.
But lo thou seest I march another pace,
    And come with truth thy falsehood to disclose:
Thy sin, revived, upbraids thy blushing face,
    Which thou long dead in silence didst suppose.

O lay up this in marking memory
    You that are wont God's judgments to forget:
In vain to others for release you fly,
    If once on you I griping fingers set.
And know the rest: my dearest worship I
    In sweet perfume of offered praise do place:
And who directs his goings orderly,
    By my conduct shall see God's saving grace.

THE FIFTY-FIRST PSALM

To the chief Musician, A Psalm of David, when Nathan the prophet came unto him, after he had gone in to Bathsheba.

~ Thomas Carew

Good God unlock thy magazines
Of mercy, and forgive my sins.

O wash and purify the foul
Pollution of my sin-stained soul.

For I confess my faults that lie
In horrid shapes before mine eye.

Against thee only, and alone
In thy sight was this evil done,
That all men might thy justice see
When thou art judged for judging me.

Even from my birth I did begin
With mothers milk to suck in sin.

But thou lovest truth, and shalt impart
Thy secret wisdom to my heart.

Thou shalt with hyssop purge me; so
Shall I seem white as mountain snow.

Thou shalt send joyful news, and then
My broken bones grow strong again.

Let not thine eyes my sins survey,
But cast those cancelled debts away.

O make my cleansed heart, a pure cell
Where a renewed spirit may dwell.

Cast me not from thy sight, nor chase
Away from me thy spirit of grace.

Send me thy saving health again,
And with thy spirit those joys maintain.

Then will I preach thy ways, and draw
Converted sinners to thy law.

O God my God of health, unseal
My blood-shut lips, and I'll reveal
What mercies in thy justice dwell,
And with loud voice thy praises tell.

Could sacrifice have purged my vice
Lord I had brought thee sacrifice:
But though burnt offerings are refused
Thou shalt accept the heart that's bruised;
The humbled soul, the spirit oppressed,
Lord such oblations please thee best.

Bless Sion Lord, repair with pity
The ruins of thy holy city.

Then will we holy vows present thee,
And peace offerings that content thee,
And then thine altars shall be pressed
With many a sacrificed beast.

THE FIFTY-SECOND PSALM

To the chief Musician, Maschil, A Psalm of David, when Doeg the Edomite came and told Saul, and said unto him, David is come to the house of Ahimelech.

~ *Mary Sidney Herbert*

Tyrant, why swellst thou thus,
  Of mischief vaunting?
Since help from God to us,
  Is never wanting?

Lewd lies thy tongue contrives,
  Loud lies it soundeth:
Sharper than sharpest knives
  With lies it woundeth.

Falsehood thy wit approves,
  All truth rejected:
Thy will all vices loves,
  Virtue neglected.

Not words from cursed thee,
  But gulfs are poured;
Gulfs wherein daily be
  Good men devoured.

Thinkst thou to bear it so?
  God shall displace thee;
God shall thee overthrow,
  Crush thee, deface thee.

The just shall fearing see
   These fearful chances:
And laughing shoot at thee
   With scornful glances.

Lo, lo, the wretched wight,
   Who God disdaining,
His mischief made his might,
   His guard his gaining.

I as an olive tree,
   Still green shall flourish:
God's house the soil shall be
   My roots to nourish.

My trust on his true love
   Truly attending,
Shall never thence remove,
   Never see ending.

Thee will I honor still
   Lord, for this justice:
There fix my hopes I will
   Where thy saints' trust is.

Thy saints trust in thy name,
   Therein they joy them:
Protected by the same
   Nought can annoy them.

THE FIFTY-THIRD PSALM

To the chief Musician, upon Mahalath, Maschil, A Psalm of David.

Laurance Wieder

The fool says to himself, What God?
And takes, and breaks his word, and does
No good, no, none, not anyone. Such rot
In fruit would sicken flies.

God peered down through his window
In the sky, to see his children
At their lives, the men and women,
To find if even one still tried to know

Life and good from death and evil,
But they'd all gone back to witches'

Days, and gold greed blood haphazard couples
And no one knows, does, good, or teaches.

Don't they have an inkling of their doing,
Dying without shame and chewing
Up the people (who would, could they, love
The lore) like bakers' crusty loaves?

The bad have not called God by any name, not even
When the fear came on them, fear that floats
Like bone ash puffed by chimneys in the air, spouts
Of naked ignorance despised shamed by no God.

If only someone would save us from
The blind, our selves, the bloated, come
He from Jerusalem or nearer home

To sunder what has hindered us
From freedom and from happiness,
Then Israel, who wrestled, shall rejoice.

THE FIFTY-FOURTH PSALM

To the chief Musician on Neginoth, Maschil, A Psalm of David, when the Ziphims came and said to Saul, Doth not David hide himself with us?

~ John Hall

O God, I call to thee for help
In my distress and need,
For thy name's sake, and in thy strength,
Avenge my cause with speed.

For strangers full of tyranny
Against me rise and rave:
Such foolish folk as fear not God
Do seek my life to have.

But lo God is my help at need,
Yea only it is he,
That doth my soul uphold and save,
From their iniquity.

And evil shall the Lord reward
Upon mine enemies,
And in his truth destroy them all
That virtue do despise.

With offerings of an heart most free,
Now will I praise thy name:
Because, O Lord, my comfort still
Consisteth in the same.

For thou Lord didst deliver me,
From troubles manifold:
So that upon my foes mine eye
Doth his desire behold.

For this to give glory to God
Shall be my heart's delight,
To the father, and to the son,
And to the holy sprite:

As it from the beginning was,
And at this time is sure,
And as it shall world without end
Continue and endure.

THE FIFTY-FIFTH PSALM

To the chief Musician on Neginoth, Maschil, A Psalm of David.

Henry Howard of Surrey

Give ear to my suit, Lord, fromward hide not thy face.
Behold, harking in grief, lamenting how I pray.
My foes they bray so loud, and eke threap on so fast,
Buckled to do me scathe, so is their malice bent.
Care pierceth my entrails and travaileth my sprite;
The grisly fear of death environeth my breast;
A trembling cold of dread clean overwhelmeth my heart.
'O,' think I, 'had I wings like to the simple dove,
This peril might I fly, and seek some place of rest
In wilder woods, where I might dwell far from these cares.'
What speedy way of wing my plaints should they lay on,
To scape the stormy blast that threatened is to me!
Rein those unbridled tongues! break that conjured league!
For I deciphered have amid our town the strife:
Guile and wrong kept the walls, they ward both day and night;
And while mischief with care doth keep the market stead;
Whilst wickedness with craft in heaps swarm through the street
Not my declared foe wrought me all this reproach;
By harm so looked for, it weigheth half the less.
For though mine enemy's hap had been for to prevail.

I could have hid my face   from venom of his eye.
It was a friendly foe,   by shadow of good will,
Mine old fere and dear friend,   my guide, that trapped me;
Where I was wont to fetch   the cure of all my care,
And in his bosom hide   my secret zeal to God.
Such sudden surprise quick   may them hell devour,
Whilst I invoke the Lord,   whose power shall me defend.
My prayer shall not cease   from that the son descends
Till he his hauteur win   and hide them in the sea.
With words of hot effect,   that moveth from heart contrite,
Such humble suit, O Lord,   doth pierce thy patient ear.
It was the Lord that brake   the bloody compacts of those
That pricked on with ire   to slaughter me and mine.
The everlasting God   whose kingdom hath no end,
Whom, by no tale to dread   he could divert from sin,
The conscience unquiet   he strikes with heavy hand,
And proves their force in faith   whom he swore to defend.
Butter falls not so soft   as doth his patience long,
And overpasseth fine oil,   running not half so smooth.
But when his sufferance finds   that bridled wrath provokes,
He threatens wrath, he whets more sharp   than any tool can file.
Friar, whose harm and tongue   presents the wicked sort
Of those false wolves, with coats   which do their ravin hide,
That swear to me by heaven,   the footstool of the Lord,
Who though force had hurt my fame,   they did not touch my life:
Such patching care I loathe   as feeds the wealth with lies.
But in the other Psalm   of David find I ease.

THE FIFTY-SIXTH PSALM

To the chief Musician upon Jonath-elem-rechokim, Michtam of David, when the Philistines took him in Gath.

~ Mary Sidney Herbert

Fountain of pity now with pity flow:
These monsters on me daily gaping go,
    Daily me devour these spies,
    Swarms of foes against me rise,
O God that art more high than I am low.

Still when I fear, yet will I trust in thee:
Thy word, O God, my boast shall ever be;
    God shall be my hopeful stay,
    Fear shall not that hope dismay
For what can feeble flesh do unto me?

I, as I can, think, speak, and do the best:
They to the worst my thoughts, words, doings wrest.
  All their hearts with one consent
  Are to work my ruin bent,
From plotting which, they give their heads no rest.

To that intent they secret meetings make,
They press me near my soul in snare to take,
  Thinking slight shall keep them safe.
  But thou, Lord, in wrathful chafe,
Their league so surely linked, in sunder shake.

Thou didst, O Lord, with careful counting, look
On every journey I, poor exile, took:
  Every tear from my sad eyes
  Saved in thy bottle lies,
These matters are all entered in thy book.

Then whensoever my distressed sprite
Crying to thee, brings these unto thy sight,
  What remaineth for my foes?
  Blames, and shames, and overthrows,
For God himself I know for me will fight.

God's never-falsed word my boast shall be,
My boast shall be his word to set me free,
  God shall be my hopeful stay;
  Fear shall not that hope dismay,
For what can mortal men do unto me?

For this, to thee, how deeply stand I bound
Lord, that my soul dost save, my foes confound?
  Ah, I can no payment make,
  But if thou for payment take
The vows I pay, thy praises I resound:

Thy praises who from death hast set me free
Whither my feet did, headlong, carry me;
  Making me, of thy free grace,
  There again to take my place,
Where light of life, with living men, I see.

THE FIFTY-SEVENTH PSALM

To the chief Musician, Altaschith, Michtam of David, when he fled from Saul in the cave.

~ P. Hately Waddell

Be gude till me, God, be gude till me;
For my life lippens a' till yerlane:
I' the sconce o' yer wings I sal bide a-wee,
Till a' thir mischieffs are gane.
Till the God that's fu' heigh, I sal skreigh;
Till God that rights a' for mysel:
He sal rax frae the lift, an' sal redd me free,
Frae the haughty carl that wad glaum at me: *Selah.*

His rewth an' his trewth God can sen' far eneugh, himsel.
My life's amang lyouns its lane;
I lye amang bleezan bran's:
Sons o' the yird, their teeth pikes an' flanes;
An' their tongue, a swurd sae snell.
O God, be thou liftit abune the lift;
Thy gloiry, owre yirth itsel!
A net they set for my feet,
Whan my life sae laigh was laid;
A sheugh they howkit afore my face;
I' the heart o't, themsels they slade: *Selah.*

My heart, it's set, O God;
My heart, it's set fu' stieve;
Till thee I maun lilt an' sing:
Wauken, my gloiry, wauken heigh;
Langspiel an' harp, fy haste ye, baith:
Mysel I maun wauken or morning.

I sal lilt till ye, Lord, amang a' the folk;
I sal lilt till yersel, amang a' their kin:
For heigh till the hevins is that rewth o' thine;
An' abune the cluds your trewth can win.
O God, be thou liftit abune the lift;
Owre a' the yirth, thy gloiry seen.

THE FIFTY-EIGHTH PSALM

To the chief Musician, Altaschith, Michtam of David.

David Rosenberg

Can this be justice
this pen to hold
they that move my arm

to follow them—blind stars?
They think I have submitted
to the vicious decorum of fame?

O generation come from dust
O no: you steel yourselves
to write; your hands

weigh, like a primitive scale,
selfish desire unfulfilled . . .
strangers from the womb

no sooner born and here
than chasing after
impulsive wishes

for which they will lie, cheat, kill.
Cancerous cold desire
gnaws in their brain

as the doctor
the greatest virtuoso specialist
numbs their consciousness

cutting into the chest
exposing the vital organ
totally blind to the truth.

Lord, cramp their fingers
till the arms hang limp like sausage,
grind down to sand

the teeth of the power hungry
and let their selves dissolve into it
like ebbing tide on a junk strewn beach

and when they in profound bitterness
unsheathe the sharpened thought
cut it out of their brain, Love!

make them disappear like snails
slime of their bodies melting away
or like babies, cord cut in abortion

to be thrown out as discharge
eyes withered in the daylight
though they never looked at it.

And let the children of greed like weeds
be pulled from their homes
and their parents blown away like milkweed . . .

The loving man will be revived
by this revenge and step ashore
from the bloodlust of the self-righteous

so that every man can say
there is justice so deep
a loving man has cause to sing.

THE FIFTY-NINTH PSALM

To the chief Musician, Altaschith, Michtam of David; when Saul sent, and they watched the house to kill him.

~ *Mary Sidney Herbert*

Save me from such as me assail:
  Let not my foes,
O God, against my life prevail:
  Save me from those,
Who make a trade of cursed wrong
And, bred in blood, for blood do long.

Of these one sort do seek by slight
  My overthrow:
The stronger part with open might
  Against me go
And yet thou God, my witness be
From all offence my soul is free.

But what if I from fault am free?
  Yet they are bent,
To band and stand against poor me,
  Poor innocent.
Rise God, and see how these things go:
And rescue me from instant woe.

Rise, God of armies, mighty God
   Of Israel
Look on them all who spread abroad
   On earth do dwell
And let thy hand no longer spare
Such as of malice wicked are.

When golden sun in west doth set,
   Returned again,
As hounds that howl their food to get,
   They run amain
The city through from street to street,
With hungry maw some prey to meet.

Night elder grown, their fittest day,
   They babbling prate,
How my lost life extinguish may
   Their deadly hate.
They prate and babble void of fear,
For, tush, say they, who now can hear?

Even thou canst hear, and hearing scorn,
   All that they say;
For them (if not by thee upborne)
   What props do stay?
Then will I, as they wait for me
O God my fortress, wait on thee.

Thou ever me with thy free grace
   Prevented hast:
With thee my prayer shall take place
   Ere from me past,
And I shall see who me do hate
Beyond my wish in woeful state.

For fear my people it forget
   Slay not outright
But scatter them and so them set
   In open sight
That by thy might they may be known,
Disgraced, debased, and overthrown.

No witness of their wickedness
   I need produce
But their own lips, fit to express
   Each vile abuse:
In cursing proud, proud when they lie
O let them dear such pride a-buy.

At length in rage consume them so,
That nought remain:
Let them all being quite forego,
And make it plain,
That God who Jacob's rule upholds,
Rules all, all-bearing earth enfolds.

Now thus they fare: when sun doth set,
Returned again,
As hounds that howl their food to get,
They run amain
The city through from street to street
With hungry maws some prey to meet.

Abroad they range and hunt apace
Now that, now this,
As famine trails a hungry trace;
And though they miss,
Yet will they not to kennel hie,
But all the night at bay do lie.

But I will of thy goodness sing
And of thy might,
When early sun again shall bring
His cheerful light;
For thou my refuge and my fort
In all distress dost me support.

My strength doth of thy strength depend:
To thee I sing
Thou art my fort, me to defend.
My God, my king,
To thee I owe, and thy free grace,
That free I rest in fearless place.

THE SIXTIETH PSALM

To the chief Musician, upon Shushaneduth, Michtam of David, to teach; when he strove with Aramnaharaim and with Aramzobah, when Joab returned, and smote of Edom in the valley of salt twelve thousand.

~ Laurance Wieder

O God, the cup
You pass to us
Is crazed, is cracked.
We drink it up.

God said, On earth
I'll rest my sandal.
Jordan is my
Fingerbowl,
Zion's sky
An empty doorway
To my city.

We said, But dip
And we will sip, Lord.
Always angry?
Always praised.

THE SIXTY-FIRST PSALM

To the chief Musician upon Neginah, A Psalm of David.

Christopher Smart

O God, thy gracious ear apply,
And keep me from despair,
Look down upon my streaming eye,
Give audience to the bursting sigh,
Which interrupts my plaintive prayer.

Where'er on earth I pitch my tent,
I will thy name invoke,
To soothe me when my strength is spent,
And toilsome heaviness has bent
My heart and members to her yoke.

O land me on some rocky shore
Above my helpless height;
Thou art my hope from long before,
The fortress that mine eyes explore,
As spoilers for my shipwreck wait.

I will within thy temple dwell
And there for ever sing;
There likewise all the choir compel,
For mine infirmities are well
Beneath the shadow of thy wing.

For thou, O righteous Lord, hast heard
My soul's supreme desires;
And hast in covenant appeared
To those that have thy name revered,
And act as thy blessed word inspires.

Thou shalt unto thy king extend
The number of his days,
So that his reign shall have no end,
And to his years thou shalt commend
The lot of everlasting praise.

He shall before God's face abide
In sempiternal youth,
O thou whose hosts in heaven reside,
For his reception there provide
Thy loving mercy—and thy truth.

So shall I never cease to bless
The glory of thy name,
To that in penitence confess,
To that in gratitude address,
By goodly pride and honest shame.

THE SIXTY-SECOND PSALM

To the chief Musician, to Jeduthun, A Psalm of David.

Mary Sidney Herbert

Yet shall my soul in silence still
On God, my help, attentive stay:
Yet he my fort, my health, my hill,
Remove I may not, move I may.
How long then shall your fruitless will
An enemy so far from fall,
With weak endeavor strive to kill,
You rotten hedge, you broken wall?

Forsooth, that he no more may rise,
Advanced eft to throne and crown:
To headlong him their thoughts devise,
And, past relief, to tread him down.
Their love is only love of lies:
Their words and deeds dissenting so,
When from their lips most blessing flies,
Then deepest curse in heart doth grow.

Yet shall my soul in silence still
On God, my hope, attentive stay:
Yet he my fort, my health, my hill,
Remove? O no: not move I may.
My God doth me with glory fill,

Not only shield me safe from harm:
To shun distress, to conquer ill,
To him I climb, in him I arm.

O then, on God, our certain stay,
All people in all times rely,
Your hearts before him naked lay:
To Adam's sons 'tis vain to fly,
So vain so false, so frail are they;
Even he that seemeth most of might
With lightness self if him you weigh,
Then lightness self will weigh more light.

In fraud, and force, no trust repose:
Such idle hopes from thoughts expel,
And take good heed, when riches grows
Let not your heart on riches dwell.
All power is God's, his own word shows,
Once said by him, twice heard by me:
Yet from thee, Lord, all mercy flows,
And each man's work is paid by thee.

THE SIXTY-THIRD PSALM

A Psalm of David, when he was in the wilderness of Judah.

~ *P. Hately Waddell*

O God, ye are God o' my ain;
Wi' the glintin I sought yersel:
My saul, it maun win till thee;
My bouk, it clings for yerlane;
In a dry drowthy lan', whar nae watirs be:

Till see ye again i' yer halie howff;
Till leuk on yer might an' yer gloiry syne.
For yer gudeness is mair nor life,
My lips sal gie laud till thee:
Sae blythe maun I bid thee, ay while I live;
My loov's I maun lift till that name o' thine.

As wi' creesh an' wi' talch, sal my saul be sta't;
An' wi' liltin lips sal my mouthe gang free:
Whan I think o' yersel on my bed o' dule;
Whan I wauken at night, I sal mind on thee.
For ye 'been a stoop till mysel;
I' the scaum o' yer wings I sal lilt an' laud.

My saul, it hauds eftir ye close;
  Yer right han', till me it's a gad.
Bot, my life wha wad herry till dead,
  Lat them gang till yirthes laighest line:
Lat them stoit on the nieve o' the swurd;
  An' be glaum for the foxes syne.

Bot the king sal be blythe in God;
  A' that swear by him, fu' blythe sal they be:
Sae the gab sal be steekit for ay,
  O' them wha can yammir a lie.

90

THE SIXTY-FOURTH PSALM

To the chief Musician, A Psalm of David.

Christopher Smart

Hear, O my God, my voice accept
My wailings, and the tears I wept
  In agony of prayer,
Preserve my soul from those that deal
In death, who have not sense to feel,
  Nor pity to forbear.

Prevent me from the secret mines,
And rescue from the dark designs
  Of guilt combined with rage;
From those who rising in a band
To do the work that Satan planned,
  By mutual ties engage.

Their tongues exasperate with spite,
Like falchions whetted for the fight,
  Are eager to defame;
They bend their bows, and strain their strings,
And give their poisoned arrows wings,
  Even bitter words of shame.

That they may from an ambush shoot
At those that yield abundant fruit,
  The godly and the just;
And swift the desperate archers dart
The pointed mischief to the heart
  Of men without mistrust.

To wickedness they plight their troth,
And work each other up to wrath,
  And in their crimes agree;
They privily by stealth convene,
And sneak to lay their snares unseen,
  Blaspheming "who shall see!"

In malice mischief they conceive,
And then to murder and to thieve,
  Their several bands they file;
Each on his fellow's guilt relies,
And all their practices disguise
  In subtlety and guile.

But God, their treason to detect,
Against the traitors shall direct
  His arrows swift as thought;
And terror shall their conscience wound,
And all the schemes that they propound
  Be to confusion brought.

Yea, they their dealings shall impeach
With their own tongues, and make a breach
  Upon the webs they spun;
And they that their event behold,
And those that hear their story told,
  Their deeds shall scorn and shun.

And they that their event behold,
And those that hear their story told
  Shall praise the Lord alone;—
"It is the Lord's resistless power,
That saved us in the dreadful hour,
  The people and the throne."

Inspired with mercies so profuse,
The wise and good shall give a loose
  To transport and delight;
And every man, whose heart is whole
From treason, shall with all his soul
  This song of joy recite.

THE SIXTY-FIFTH PSALM

To the chief Musician, A Psalm and Song of David.

~ *Henry Vaughan*

Sion's true, glorious God! on thee
Praise waits in all humility.
All flesh shall unto thee repair,
To thee, O thou that hearest prayer!
But sinful words and works still spread
And overrun my heart and head;
Transgressions make me foul each day,
O purge them, purge them all away!

Happy is he! whom thou wilt choose
To serve thee in thy blessed house!
Who in thy holy temple dwells,
And filled with joy, thy goodness tells!
King of salvation! by strange things
And terrible, thy justice brings
Man to his duty. Thou alone
Art the world's hope, and but thee, none.
Sailors that float on flowing seas
Stand firm by thee, and have sure peace.
Thou stillst the loud waves, when most wild
And makest the raging people mild.
Thy arm did first the mountains lay
And girds their rocky heads this day.
The most remote, who know not thee,
At thy great works astonished be.

The outgoings of the even and dawn,
In antiphones sing to thy name.
Thou visitst the low earth, and then
Waterst it for the sons of men,
Thy upper river, which abounds
With fertile streams makes rich all grounds,
And by thy mercies still supplied
The sower doth his bread provide.
Thou waterst every ridge of land
And settlest with thy secret hand
The furrows of it; then thy warm
And opening showers (restrained from harm)
Soften the mold, while all unseen
The blade grows up alive and green.
The year is with thy goodness crowned,

And all thy paths drop fatness round,
They drop upon the wilderness,
For thou dost even the deserts bless,
And hills full of springing pride
Wear fresh adornments on each side.
The fruitful flocks fill every dale,
And purling corn doth clothe the vale;
They shout for joy, and jointly sing,
Glory to the eternal king!

THE SIXTY-SIXTH PSALM

To the chief Musician, A Song or Psalm.

~ *Mary Sidney Herbert*

All lands, the limbs of earthy round,
With triumph tunes God's honor sound:
Sing of his name the praiseful glory,
And glorious make his praises' story.
Tell God: O God, what frightful wonder
  Thy works do witness, whose great might
Thy enemies so bringeth under,
  Though frown in heart, they fawn in sight.

All earth, and every land therefore
Sing to this God, this God adore:
All earth, I say, and all earth dwellers,
Be of his worth the singing tellers.
O come, behold, O note beholding,
  What dreadful wonders from him flow:
More height, more weight, more force enfolding,
  Than Adam's earthy brood can show.

The sea up-dried by his hand,
Became a field of dusty sand:
Through Jordan's streams we dryshod waded,
The joy whereof not yet is faded.
His throne of strength unmoved standeth:
  His eye on every coast is cast:
The rebel who against him bandeth
  Of ruin's cup shall quickly taste.

You folk his flock, come then employ
In lauding him your songs of joy
On God, our God, your voices spending,

Still praying, praising, never ending.
For he our life hath us re-given,
Nor would he let our goings slide:
Though for our trial nearly driven,
Yea silver like in furnace tried.

For God thou didst our feet in-net,
And pinching saddles, on us set
Nay (which is worse to be abidden),
Even on our heads a man hath ridden.
He rode us through where fires flashed;
Where swelling streams did rudely roar:
Yet scorched thus, yet we thus washed,
Were set by thee on plenteous shore.

I therefore to thy house will go,
To pay and offer what I owe:
To pay my vows, my lips then vowed
When under grief my body bowed;
To offer whole burnt sacrifices,
The fat of rams with sweet perfume:
Nay goats, nay bulls, of greater sizes,
And greater prices to consume.

O come, all ye that God do fear,
O come, and lend attentive ear;
While by my tongue shall be expressed,
How blessed he my soul hath blessed.
I cried to him, my cry procured
My free discharge from all my bands:
His ear had not my voice endured,
But that my heart unstained stands.

Now as my heart was innocent,
God heard the hearty sighs I spent:
What I to prayers recommended,
Was graciously by him attended.
Praise, praise him then, for what is left me,
But praise to him: who what I prayed
Rejected not, nor hath bereft me
My hopeful help, his mercy's aid.

THE SIXTY-SEVENTH PSALM

To the chief Musician on Neginoth, A Psalm or Song.

John Davies

Show us thy mercy, Lord, and grace divine;
Turn thy bright face, that it on us may shine,
That all the men on earth enlightened so,
Their own salvation, and thy ways may know.
O let thy people praise thy blessed name,
And let all tongues and nations do the same,
And let all mortal men rejoice in this,
That God their judge and just his judgment is.
O let thy people praise thy blessed name,
And let all tongues and nations do the same,
Then shall the earth bring forth a rich increase,
And God shall bless us with a fruitful peace;
Even God shall bless us and his holy fear
Possess the hearts of all men everywhere.

THE SIXTY-EIGHTH PSALM

To the chief Musician, A Psalm or Song of David.

Christopher Smart

Arouse—and let thy foes disperse,
Thou master of the universe,
Arouse thee from on high;
Take up the trumpet and alarm,
And at the terror of thine arm
Let those that hate thee fly.

Like as afflicting smoke's dispelled,
Let them be driven away and quelled,
As wax before the fire,
Let fraud at thine effulgence fail,
And let the multitudes in mail
Before my God retire.

But let the men of righteous seed,
Accepted in their father's deed,
Rejoice before the shrine;
Yea, let them shout till heaven resounds,
There is no need of end or bounds
To joyfulness divine.

Give praise—with songs your praises blend,
And as your thoughts to heaven ascend,
   And leave the world beneath,
Extol his universal name,
Who rides on the celestial flame,
   In Jah, which all things breathe.

The father of the friendless child,
To keep the damsel undefiled,
   And judge the widow's cause,
Is God upon his righteous throne,
Whence he the hands to rapine prone
   O'ersees and overawes.

Thy Lord domestic peace creates,
And those his mercy congregates,
   Who solitary dwell;
The slave delivers from his chain,
But rebels in dry wastes remain,
   And where no waters well.

When thou Jehovah led the way,
Before thy people in array,
   From Egypt's barbarous coast;
Through boundless wilds exposed and parched,
In pillared majesty thou marched
   The captain of the host.

The earth in ecstasy gave place,
With vast vibrations on her base
   The present God she found;
Even Israel's God—the heavens dissolved,
And Sinai's mount in clouds involved,
   Felt all his rocks rebound.

O God, thou badest the heavens dispense
The bread of thy benevolence,
   Down with the daily dew;
And fixed the people of thy power,
Amidst their doubtings by a shower
   Miraculous and new.

Therein thy congregation dwelt,
Even midst the manna, which thou dealt
   So plentiful and pure;
Thy goodness to confirm the weak,
Thy charity to bless and break
   The largess for the poor.

God, in stupendous glory decked,
His gracious covenant direct,
   Came down from heaven to teach;
Great was the trembling and the fear
Of crowds, that rushed that word to hear,
   They were enjoined to preach.

Each talking tyrant at the head
Of thousands and ten thousands fled,
   They fled with all their might;
And all Judea's blooming pride,
The spouse, the damsel and the bride,
   Disposed the spoil at night.

Though ye the bitter bondage wept,
And midst Rhamnesian tripods slept,
   Hereafter is your own;
Ye shall as turtle-doves unfold
The silver plumage winged with gold,
   And make melodious moan.

When kings were scattered for our sake,
And God alarmed his host to take
   His vengeance on the foe;
On Israel's countenance benign
He made his radiant grace to shine
   As bright as Salmon's snow.

Jehovah's hill's a noble heap,
And even as Bashan's spiry steep,
   From which the cedars nod;
And Zion's mount herself sublimes,
And swells her goodly crest and climbs
   To meet descending God.

Ye haughty hills that leap so high,
What is the exertion that ye try?
   This is God's hallowed mount,
On whose blessed top the glories play,
And where the Lord desires to stay
   While we his praise recount.

The chariots of the Lord are made
Of angels in a cavalcade
   Even twenty thousand strong,
Those thousands of the first degree,
O'er Sinai—in the midst is He,
   And bears the pomp along.

God is gone up from whence he rose;
With gifts accepted for his foes,
His loaded altars smoke;
Captivity, from chains reprieved,
Is made his captive, and received
To thy most blessed yoke.

God is our help from every ill,
And gives to every want its fill,
For us and all our race;
By him we're every hour reviewed,
To him the daily prayer's renewed
For daily bread and grace.

God, that great God whom we profess,
Is all-benevolent to bless,
Omnipotent to save;
In God alone is our escape,
From death and all the gulfs that gape,
From terror and the grave.

God shall not send his blessing down
To rest upon the hoary crown
Of those which grace resist;
But shall afflict the heads of all,
That after his repeated call
To penitence, persist.

From Bashan, which they passed of yore,
Said God, I will my tribes restore,
And bring them back again;
Where Abraham worshipped and was blessed,
Of Canaan they shall be possessed,
Emerging from the main.

That thy baptized foot may tread,
Where proud blasphemers laid their head,
By judgments unreclaimed;
And that thy shepherd's dogs may chase
Thy flocks into their pleasant place,
Who made the earth ashamed.

They've seen (their errors to disprove)
My God in blessed procession move,
The pomp of God my king;
Accordant to the train below,
The dances rise, the streamers flow,
And holy flowers they fling.

The goodly show the singers lead,
The minstrels next in place proceed,
With music sweet and loud;
The damsels, that with wild delight
The brisk-resounding timbrels smite,
Are in the mid-most crowd.

O thou Jeshurun, yield thy thanks,
All ages, sexes, tribes and ranks,
In congregated bands;
To God united thanks restore,
Brought from the heart its inmost core,
And with protesting hands.

There Benjamin in triumph goes,
Least, but in love the Lord, of those
That dwell in tents and bowers;
And Judah next to the most high,
With Zebulon and Naphtali
Their princedoms and their powers.

God to the sires of all the tribes
Some great peculiar gift ascribes,
To each his talents told;
The loan with such long-suffering lent,
Do thou establish and augment
Ten thousand thousand fold.

From this thy temple which we lay,
To thee the homage they shall pay,
To thee the praise impute;
Kings shall their annual gifts renew,
And give Melchisedec his due,
The glory and the fruit.

Rebuke the spearmen with thy word,
Those calves and bulls of Bashan's herd,
Which from our ways abhor;
Let them pay toll, and hue the wood,
Which are at enmity with good,
And love the voice of war.

The nobles from the sons of Ham,
Shall bring the bullock and the ram,
Idolatrous no more;
The Morians soon shall offer alms,
And bow their heads, and spread their palms,
God's mercy to implore.

Ye blessed angels of the Lord,
Of nations and of kings the ward,
That further thanks and prayer,
To Jesus Christ your praise resound,
Collected from the regions round
Your tutelary care.

In other days before the seven,
Upon that ante-mundane heaven,
In glorious pomp he rode—
He sends a voice, which voice is might,
In inconceivable delight
The acknowledged word of God.

Ye heroes foremost in the field
That couch the spear, or bear the shield,
Bless God that ye prevail;
His splendor is on Israel's brow,
He stands all-powerful on the prow
Midst all the clouds that sail.

O God, all miracle thou art,
Even thou the God of Israel's heart
Within thy holy shrine,
Thou shalt with strength and power protect,
Thy people in the Lord elect,
Praise, endless praise be thine.

THE SIXTY-NINTH PSALM

To the chief Musician upon Shoshannim, A Psalm of David.

~ *Mary Sidney Herbert*

Troublous seas my soul surround:
Save, O God, my sinking soul,
Sinking, where it feels no ground,
In this gulf, this whirling hole.
Waiting aid, with earnest eyeing,
Calling God with bootless crying:
Dim and dry in me are found
Eye to see, and throat to sound.

Wrongly set to work my woe
Haters have I, more than hairs:
Force in my afflicting foe
Bettering still, in me impairs

Thus to pay, and loss constrained,
What I never ought or gained;
Yet say I: thou God dost know
How my faults and follies go.

Mighty Lord, let not my case
   Blank the rest that hope on thee:
Let not Jacob's God deface
   All his friends in blush of me.
Thine it is, thine only quarrel
Dights me thus in shame's apparel:
Mote, nor spot, nor least disgrace,
But for thee, could taint my face.

To my kin a stranger quite,
   Quite an alien am I grown:
In my very brethren's sight
   Most uncared for, most unknown;
With thy temples zeal out-eaten,
With thy slanders scourges beaten,
While the shot of piercing spite
Bent at thee, on me doth light.

If I weep, and weeping fast,
   If in sackcloth sad I mourn,
In my teeth the first they cast,
   All to jest the last they turn;
Now in streets, with public prating,
Pouring out their inward hating:
Private now at banquets placed,
Singing songs of winy taste.

As for me to thee I pray,
   Lord, in time of grace assigned:
Gracious God, my kindest stay,
   In my aid be truly kind.
Keep me safe unsunk, unmired
Safe from flowing foes retired:
Calm these waves, these waters bay,
Leave me not this whirlpool's prey.

In the goodness of thy grace,
   Lord, make answer to my moan:
Eye my ill, and rue my case,
   In those mercies told by none.
Let not by thy absence languish

Thy true server drowned in anguish.
Haste, and hear, come, come apace,
Free my soul from foemen's chase.

Unto thee what needs be told
  My reproach, my blot, my blame?
Sith both these thou didst behold,
  And canst all my haters name.
While afflicted, while heart-broken,
Waiting yet some friendship's token,
Some I looked would me uphold,
Looked: but found all comfort cold.

Comfort? nay (not seen before)
  Needing food they set me gall:
Vinegar they filled me store,
  When for drink my thirst did call.
O then snare them in their pleasures,
Make them, trapped even in their treasures,
Gladly sad, and richly poor,
Sightless most, yet mightless more.

Down upon them fury rain
  Lighten indignation down:
Turn to waste, and desert plain,
  House and palace, field and town.
Let not one be left abiding
Where such rancor had residing;
Whom thou painest, more they pain:
Hurt by thee, by them is slain.

Causing sin on sin to grow,
  Add still ciphers to their sum.
Righter let them never go,
  Never to thy justice come
But from out the book be crossed,
Where the good men live engrossed:
While my God, me poor and low,
High shall mount from need and woe.

Then by me his name with praise,
  Gladsome praise, shall be upborne
That shall more Jehovah please
  Than the beast with hoof and horn.
With what joy, ye godly grieved
Shall your hearts be then relieved?

When Jehovah takes such ways
Bound to loose, and fallen to raise?

Laud him then O heavenly skies,
   Earth with thine, and seas with yours:
For by him shall Sion rise,
   He shall build up Judah's towers.
There his servants, and their races,
Shall in fee possess the places:
There his name who love and prize,
Stable stay shall eternize.

THE SEVENTIETH PSALM

To the chief Musician, A Psalm of David to bring to remembrance.

~ P. Hately Waddell

O God, till be skowth to me;
Lord, till be stoop to me,
   Haste ye an' gang:
Blate an' be-fule'd be they,
Wha seek the life o' me;
Hame'ard an' gyte gae they,
   Wha wiss me wrang.
Wha cry Ha, ha! till me,
Fee for their scorn o' me,
   Turn'd bak lat them be:
Bot fyke an' be fain in thee,
A' wha spier eftir thee:
An' wha lo'e that health o' thine,
Ay lat them cry fu' fain,
   God be on hie!
Bot puir an' forfairn am I;
O God, make haste to me:
Strenth o' mine, yett o' mine,
   Ye are yerlane;
Lord God Almighty,
   Taigle ye nane!

THE SEVENTY-FIRST PSALM

~ Mary Sidney Herbert

Lord, on thee my trust is grounded:
Leave me not with shame confounded;
But in justice bring me aid.
Let thine ear to me be bended:
Let my life from death defended
Be by thee in safety stayed.

Be my rock, my refuge tower,
Show thy unresisted power,
Working now thy wonted will:
Thou, I say, that never feignest
In thy biddings but remainest
Still my rock, my refuge still.

O my God, my sole help-giver,
From this wicked me deliver,
From this wrongful spiteful man:
In thee trusting, on thee standing,
With my childish understanding,
Nay with life my hopes began.

Since imprisoned in my mother
Thou me freedst, whom have I other
Held my stay, or made my song?
Yea, when all me so misdeemed,
I to most a monster seemed,
Yet in thee my hope was strong.

Yet of thee the thankful story
Filled my mouth, thy gracious glory
Was my ditty long the day.
No not then, now age assaileth,
Courage, verdure, virtue faileth,
Do not leave me cast away.

They by whom my life is hated,
With their spies have now debated,
Of their talk; and lo the sum:
God say they hath him forsaken
Now pursue, he must be taken,
None will to his rescue come.

O my God be not absented:
O my God, now, now, presented

Let in haste thy succors be,
Make them full disgraced, shamed,
All dismighted, all defamed,
Who this ill intend to me.

As for me, resolved to tarry
In my trust, and not to vary:
I will heap thy praise with praise
Still with mouth thy truths recounting,
Still thy aids, though much surmounting
Greatest sum that number lays.

Nay, my God, by thee secured
Where will I not march assured?
But thy truth what will I hold,
Who by thee from infant cradle
Taught still more, as still more able,
Have till now thy wonders told?

Now that age hath me attainted,
Age's snow my head hath painted,
Leave me not, my God, forlorn.
Let me make thy might's relation,
To this coming generation,
To this age as yet unborn.

God, thy justice highest raised,
Thy great works as highly praised:
Who thy peer, O God, doth reign?
Thou into these woes dost drive me:
Thou again shalt hence revive me:
Lift me from this deep again.

Thou shalt make my greatness greater,
Make my good with comfort better,
Thee my lute, my harp shall ring:
Thee my God that never slidest
From thy word but constant bidest,
Jacob's holy heavenly king.

So my lips all joy declaring,
So my soul no honor sparing,
Shall thee sing, by thee secure;
So my tongue all turns, all places,
Tell thy wreaks and their disgraces,
Who this ill to me procure.

THE SEVENTY-SECOND PSALM

A Psalm for Solomon.

~ *Laurance Wieder*

Give this child judgment, and more children
  So that he, and they, can govern
One another, face-to-face, like Moses talking
  To the well-spring wished
That all the offspring might be prophets.
  That mountain shadow
Lengthened in the wilderness. It touched
  Our cities, made the far
Ends of the earth, lands beyond the sea
  Remember what life might be
Like, if wanting didn't make us bow to idols,
  Power, money, safety, famous
For a time, then ground and scattered by a wind.
  If not this one, let someone
Come and lead us to ourselves. We lift our hand
  To fend the needless blow,
Will feed the needy then. We show the blossom,
  Trunk, limb, fruit, sow
Grain, and knead the bread. We think the sunlight
  Gold on the west wall
Is afternoon. Let us know more than can be said.

BOOK THREE

Though, Lord, to Israel

THE SEVENTY-THIRD PSALM

A Psalm of Asaph.

Henry Howard of Surrey

Though, Lord, to Israel thy graces plenteous be:
I mean to such with pure intent as fix their trust in thee;
Yet while the faith did faint that should have been my guide,
Like them that walk in slipper paths my feet began to slide,
While I did grudge at those that glory in their gold,
Whose loathsome pride enjoyeth wealth, in quiet as they would.
To see by course of years what nature doth appear,
The palaces of princely form succeed from heir to heir;
From all such travails free as long to Adam's seed;
Neither withdrawn from wicked works by danger nor by dread
Whereof their scornful pride; and gloried with their eyes,
As garments clothe the naked man, thus are they clad in vice.
Thus as they wish succeeds the mischief that they mean,
Whose glutton cheeks sloth feeds so fat as scant their eyes be seen.
Unto whose cruel power most men for dread are fain
To bend and bow with lofty looks, while they vaunt in their reign
And in their bloody hands, whose cruelty doth frame
The wailful works that scourge the poor without regard of blame.
To tempt the living God they think it no offence,
And pierce the simple with their tongues that can make no defence.
Such proofs before the just, to cause the hearts to waver,
Be set like cups mingled with gall, of bitter taste and savor.
Then say thy foes in scorn, that taste no other food,
But suck the flesh of thy elect and bathe them in their blood:
"Should we believe the Lord doth know and suffer this?
Fooled be he with fables vain that so abused is."
In terror of the just thus reigns iniquity,
Armed with power, laden with gold, and dread for cruelty.
Then vain the war might seem that I by faith maintain
Against the flesh, whose false effects my pure heart would disdain.

For I am scourged still, that no offence have done,
By wrath's children; and from my birth my chastising begun.
When I beheld their pride and slackness of thy hand,
I gan bewail the woeful state wherein thy chosen stand.
And as I sought whereof thy sufferance, Lord, should grow,
I found no wit could pierce so far, thy holy dooms to know,
And that no mysteries nor doubt could be distrust
Till I come to the holy place, the mansion of the just,
Where I shall see what end thy justice shall prepare

For such as build on worldly wealth, and dye their colors fair.
O, how their ground is false and all their building vain!
And they shall fall, their power shall fail that did their pride maintain.
As charged hearts with care, that dream some pleasant turn,
After their sleep find their abuse, and to their plaint return,
So shall their glory fade; thy sword of vengeance shall
Unto their drunken eyes, in blood disclose their errors all.
And when their golden fleece is from their back yshorn,
The spots that underneath were hid, thy chosen sheep shall scorn.
And till that happy day my heart shall swell in care,
My eyes yield tears, my years consume between hope and despair.
Lo, how my sprites are dull, and all thy judgments dark;
No mortal head may scale so high, but wonder at thy work.
Alas, how oft my foes have framed my decay;
But when I stood in dread to drench, thy hands still did me stay.
And in each voyage that I took to conquer sin,
Thou wert my guide, and gave me grace to comfort me therein.
And when my withered skin unto my bones did cleave,
And flesh did waste, thy grace did then my simple sprites relieve.
In other succor then, O Lord, why should I trust,
But only thine, whom I have found in thy behight so just.
And such for dread or gain, as shall thy name refuse,
Shall perish with their golden gods that did their hearts seduce.
Where I, that in thy word have set my trust and joy,
The high reward that longs thereto shall quietly enjoy.
And my unworthy lips, inspired with thy grace,
Shall thus forespeak thy secret works in sight of Adam's race.

THE SEVENTY-FOURTH PSALM

Maschil of Asaph.

~ Laurance Wieder

Why always angry, God? Why smoke against us and inhale
Sacrifices? Zion's rubble. Temple hacked
To splinters, they burn children with their teachers.
No sign, no prophet here to read
A dream or point to ashes traces of some promised justice.
They mock the name that I can't
Speak, and gingerly pluck baubles from the coals.
Destroy them, Lord.
Return us. You once crushed
The seven headed ocean haunting twisted beast Leviathan
And fed his brains as manna cake

To children in the desert. You opened springs from rocks,
You raised silt islands from deep
River beds, and dried them. You set sun and moon, the different
Bodies of the day and night, you
Flickered lightning bugs in summer garden spaces between trees,
Made standing puddles glinting ice.
You taught us, now deliver us
From those who worship templed darkness. Look,
We blush for you, your name,
Though we are poor, and weak, and strangers roar.

THE SEVENTY-FIFTH PSALM

To the chief Musician, Altaschith,
A Psalm or Song of Asaph.

~ Mary Sidney Herbert

Thee, God, O thee, we sing, we celebrate:
Thy acts with wonder who but doth relate?
So kindly nigh thy name our need attendeth.
Sure I, when once the charge I undergo
Of this assembly, will not fail to show
My judgments such, as justest rule commendeth.

The people loose, the land I shaken find:
This will I firmly prop, that straitly bind;
And then denounce my uncontrolled pleasure:
Brag not you braggarts, you your saucy horn
Lift not, lewd mates: no more with heaven's scorn
Dance on in words your old repining measure.

Where sun first shows; or last enshades his light;
Divides the day, or pricks the midst of night;
Seek not the fountain whence preferment springeth.
God's only fixed course that all doth sway,
Limits dishonors night, and honors day,
The king his crown, the slave his fetters bringeth.

A troubled cup is in Jehovah's hand,
Where wine and winy lees compounded stand,
Which frankly filled, as freely he bestoweth;
Yet for their draught ungodly men doth give,
Gives all (not one except) that lewdly live,
Only what from the dregs by wringing floweth.

And I, secure, shall spend my happy times
In my, though lowly, never-dying rhymes,
    Singing with praise the God that Jacob loveth.
My princely care shall crop ill-doers low,
In glory plant, and make with glory grow
    Who right approves, and doth what right approveth.

THE SEVENTY-SIXTH PSALM

To the chief Musician on Neginoth,
A Psalm or Song of Asaph.

~ *Mary Sidney Herbert*

Only to Judah God his will doth signify;
    Only in Jacob is his name notorious;
His restful tent doth only Salem dignify;
    On Sion only stands his dwelling glorious;
Their bow, and shaft, and shield, and sword he shivered,
Drave war from us, and us from war delivered.

Above proud princes, proudest in their thievery,
    Thou art exalted high, and highly glorified:
Their weak attempt, thy valiant delivery,
    Their spoil, thy conquest meet to be historified.
The mighty handless grew as men that slumbered,
For hands grew mightless, sense and life encumbered.

Nay, God, O God, true Jacob's sole devotion,
    Thy check the very cars and horses mortified,
Cast in dull sleep, and quite deprived of motion.
    Most fearful God, O how must he be fortified!
Whose fearless foot to bide thy onset tarrieth,
When once thy wrath displayed ensign carrieth.

From out of heaven thy justice judgment thundered
    When good by thee were saved, and bad were punished,
While earth at heaven with fear and silence wondered.
    Yea, the most rageful in their rage astonished
Fell to praise thee: whom thou, how ever furious
Shall eft restrain, if fury prove injurious.

Then let your vows be paid, your offerings offered
    Unto the Lord, O you of his protection:
Unto the fearful let your gifts be proffered,
    Who loppeth princes' thoughts, prunes their affection,
And so himself most terrible doth verify,
In terrifying kings, that earth do terrify.

THE SEVENTY-SEVENTH PSALM

To the chief Musician, to Jeduthun,
A Psalm of Asaph.

George Sandys

To God I cried. He heard my cries
Again, when plunged in miseries,
Renewed with raised hands and eyes.

My festered wounds ran all the night,
No comfort could my soul invite
To relish long outworn delight.

I called upon the ever-blessed,
And yet my troubles still increased,
Almost to death by sorrow pressed.

Thou keepst my galled eyes awake;
Words fail my grief; sighs only spake,
Which from my panting bosom brake.

Then did my memory unfold
The wonders which thou wroughtst of old,
By our admiring fathers told.

The songs which in the night I sung,
When deeply by affliction stung,
These thoughts thus moved my desperate tongue:

Wilt thou for ever, Lord, forsake?
Nor pity on the afflicted take?
O shall thy mercy never wake?

Wilt thou thy promise falsify?
Must I in thy displeasure die?
Shall grace before thy fury fly?

This said, I thus my passions checked,
His changes on their ends reflect,
To punish and restore the elect.

His great deliverance shall dwell
In my remembrance; I will tell
What in our fathers' days befell.

His counsels from our reach are set,
Hid in his sacred cabinet.
What God like ours, so good, so great?

Who wonders can effect alone
His people's great redemption,
To Jacob's seed, and Joseph's known.

The yielding floods confess thy might,
The deeps were troubled at thy sight,
And seas recoiled in their affright.

The clouds in storms of rain descend,
The air thy hideous fragors rend,
Thy arrows dreadful flames extend.

Thy thunders roaring rake the skies,
Thy fatal lightning swiftly flies,
Earth trembles in her agonies.

Thy ways even through the billows lie,
The floods then left their channels dry,
No mortal can thy steps descry.

Like flocks, through wilderness of sand,
Thou led us to this pleasant land,
By Moses' and by Aaron's hand.

THE SEVENTY-EIGHTH PSALM

Maschil of Asaph.

Laurance Wieder

The past is riddled with old stories
Told by grandparents to children:
Remember how the people came
To be called chosen, and no sooner
Hoped than were forgotten?
God
Reminded Jacob's children's children
Of their nomad fathers' deep confusion:
Who were they? where did they come from?
How sea water stood like dikes
Against the flood of Pharaoh's army,
How day cloud and night fire made a pillar
Signpost where there was no road,
How bare rock spouted rivers through
The wasteland, and how people spoke
Against what saved them, asked for meat
To go with water, asked for bread,
For table service where there was no table.

God heard them, rumbled heaven open,
Tumbled manna from the sky, threw wheat
For angel cake, sent dust storms stocked
With quail dropped around their tents.
They ate what cravings made them. Full,
They pushed back from the table
And complained. God cut them down.

For all this they believed no more
In providence than in their own days:
Water poured on rock at noon.
Seeing shadows overtake them
They remembered what made mountains
Mumble, staggered by the burden
Of just being's vacant lot.
God remembered flesh was made
Of knowing, life a ripple shortly
Smoothed on doldrum waters. If not
Miracles, why not believe
In plagues? Blood clotted Nile
Swarming flies, frogs, fields rattling
Clouds of grasshoppers and locusts,
Hail-beaten grapevines, frost
Nipped sycamores, sheep and cattle
Lightning spitted, epidemic, last
The first-born of all Egypt
Taken on the dark wing as they slept.

God led his children out of bondage,
Through the sea and into emptiness,
Sat them around the holy mountain,
Read them stony laws, shook out
Nations from the skirting lands
Time promised them, and pitched their tents.

Children, grown to be their fathers,
Praised statues, groves in hillside shrines.
A fair breeze folded Jacob's tents
Among their enemies: no ark,
No promise left, the young men burned
Or butchered, virgins taken without
Ceremony, priests erased,
And widows did not mourn at all.

That silence shook the Lord awake, and
David chosen from his pastures toppled

Giant idols with a sling. He built
A court in Zion. People followed him.
He shepherded the children skillfully.

THE SEVENTY-NINTH PSALM

A Psalm of Asaph.

~ Christopher Smart

From afar, O God, the nations
Thy possessions storm and sweep,
Churches now are desolations,
And Jerusalem an heap.

These unformed barbarian forces
Birds with our dead bodies feast,
And thy saints dismembered corses
Give they to each savage beast.

Human blood, like wasted water,
Round about the wall is shed,
And such universal slaughter
Leaves no burial for the dead.

Us of God's own circumcision,
All our adversaries brand;
Scorned we are, the trite derision
Even for outcasts of the land.

Lord, how long shall thy displeasure
Punish our perverted ways;
Fed and fanned beyond all measure
Shall thy jealous fury blaze?

Let the bolts of thy correction
Those who know thee not chastise;
Realms and kings in disaffection
Who thy glorious name despise.

For revengeful and voracious
They have preyed on Jacob's race,
And have laid their hands rapacious
On his goodly dwelling place.

O remember not how grievous
Were thy servants' sins of old,
But in mercy soon relieve us
To such fell destroyers sold.

Help us, O thou blessed redeemer,
For the glory of thy name;
Ward the ruffian, foil the schemer,
And have mercy on our shame.

Wherefore should the heathen scoffer
Say with supercilious brow,
Where is he to whom they offer,
Where is God their helper now?

O let vengeance now be sated,
Let the blood that's shed atone,
And from those who thus have hated
Take away the hearts of stone.

From the dungeon deep resounding
Hear the prisoners as they sigh;
O let grace to power abounding,
Save the poor, condemned to die!

For their words of foul expression,
Which our evil neighbors urge;
Give them grace unto confession,
With thy blood blasphemers purge.

So shall they thou chose to sever
To thyself a special stock,
Yield thee thanks and praise for ever,
Blessed pastor of our flock.

THE EIGHTIETH PSALM

To the chief Musician upon Shoshannim-Eduth,
A Psalm of Asaph.

~ *John Milton*

Thou shepherd that dost Israel keep
Give ear in time of need,
Who leadest like a flock of sheep
Thy loved Joseph's seed,
That sitt'st between the cherubs bright
Between their wings outspread,
Shine forth, and from thy cloud give light,
And on our foes thy dread.
In Ephraim's view and Benjamin's,
And in Manasseh's sight

Awake thy strength, come, and be seen
   To save us by thy might.
Turn us again, thy grace divine
   To us O God vouchsafe;
Cause thou thy face on us to shine,
   And then we shall be safe.
Lord God of hosts, how long wilt thou,
   How long wilt thou declare
Thy smoking wrath and angry brow
   Against thy people's prayer?
Thou feedst them with the bread of tears,
   Their bread with tears they eat,
And makest them largely drink the tears
   Wherewith their cheeks are wet.
A strife thou makest us and a prey
   To every neighbor foe,
Among themselves they laugh, they play,
   And flouts at us they throw.
Return us, and thy grace divine,
   O God of hosts vouchsafe;
Cause thou thy face on us to shine,
   And then we shall be safe.
A vine from Egypt thou hast brought,
   Thy free love made it thine,
And drovest out nations proud and haut
   To plant this lovely vine.
Thou didst prepare for it a place
   And root it deep and fast,
That it began to grow apace
   And filled the land at last.
With her green shade that covered all,
   The hills were overspread,
Her bows as high as cedars tall
   Advanced their lofty head.
Her branches on the western side
   Down to the sea she sent,
And upward to that river wide
   Her other branches went.
Why hast thou laid her hedges low
   And broken down her fence,
That all may pluck her, as they go,
   With rudest violence?
The tusked boar out of the wood
   Upturns it by the roots,

Wild beasts there browse, and make their food
Her grapes and tender shoots.
Return now, God of hosts, look down
From heaven, thy seat divine,
Behold us, but without a frown,
And visit this thy vine.
Visit this vine which thy right hand
Hath set and planted long,
And the young branch, that for thyself
Thou hast made firm and strong.
But now it is consumed with fire
And cut with axes down,
They perish at thy dreadful ire,
At thy rebuke and frown.
Upon the man of thy right hand
Let thy good hand be laid,
Upon the son of man, whom thou
Strong for thyself hast made.
So shall we not go back from thee
To ways of sin and shame,
Quicken us thou, then gladly we
Shall call upon thy name.
Return us, and thy grace divine
Lord God of hosts vouchsafe,
Cause thou thy face on us to shine,
And then we shall be safe.

THE EIGHTY-FIRST PSALM

To the chief Musician upon Gittith,
A Psalm of Asaph.

George Wither

In God our strength, let us rejoice;
To Jacob's God, let us now sing,
And in our psalms, to help the voice,
The timbrel, harp, and psaltery bring.
The moon renewing, trumpets blow,
And when the solemn feastings be:
For Jacob's God, long time ago,
In Israel did this law decree.

This testimony he prepared,
When Joseph came from Egypt land

And lived where he a language heard,
Whose words he did not understand.
From burdens, and the potters task,
Thy hands and shoulders I did free,
I helped, when thou for help didst ask,
  And heard thee from the storm, said he. *Selah.*

Even at the waters of debate
I said (that I might prove thee there)
O Israel mark, what I relate,
And to my words incline thine ear.
Thou shalt no other gods at all,
But me the Lord thy God, receive;
For thee I brought from Egypt's thrall,
  And will thy largest askings give.

But Israel did my words contemn;
Of me, my people would have none:
So, to their pleasures left I them,
Who after their own lusts are gone.
O! had my people me obeyed,
If Israel had my ways pursued,
I on their foes my hand had laid:
  Their haters I had soon subdued.

My foes had then obeyed my power,
And, I had still my folk upheld:
I then had fed with purest flour
  And, with rock-honey, them had filled.

THE EIGHTY-SECOND PSALM

A Psalm of Asaph.

David Rosenberg

My Lord is the judge
at the heart
in the infinite

speaking through time and space
to all gods
he let be

"instead of lips
smoothed by success
and appearances

defend your silent critic
locked in barred categories
his conscience

painfully opened
by vicious systems
release him

let him speak
break the grip
of the prosperous

whose things enclose them
from the lightness of knowledge
the openness of understanding

they build in darkness
burying justice
digging at the foundation

of earth and men
the orbit
of trust"

I was thinking
you too are gods
heads of nations

thoughts of My Lord
but you will disappear
like the spirit you silence

your heads fall
like great nations
in ruins

My Lord, open
their consciousness
to share your judgment

all nations are men
you hear
beyond categories.

THE EIGHTY-THIRD PSALM

A Song or Psalm of Asaph.

~ P. Hately Waddell

O God, be-na whush; be-na quaiet;
  Be-na lown, O God.
For leuk, yer ill-willers wauken a din;
  An' yer haters rax up the head:
Again yer ain folk, they 'taen canny thought;
  An' ettle mischieff on wha lye i' that neuk o' thine.
Quo' they, "Come awa; lat 's sned them by, frae amang the folk;
  That the name o' Isra'l be nae langer in mind!"
For their heart they hae packit thegither;
  Again thee, they hae snedden a tryst:
Edom's howffs an' the Ishma'lites;
  Moab an' the Hagarenes:
Gebal, an' Ammon, an' Amalek;
  Philistins, wi' dwallers in Tyre:
Assyr as weel, was in pack wi' them;
  An' they stoopit the bairns o' Lot. *Selah.*

Bot do ye until them, as till Midian, as till Sisera,
  As till Jabin, awa by the Kison flude:
They war clean done awa at Endor;
  They war dang like dung on the yird.
Mak the best amang them, like Oreb, an' like Zeeb;
  An' like Zebah, an' e'en like Zalmunnah, their foremaist ilk ane.
Wha said, "Lat us glaum for oursels,
  The hirsel an' a' o' God."
My God, mak them a' like a trinnle;
  Like fothir afore the win'.
As low licks up the wood;
  An' a bleeze, as it kennles the hills:
Sae drive ye them wi' yer onding;
  An' wi' yer swirlin blast, gar them cling.
Fill-fu' their faces wi' scorn,
  Or they seek for yer name, O Lord.
Scham'd lat them be, an' lang frightit;
  An' daiver'd, an' whamml'd dune.
Syne sal they ken that yersel, wi' that name o' yer ain,
  Jehovah, are heighest the hail yirth abune!

THE EIGHTY-FOURTH PSALM

To the chief Musician upon Gittith,
A Psalm for the sons of Korah.

Mary Sidney Herbert

How lovely is thy dwelling,
  Great God, to whom all greatness is belonging!
To view thy courts far, far from any telling,
  My soul doth long, and pine with longing.
    Unto the God that liveth
    The God that all life giveth
  My heart and body both aspire,
  Above delight, beyond desire.

Alas! the sparrow knoweth
  The house where free and fearless she resideth:
Directly to the nest the swallow goeth,
  Where with her sons she safe abideth.
    O altars thine, most mighty
    In war, yea most almighty:
  Thy altars, Lord! ah! why should I
  From altars thine, excluded lie?

O happy who remaineth
  Thy household-man, and still thy praise unfoldeth;
O happy who himself on thee sustaineth,
  Who to thy house his journey holdeth!
    Meseems I see them going
    Where mulberries are growing:
  How wells they dig in thirsty plain,
  And cisterns make, for falling rain.

Meseems I see augmented
  Still troop with troop, till all at length discover
Sion, whereto their sight is represented
  The Lord of hosts, the Sion lover.
    O Lord, O God, most mighty
    In war, yea most almighty:
  Hear what I beg, harken I say,
  O Jacob's God, to what I pray.

Thou art the shield us shieldeth:
  Then Lord, behold the face of thine anointed:
One day spent in thy courts more comfort yieldeth,
  Than thousands otherwise appointed.
    I count it clearer pleasure

To spend my age's treasure
Waiting a porter at thy gates,
Than dwell a lord with wicked mates.

Thou art the sun that shineth,
Thou art the buckler, Lord, that us defendeth:
Glory and grace Jehovah's hand assigneth:
And good, without refusal, sendeth
To him who truly treadeth
The path to pureness leadeth.
O Lord of might, thrice blessed he,
Whose confidence is built on thee.

THE EIGHTY-FIFTH PSALM

To the chief Musician,
A Psalm for the sons of Korah.

~ *John Milton*

Thy land to favor graciously
Thou hast not Lord been slack,
Thou hast from hard captivity
Returned Jacob back.
The iniquity thou didst forgive
That wrought thy people woe,
And all their sin that did thee grieve
Hast hid where none shall know.
Thine anger all thou hadst removed,
And calmly didst return
From thy fierce wrath which we had proved
Far worse than fire to burn.
God of our saving health and peace,
Turn us, and us restore,
Thine indignation cause to cease
Toward us, and chide no more.
Wilt thou be angry without end,
Forever angry thus?
Wilt thou thy frowning ire extend
From age to age on us?
Wilt thou not turn and hear our voice
And us again revive,
That so thy people may rejoice
By thee preserved alive.
Cause us to see thy goodness Lord,

To us thy mercy show,
Thy saving health to us afford
And life in us renew.
And now what God the Lord will speak
I will go straight and hear,
For to his people he speaks peace
And to his saints full dear,
To his dear saints he will speak peace,
But let them never more
Return to folly, but surcease
To trespass as before.
Surely to such as do him fear
Salvation is at hand
And glory shall ere long appear
To dwell within our Land.
Mercy and truth that long were missed
Now joyfully are met;
Sweet peace and righteousness have kissed
And hand in hand are set.
Truth from the earth like to a flower
Shall bud and blossom then,
And justice from her heavenly bower
Look down on mortal men.
The Lord will also then bestow
Whatever thing is good;
Our land shall forth in plenty throw
Her fruits to be our food.
Before him righteousness shall go
His royal harbinger,
Then will he come, and not be slow,
His footsteps cannot err.

THE EIGHTY-SIXTH PSALM

A Prayer of David.

Christopher Smart

O Lord, thy supplicant receive
His wishes to obtain,
With favoring ear indulge thy leave
To poverty and pain.

My God for my defence prepare,
For I am sound and pure;

And of thy providential care
I still myself assure.

O Lord, in mercy condescend
My fervent prayer to meet.
For day by day my knees shall bend
While I thy grace entreat.

O Lord, thy servant's soul refresh,
Which heaviness dismays;
For unto thee from out my flesh
That soul by prayer I raise.

For thou, O Lord, art good to all,
And gracious in excess;
And great in mercy at the call
Of such as kneel and bless.

Attend, O Lord, while thus I pray,
And as my voice aspires,
From humbled members hear and weigh
The drift of my desires.

What time adversities deject,
And anguish is severe,
I will mine orisons direct
To thine attentive ear.

Midst angels and the thrones above,
There is no God like thee;
Nor is there any power, but love,
That can such deeds decree.

All nations, whose stupendous sum
Thy word came forth to frame,
O Lord, shall to thine altar come,
And glorify thy name.

For thou art magnitude and might,
All wonders are thine own;
In love, in omnipresent light,
Art very God alone.

Lord, thine instructive grace impart,
That I may keep thy law;
O to thy nature knit my heart,
And to thine honor awe.

O Lord, my God, I will restore
The thanks so justly due;
And from my heart for evermore
The songs of praise renew.

For thy compassion is extreme
My sorrows to dispel,
And thou my spirit shalt redeem
From out the depths of hell.

O God, the proud in armies rise,
And men of guile profound,
Who have not thee before their eyes,
Attempt my soul to wound.

But thou, O Lord our God, art fraught
With clemency divine,
Long-suffering, and surpassing thought
As faithful and benign.

O with thy mercy turn at length,
Nor my petition shun,
And as a servant give me strength,
And bless me as a son.

O show some token of thy grace
My slanderers to refute,
For all my griefs thy words solace,
And my fatigues recruit.

THE EIGHTY-SEVENTH PSALM

A Psalm or Song for the sons of Korah.

~ John Milton

Among the holy mountains high
Is his foundation fast,
There seated in his sanctuary,
His temple there is placed.
Sion's fair gates the Lord loves more
Than all the dwellings fair
Of Jacob's land, though there be store
And all within his care.
City of God, most glorious things
Of thee abroad are spoke;
I mention Egypt, where proud kings

Did our forefathers yoke,
I mention Babel to my friends,
Philistia full of scorn,
And Tyre with Ethiop's utmost ends,
Lo this man there was born:
But twice that praise shall in our ear
Be said of Sion last:
This and this man was born in her,
High God shall fix her fast.
The Lord shall write it in a scroll
That ne'er shall be outworn
When he the nations doth enroll
That this man there was born.
Both they who sing and they who dance
With sacred songs are there,
In thee fresh brooks, and soft streams glance
And all my fountains clear.

THE EIGHTY-EIGHTH PSALM

A Song or Psalm for the sons of Korah, to the chief Musician upon Mahalath Leanoth, Maschil of Heman the Ezrahite.

Henry Howard of Surrey

O Lord, upon whose will dependeth my welfare.
To call upon thy holy name since day nor night I spare,
Grant that the just request of this repentant mind
So pierce thine ears that in thy sight some favor it may find.
My soul is freighted full with grief of follies past;
My restless body doth consume and death approacheth fast;
Like them whose fatal thread thy hand hath cut in twain,
Of whom there is no further bruit, which in their graves remain.
O Lord, thou hast cast me headlong to please my foe,
Into a pit all bottomless, where as I plain my woe
The burden of thy wrath it doth me sore oppress,
And sundry storms thou hast me sent of terror and distress.
The faithful friends are fled and banished from my sight,
And such as I have held full dear have set my friendship light.
My durance doth persuade of freedom such despair
That, by the tears that bane my breast, mine eye sight doth impair.
Yet did I never cease thine aid for to desire,
With humble heart and stretched hands for to appease thy ire.
Wherefore dost thou forbear, in the defence of thine,

To show such tokens of thy power, in sight of Adam's line,
Whereby each feeble heart with faith might so be fed
That in the mouth of thy elect thy mercies might be spread?
The flesh that feedeth worms can not thy love declare,
Nor such set forth thy faith as dwell in the land of despair.
In blind indurate hearts light of thy lively name
Can not appear, as can not judge the brightness of the same.
Nor blasted may thy name be by the mouth of those
Whom death hath shut in silence, so as they may not disclose.
The lively voice of them that in thy word delight
Must be the trump that must resound the glory of thy might.
Wherefore I shall not cease, in chief of my distress,
To call on thee till that the sleep my wearied limbs oppress.
And in the morning eke, when that the sleep is fled,
With floods of salt repentant tears to wash my restless bed.
Within this careful mind, burdened with care and grief,
Why dost thou not appear, O Lord, that shouldst be his relief?
My wretched state behold, whom death shall strait assail;
Of one from youth afflicted still, that never did but wail.
The dread, lo, of thine ire hath trod me under feet;
The scourges of thine angry hand hath made death seem full sweet.
Like to the roaring waves the sunken ship surround,
Great heaps of care did swallow me and I no succor found.
For they whom no mischance could from my love divide
Are forced, for my greater grief, from me their face to hide.

THE EIGHTY-NINTH PSALM

Maschil of Ethan the Ezrahite.

~ Christopher Smart

The loving-kindness of the Lord
Shall grace the sacred page;
His truth the Psalmist shall record
From age to rising age.

For I have said that mercy's reign
Henceforward shall commence;
And fed by faithfulness maintain
Her infinite expense.

I have renewed with mine elect
My covenant of peace,
And sworn to this benign effect
To him that kept the fleece.

Thy house I will for ever build,
And in thy seed descend;
The throne of David shall be filled
And flourish without end.

O Lord, the heavens with sapphire cieled,
And all the lights that blaze,
Their truth affords a beauteous field
For social saints to praise.

For who is he to heaven referred,
Intelligence or form,
That can be named with God the word,
In whom all life is warm?

Or what is he of most account
Amongst the powers below,
That can be likened to the fount
From whence all honors flow?

Amidst the synod of the blessed,
The Lord is greatly feared;
And with incessant prayer addressed
By souls of saints ensphered.

O Lord, incomparable God,
Thy truth around we hail,
From heaven's first convex to the sod
That sheathes the humble vale.

Thou rulest the raging of the sea,
When surges foam and chafe;
Thou biddest contending waves agree,
To send the navy safe.

Thou hast upon the Egyptian land
Thy dreadful vengeance hurled;
And scattered with thy mighty hand
Their host throughout the world.

Thine are the heavens, and bright array
That in succession shine,
The earth, thy firm foundations stay,
And all therein is thine.

Thou hast divided north and south,
Bleak wind and genial flame;
And fragrant Hermon finds a mouth,
And Tabor sings thy name.

Strong is thine arm in deeds of love,
Thy hand of peerless proof;
Thy right hand brandishes above
The heaven's interior roof.

Justice and equity beneath
Thy throne have placed their seat;
But truth and love thy spirit breathe,
And thy bright presence greet.

Blessed is the people, whom the voice
Of conscience calls thine own;
Lord, in thy light they shall rejoice,
And seek towards thy throne.

They in thy name shall take delight,
Each consecrated hour;
And make their boast, as they recite
Thy deeds of righteous power.

Thou art the glory of our strength,
In safeguard or assault;
And in the blessed Lamb at length
Our horn thou shalt exalt.

For God is our redoubted fort,
And our defence sustains,
And o'er each province, coast and port
The Lord Jehovah reigns.

Thy visionary word of late
Thou deignedst to disclose;
A man by grace and nature great
I have prepared and chose.

My servant David have I tried,
And his good deeds allow;
My holy cruse I have applied
To bless his honored brow.

My hand his scepter shall uphold,
And keep him in his seat;
And my right arm shall make him bold
Opposers to defeat.

Invidious foes shall have no force
When he his troops alarms,
The son of fraud shall have recourse
To flight before his arms.

I will his enemies destroy
   Myself before his eyes;
And with my bitterest plagues annoy
   Whoever his worth despise.

My mercy shall be with his sword,
   My truth his acts adorn;
And by his fervent prayer implored,
   I will exalt his horn.

I likewise will advance his realm
   Where distant oceans roll;
And his right hand shall hold the helm
   The billows to control.

He shall invoke my name in prayer,
   And in my service live;
'My God omnipotent to spare,
   My father to forgive.'

And I his pedigree will fix
   Amongst celestial things,
Whose race and rank with angels mix
   Above all earthly kings.

My mercy and mine aid shall be
   For ever on his side;
And by the grant I now decree
   I surely will abide.

Son after son he shall endure,
   His offspring will I raise;
And his succession will secure
   As heavens eternal days,

But if the shoots of such a stem
   My dictate should refuse;
And in their lives that way condemn,
   Which grace to faith foreshows;

If they should break the holy laws
   Which my commandments urge,
I will my zealous angel cause
   Their dire offence to scourge.

But yet I will not wholly take
   My kindness from his seed;
Nor void that blessed promise make
   To which my truth agreed.

I will for my own glory care,
  Nor change the word I past;
Once by my holiness I swore
  That David's house should last.

The line of his descent shall run
  With deathless heroes crowned;
Before my presence, as the sun,
  His throne shall be renowned.

His daughters shall be sweet and fair,
  As is the lunar light;
That faithful type of heavenly care,
  And blessing of the night.

But thou hast with abhorrence spur
  And thine anointed left;
Thy love to indignation turned,
  And of thy grace bereft.

The covenant is of no trust,
  If thus his days he drag;
And o'er his crown, defiled in dust,
  His foes blaspheme and brag.

Around his borders are infringed,
  And all the towers he barred;
The moats filled up, the gates unhinged
  The strong munitions marred.

All those that pass along the road,
  Upon his goods encroach;
And every neighbor comes to goad
  His conscience with reproach.

Thou liftest up the hand that throws
  The spear against his breast;
Thou hast delighted all his foes
  Which his domains infest.

No longer is his weapon edged
  To boast ten thousands slain,
And victory no more is fledged
  For his renowned campaign.

No more his blooming honors glow
  With heavens effulgent beam;
His eminence is levelled low,
  And made of none esteem.

The riper days thou hast cut off
   Of all his better age,
And given his glory to the scoff
   Of obloquy and rage.

For ever, Lord, wilt thou retire
   From my submissive suit,
And shall thine anger burn like fire
   In this my disrepute?

Remember how my time is brief,
   How urgent nature's debt;
Why hast thou fashioned man for grief,
   And unavailing sweat?

What man is he, whose strength or art
   Shall his own spirit save,
Or who, when gasping to depart,
   Can countermine the grave?

Lord, where is thine indulgent oath
   That David should despond,
And thy good truth engaged to both
   His truncheon and his wand?

Remember how thy gallant tribes
   Are with invectives stung,
And how my loathing ear imbibes
   The taunts of many a tongue,

Wherewith thine enemies insult,
   And call our ways perverse;
And o'er thy servants faults exult,
   And their good fame asperse.

Hosanna to the throne of grace—
   Amen from all the throng;
Amen from him that holds his place
   To lead the choir in song.

BOOK FOUR

Our Home, to Whom We Fly

THE NINETIETH PSALM

A Prayer of Moses the man of God.

~ Francis Bacon

O Lord, thou art our home, to whom we fly,
And so hast always been from age to age:
Before the hills did intercept the eye,
Or that the frame was up of earthly stage,
One God thou wert, and art, and still shall be;
The line of time, it doth not measure thee.

Both death and life obey thy holy lore,
And visit in their turns, as they are sent;
A thousand years with thee they are no more
Than yesterday, which, ere it is, is spent:
Or as a watch by night, that course doth keep,
And goes, and comes, unwares to them that sleep.

Thou carriest man away as with a tide:
Then down swim all his thoughts that mounted high;
Much like a mocking dream, that will not bide,
But flies before the sight of waking eye;
Or as the grass, that cannot term obtain
To see the summer come about again.

At morning, fair it musters on the ground;
At even, it is cut down and laid along:
And though it spared were and favor found,
The weather would perform the mower's wrong:
Thus hast thou hanged our life on brittle pins,
To let us know it will not bear our sins.

Thou buriest not within oblivion's tomb
Our trespasses, but enterest them aright;
Even those that are conceived in darkness' womb,
To thee appear as done at broad daylight.
As a tale told, which sometimes men attend,
And sometimes not, our life steals to an end.

The life of man is threescore years and ten,
Or, that if he be strong, perhaps fourscore;
Yet all things are but labor to him then,
New sorrows still come on, pleasures no more.
Why should there be such turmoil and such strife,
To spin in length this feeble line of life?

But who considers duly of thine ire?
Or doth the thoughts thereof wisely embrace?
For thou, O God, art a consuming fire:
Frail man, how can he stand before thy face?
If thy displeasure thou dost not refrain,
A moment brings all back to dust again.

Teach us, O Lord, to number well our days,
Thereby our hearts to wisdom to apply;
For that which guides man best in all his ways,
Is meditation of mortality.
This bubble light, this vapor of our breath,
Teach us to consecrate to hour of death.

Return unto us, Lord, and balance now
With days of joy our days of misery;
Help us right soon, our knees to thee we bow,
Depending wholly on thy clemency;
Then shall thy servants both with heart and voice,
All the days of their life in thee rejoice.

Begin thy work, O Lord, in this our age,
Show it unto thy servants that now live;
But to our children raise it many a stage,
That all the world to thee may glory give.
Our handiwork likewise, as fruitful tree,
Let it, O Lord, blessed, not blasted be.

THE NINETY-FIRST PSALM

~ Thomas Carew

Make the great God thy fort, and dwell
In him by faith, and do not care
(So shaded) for the power of hell
Or for the cunning fowler's snare
Or poison of the infected air.

His plumes shall make a downy bed
Where thou shalt rest, he shall display
His wings of truth over thy head,
Which like a shield shall drive away
The fears of night, the darts of day.

The winged plague that flies by night,
The murdering sword that kills by day,

Shall not thy peaceful sleeps affright
   Though on thy right and left hand they
   A thousand and ten thousand slay.

Yet shall thine eyes behold the fall
   Of sinners, but because thy heart
Dwells with the Lord, not one of all
   Those ills, nor yet the plaguey dart
   Shall dare approach near where thou art.

His angels shall direct thy legs
   And guard them in the stony street;
On lions' whelps, and adders' eggs
   Thy steps shall march, and if thou meet
   With dragons, they shall kiss thy feet.

When thou art troubled, he shall hear
   And help thee, for thy love embraced
And knew his name. Therefore he'll rear
   Thy honors high, and when thou hast
   Enjoyed them long, save thee at last.

THE NINETY-SECOND PSALM

A Psalm or Song for the sabbath day.

Mary Sidney Herbert

O lovely thing
   To sing and praises frame
To thee, O Lord, and thy high name;
         With early spring
   Thy bounty to display,
Thy truth when night hath vanquished day:
         Yea so to sing,
   That ten-stringed instrument
With lute, and harp, and voice consent.

         For, Lord, my mind
   Thy works with wonder fill;
Thy doings are my comfort still.
         What wit can find,
   How bravely thou hast wrought,
Or deeply sound thy shallowest thought?
         The fool is blind,
   And blindly doth not know,
How like the grass the wicked grow.

The wicked grow
Like frail though flowery grass:
And, fallen, to wrack past help do pass.
But thou not so,
But high thou still dost stay:
And lo thy haters fall away.
Thy haters lo,
Decay and perish all;
All wicked hands to ruin fall.

Fresh oiled I
Will lively lift my horn,
And match the matchless unicorn:
Mine eye shall spy
My spies in spiteful case:
Mine ear shall hear my foes' disgrace.
Like cedar high
And like date-bearing tree,
For green, and growth the just shall be.

Where God doth dwell
Shall be his spreading place:
God's courts shall his fair bows embrace.
Even then shall swell
His blossoms fat and fair,
When aged rind the stock shall bear.
And I shall tell
How God my rock is just,
So just, with him is nought unjust.

THE NINETY-THIRD PSALM

~ Mary Sidney Herbert

Clothed in state and girt with might,
Monarch-like Jehovah reigns:
He who earth's foundation pight,
Pight at first, and yet sustains;
He whose stable throne disdains
Motion's shock, and ages' flight:
He who endless one remains,
One, the same, in changeless plight.

Rivers, yea, though rivers roar,
Roaring though sea-billows rise,

Vex the deep, and break the shore:
Stronger art thou, Lord of skies.
Firm and true thy promise lies
Now and still, as heretofore:
Holy worship never dies
In thy house where we adore.

THE NINETY-FOURTH PSALM

George Sandys

Great God of hosts, revenge our wrong
On those who are in mischief strong.
Upon thy foes
Inflict our woes,
For vengeance doth to thee belong.
Judge of the world, prevent
The proud and insolent.

How long shall they the just oppress,
And triumph in their wickedness?
How long supplant?
Ah! how long vaunt,
And glory in their dire success?
Thy saints asunder break,
Insulting o'er the weak!

Who strangers and poor widows kill,
The blood of wretched orphans spill,
And say, "Can he
Or hear or see?
Doth God regard what's good or ill?"
Brute beasts without a mind!
O fools, in knowledge blind!

Shall not the Almighty see and hear,
Who formed the eye, and framed the ear?
Who nations slew
Not punish you?
Who taught, not know? to him appear
Dark counsels, secret fires,
Vain hopes, and vast desires.

But O! thrice blessed he, whom God
Chastiseth with his gentle rod;
Informs, and awes

By sacred laws;
In storms brought to a safe abode;
While the unrighteous shall
By winged vengeance fall.

For he will not forsake the elect,
Nor who adore his name reject;
But judgment then
Shall turn again
To justice, and her throne erect.
Who are in heart upright
Shall follow that clear light.

What mortal will the afflicted aid,
Defend when impious foes invade?
Lord, hadst not thou
My soul ere now
In silent shades of death had laid;
For he my outcries heard,
And from the center reared.

When grief my laboring soul confounds,
Thou pourest balm into her wounds.
Shall tyranny
With thee comply,
Who mischief for a law propounds?
Who swarm to circumvent,
And doom the innocent.

But thou, O Lord, art my defence,
My refuge, and my recompense.
The vicious shall
By vices fall,
By their own sins be swept from hence.
God shall cut off their breath,
And give them up to death.

THE NINETY-FIFTH PSALM

~ John Davies

Come let us heartily rejoice and sing,
To God our mighty saviour and our king;
Present the praise which doth to him belong,
And show our gladness in a cheerful song;
For God our Lord, the greatest God is he,

And monarch of all gods that worshipped be.
The earth's round globe he holdeth in his hand,
And the highest mountains are at his command;
The sea is his, he hath it made of old,
And the dry land his blessed hands did mold.
Come, let us worship then, and humbly fall
Before our mighty God, which made us all.
He is our Lord and we his people be,
Our shepherd and his proper sheep are we:
This day, if you his holy voice will hear,
Let not your hearts be hardened as they were
When in the desert you his wrath did move,
And tempting him, his mighty power did prove.
Full forty years this nation grieved me so;
Their erring hearts my ways would never know:
Therefore displeased, by oath I did protest,
They never should possess my land of rest.

THE NINETY-SIXTH PSALM

Mary Sidney Herbert

Sing and let the song be new,
    Unto him that never endeth:
Sing all earth and all in you.
Sing to God and bless his name;
    Of the help, the health he sendeth,
Day by day new ditties frame.

Make each country know his worth;
    Of his acts the wondered story
Paint unto each people forth.
For Jehovah great alone
    All the gods, for awe and glory,
Far above doth hold his throne.

For but idols what are they,
    Whom besides made earth adoreth?
He the skies in frame did lay:
Grace and honor are his guides
    Majesty his temple storeth:
Might in guard about him bides.

Kindreds come Jehovah give,
    O give Jehovah all together,

Force and fame whereso you live.
Give his name the glory fit:
   Take your offerings get you thither,
Where he doth enshrined sit.

Go adore him in the place
   Where his pomp is most displayed:
Earth, O go with quaking pace,
Go proclaim Jehovah king:
   Stayless world shall now be stayed;
Righteous doom his rule shall bring.

Starry roof, and earthy floor,
   Sea, and all thy wideness yieldeth:
Now rejoice and leap and roar.
Leafy infants of the wood,
   Fields and all that on you feedeth,
Dance O dance, at such a good.

For Jehovah cometh lo!
   Lo, to reign Jehovah cometh:
Under whom you all shall go.
He the world shall rightly guide:
   Truly as a king becometh,
For the people's weal provide.

THE NINETY-SEVENTH PSALM

~ Laurance Wieder

I saw a picture of the earth afloat
In space: a solar marble, cloud
Veins in blue ore, oceans studded
With green islands, continental
Rust, capped, footed by iced poles:
Water swollen mountain glaciers
Melted in the sun's wax candle.
What chains this jewel hung
On vacuum's throat? Who knows
The name, could show a sliver
Of that shattered beaker (left
Behind when all the other shards
Swept back to nothingness) was
Creation's germ, and not be pierced
So deeply no blood flowed? Be glad

We're small, be glad no one can tell
What happens next and no returning.
Only one returns those promises
Substantial as the sands our fathers
Sifted through their fingers
For us, moments when their hearts
Felt easy, and they did not boast.

THE NINETY-EIGHTH PSALM

A Psalm.

~ Mary Sidney Herbert

O sing Jehovah, he hath wonders wrought,
  A song of praise that newness may commend:
His hand, his holy arm alone hath brought
  Conquest on all that durst with him contend.
  He that salvation doth his elect attend,
  Long hid, at length hath set in open view:
And now the unbelieving nations taught
  His heavenly justice, yielding each their due.

His bounty and his truth the motives were,
  Promised of yore to Jacob and his race
Which every margin of this earthy sphere
  Now sees performed in his saving grace.
  Then earth, and all possessing earthy place,
  O sing, O shout, O triumph, O rejoice:
Make lute a part with vocal music bear,
  And entertain this king with trumpets' noise.

Roar, sea, all that trace the briny sands:
  Thou total globe and all that thee enjoy:
You streamy rivers clap your swimming hands:
  You mountains echo each at others joy,
  See on the Lord this service you employ,
  Who comes of earth the crown and rule to take:
And shall with upright justice judge the lands,
  And equal laws among the dwellers make.

THE NINETY-NINTH PSALM

~ Mary Sidney Herbert

What if nations rage and fret?
What if earth do ruin threat?
Lo our state Jehovah guideth,
He that on the cherubs rideth.

Great Jehovah Sion holds,
High above what earth enfolds:
Thence his sacred name with terror,
Forceth truth from tongues of error.

Throned he sits a king of might,
Mighty so, as bent to right:
For how can but be maintained
Right, by him who right ordained?

O then come Jehovah sing:
Sing our God, our Lord our king:
At the footstool set before him,
(He is holy) come, adore him.

Moses erst and Aaron so,
(These did high in priesthood go)
Samuel so unto him crying,
Got their suits without denying.

But from cloudy pillar then
God did deign to talk with men:
He enacting they observing,
From his will there was no swerving.

Then our God Jehovah thou,
Unto them thy ear didst bow:
Gracious still and kindly hearted,
Though for sin they somewhile smarted.

O then come Jehovah sing:
Sing our God, our Lord, our king.
In his Sion mount before him
(He is holy) come, adore him.

THE HUNDREDTH PSALM

A Psalm of praise.

~ Laurance Wieder

It helps to make a lot of noise
When on the earth. We did not,
Were modest, too, until God made us
Enter squally bawling thank-yous
In our lifetime, children's children.

THE HUNDRED-FIRST PSALM

A Psalm of David.

~ David Rosenberg

The city of your love
sings through me
before you, My Lord

you hold my writing hand
that makes my living
creative act

won't you come to me?
I sit here in my house
with an open heart

no willful image
blocks the door,
I just won't see

the theatrics of personality
crowding
the openness you allow

this art that hurts
those with ears for only jewelry
they go far away

locked within themselves
their self-flattery
I've reduced to silence

their narrow eyes
inflated pride
blown away

I'm always looking
for your people
to share this space

the contact of imagination
inspired
by necessity

beyond the stage doors
of weak characters
cut off from real streets

no more precious actors
costumed in sound
to litter this town with cliches

every morning
I silence with your light
desperate images

they run away
from the city of your name
that calls an open heart.

THE HUNDRED-SECOND PSALM

A Prayer of the afflicted, when he is overwhelmed, and poureth out his complaint before the Lord.

~ *Thomas Wyatt*

Lord hear my prayer, and let my cry pass
Unto the Lord without impediment.
Do not from me turn thy merciful face,
Unto myself leaving my government.
In time of trouble and adversity
Incline to me thine ear and thine intent,
And when I call help my necessity;
Readily grant the effect of my desire.
These bold demands do please thy majesty,
And eke my case such haste doth well require:
For like as smoke my days been passed away,
My bones dried up as furnace with the fire,
My heart, my mind is withered up like hay,
Because I have forgot to take my bread,
My bread of life, the word of truth, I say;
And for my plaintful sighs and my dread

My bones, my strength, my very force of mind
Cleaved to the flesh, and from thy sprite were fled,
As desperate thy mercy for to find.
So made I me the solein pelican,
And like the owl that fleeth by proper kind
Light of the day, and hath herself betaken
To ruin life out of all company;
With waker care, that with this woe began,
Like the sparrow was I solitary,
That sits alone under the houses' eaves.
This while my foes conspired continually,
And did provoke the harm of my disease.
Wherefore like ashes my bread did me savor,
Of thy just word the taste might not me please;
Wherefore my drink I tempered with liquor
Of weeping tears, that from mine eyes do rain.
Because I know the wrath of thy furor,
Provoked by right, had of my pride disdain,
For thou didst lift me up to throw me down,
To teach me how to know myself again,
Whereby I knew that helpless I should drown.
My days like shadow decline, and I do dry:
And thee forever eternity doth crown,
World without end doth last thy memory.
For this frailty, that yoketh all mankind,
Thou shalt awake, and rue this misery,
Rue on Sion, Sion that as I find
Is the people that live under thy law:
For now is time, the time at hand assigned,
The time so long that doth thy servants draw
In great desire to see that pleasant day,
Day of redeeming Sion from sin's awe.
For they have ruth to see in such decay,
In dust and stones, this wretched Sion lower.
Then the Gentiles shall dread thy name alway,
All earthly kings thy glory shall honor,
Then, when thy grace thy Sion thus redeemeth,
When thus thou hast declared thy mighty power.
The Lord his servants' wishes so esteemeth
That he him turns unto the poor's request.
To our descent this to be written seemeth,
Of all comforts as consolation best,
And they that then shall be regenerate
Shall praise the Lord therefore, both most and least.

For he hath looked from the height of his estate,
The Lord from heaven in earth hath looked on us,
To hear the moan of them that are algate
In foul bondage, to loose and to discuss
The sons of death out from their deadly bond,
To give thereby occasion gracious
In this Sion his holy name to stand
And in Jerusalem his lauds lasting aye;
When in one church the people of the land
And realms been gathered to serve, to laud, to pray
The Lord alone, so just and merciful.
But to this 'semble running in the way
My strength faileth to reach it at the full.
He hath abridged my days, they may not dure
To see that term, that term so wonderful.
Although I have with hearty will and cure
Prayed to the Lord: Take me not, Lord, away,
In midst of my years, though thine ever sure
Remain eterne, whom time cannot decay.
Thou wroughtst the earth, thy hands the heavens did make;
They shall perish, and thou shalt last alway,
And all things age shall wear and overtake
Like cloth, and thou shalt change them like apparel.
Turn and translate, and they in worth it take.
But thou thyself the self remainest well
That thou wast erst, and shalt thy years extend.
Then since to this there may nothing rebel,
The greatest comfort that I can pretend
Is that the children of thy servants dear,
That in thy word are got, shall without end
Before thy face be stablished all in fere.

THE HUNDRED-THIRD PSALM

A Psalm of David.

~ John Davies

My soul, with all thy powers thy maker praise;
Forget not all his benefits to thee,
Who pardons all thy sins, and doth thee raise
When thou art fallen through any infirmity;
Who doth thee save from mischiefs that would kill thee,
And crowneth thee with mercies ever more;

And with the best of things doth feed and fill thee,
And eagle-like thy youth and strength restore.
When men oppressed do to him appeal,
He righteth every one against his foe:
He unto Moses did his laws reveal,
And unto Jacob's race his works did show.
He is more full of grace than we of sin;
To anger slow, compassionate and kind;
He doth not ever chide, and never linn,
Nor keeps displeasure always in his mind;
Nor after our misdeeds doth he us charge,
Nor takes he of our faults a strict account:
But as the space from earth to heaven is large,
So far his mercy doth our sins surmount.
As east from west is distant far away,
So far doth he from us our sins remove;
As fathers' kindness to their sons bewray,
So God, to them that fear him, shows his love.
For he that made us, and knows all, doth know
The matter whereof man was made of old:
That we were formed here on earth below
Of dust and clay, and of no better mold.
Man's age doth wither as the fading grass,
He flourisheth but as the flower in May,
Which when the south wind over it doth pass,
Is gone, and where it grew no man can say.
But God's sweet kindness ever doth consist,
His truth from age to age continue shall
To them that in his righteous laws persist,
And think upon them to perform them all.
Heaven is God's seat, there doth his glory dwell;
But over all his empire doth extend:
Praise him ye angels which in strength excel,
And his command do evermore attend.
Praise him ye hosts of heaven, which serve him there,
Whose service with his pleasure doth accord;
And praise him all his creatures everywhere,
And thou, my soul, for thy part praise the Lord.

THE HUNDRED-FOURTH PSALM

~ Henry Vaughan

Up, O my soul, and bless the Lord. O God,
My God, how great, how very great art thou!
Honor and majesty have their abode
With thee, and crown thy brow.

Thou clothest thy self with light, as with a robe,
And the high, glorious heavens thy mighty hand
Doth spread like curtains round about this globe
Of air, and sea, and land.

The beams of thy bright chambers thou dost lay
In the deep waters, which no eye can find;
The clouds thy chariots are, and thy pathway
The wings of the swift wind.

In thy celestial, gladsome messages
Dispatched to holy souls, sick with desire
And love of thee, each willing angel is
Thy minister in fire.

Thy arm unmovable forever laid
And founded the firm earth; then with the deep
As with a veil thou hidst it, thy floods played
Above the mountains steep.

At thy rebuke they fled, at the known voice
Of their Lord's thunder they retired apace:
Some up the mountains past by secret ways,
Some downwards to their place.

For thou to them a bound hast set, a bound
Which (though but sand) keeps in and curbs whole seas:
There all their fury, foam and hideous sound
Must languish and decrease.

And as thy care bounds these, so thy rich love
Doth broach the earth, and lesser brooks lets forth,
Which run from hills to valleys, and improve
Their pleasure and their worth.

These to the beasts of every field give drink;
There the wild asses swallow the cool spring:
And birds amongst the branches on their brink
Their dwellings have and sing.

Thou from thy upper springs above, from those
  Chambers of rain, where heaven's large bottles lie,
Dost water the parched hills, whose breaches close
    Healed by the showers from high.

Grass for the cattle, and herbs for man's use
  Thou makest to grow; these (blessed by thee) the earth
Brings forth, with wine, oil, bread: all which infuse
    To man's heart strength and mirth.

Thou givest the trees their greenness, even to those
  Cedars in Lebanon, in whose thick boughs
The birds their nests build; though the stork doth choose
    The fir trees for her house.

To the wild goats the high hills serve for folds,
  The rocks give conies a retiring place:
Above them the cool moon her known course holds
    And the sun runs his race.

The lions' whelps impatient of delay
  Roar in the covert of the woods, and seek
Their meat from thee, who dost appoint the prey
    And feedst them all the week.

This past, the sun shines on the earth, and they
  Retire into their dens; man goes abroad
Unto his work, and at the close of day
    Returns home with his load.

O Lord my God, how many and how rare
  Are thy great works! In wisdom hast thou made
Them all, and this the earth, and every blade
    Of grass, we tread, declare.

So doth the deep and wide sea, wherein are
  Innumerable, creeping things both small
And great: there ships go, and the shipmen's fear
    The comely spacious whale.

These all upon thee wait, that thou mayst feed
  Them in due season: what thou givest, they take;
Thy bounteous open hand helps them at need,
    And plenteous meals they make.

When thou dost hide thy face (thy face which keeps
  All things in being) they consume and mourn:
When thou withdrawst their breath, their vigor sleeps,
    And they to dust return.

Thou sendest thy spirit forth, and they revive,
The frozen earth's dead face thou dost renew.
Thus thou thy glory through the world dost drive,
And to thy works art true.

Thine eyes behold the earth, and the whole stage
Is moved and trembles, the hills melt and smoke
With thy least touch: lightnings and winds that rage
At thy rebuke are broke.

Therefore as long as thou wilt give me breath
I will in songs to thy great name employ
That gift of thine, and to my day of death
Thou shalt be all my joy.

I'll spice my thoughts with thee, and from thy word
Gather true comforts; but the wicked liver
Shall be consumed. O my soul, bless thy Lord!
Yea, bless thou him for ever!

THE HUNDRED-FIFTH PSALM

Christopher Smart

O to the Lord restore your thanks,
Invoke his name in prayer;
And to the people of all ranks
His wondrous works declare.

O let your holy songs ascend
In ecstasy of praise,
And let your conversation tend
His miracles to blaze.

With joy his hallowed name revere,
And let your mirth aspire;
And let their hearts be of good cheer
Which after him enquire.

Seek ye the Lord, and pay your court
For ever to his might;
Your bodies and your souls deport
Toward his heavenly light.

Remember his stupendous hand
The blessings it conferred;
His visitations dreadful grand,
And judgments of his word.

O ye that from his servant rose
The fruit of Abraham's loins;
Ye sons of Jacob, whom he chose,
And from the world disjoins.

He is the Lord our God alone,
And from our faithful tribes
His truth o'er all the world is sown,
And laws which he prescribes.

He has been mindful of the deed
Where love and truth engage;
To bless and raise the patriarch's seed,
Even to the thousandth age.

The grant at first for Abraham made,
Which still his oath confirms,
And then to Isaac was conveyed
Upon as easy terms.

And therewith Jacob in his turn
Was ordered to comply;
A law of infinite concern
And everlasting tie.

Importing "I will give to thee
A land of wine and oil,
And thou shalt peace and plenty see
In Canaan's pleasant soil."

And this high grace he deigned to show
To pilgrims on the road,
When Israel was yet but few,
And of no fixed abode.

What time they with their flocks and kine
Through various nations ranged;
And led by providence divine
So many climes they changed.

No man could hurt their goods or lives
As they their tents removed,
And for the virtue of their wives
He mighty kings reproved.

"Touch not mine elders, on whose head
I've poured my hallowed cruse,
And save my prophets from the dread
Of insult and abuse."

Moreover, he the famine sent,
  Which in their coasts prevailed;
Till all their corn and bread was spent,
  And their provision failed.

But still extremities to stave
  He sped a man before,
In Joseph, who was made a slave
  The plenty to restore.

Whose feet they in the stocks enthralled,
  And to the soul they pierced;
For in the spirit he was galled
  To find himself amerced.

Until his hardship in his youth
  Was weighed, and cause was heard;
And by the Lord's prophetic truth
  His innocence appeared.

His words of peace the king convince—
  Who straight his bounds enlarged,
And Egypt's fierce despotic prince
  His jeopardy discharged.

And as he took him from his ward
  Proceeded to console
By making him a mighty lord
  All Egypt to control.

To teach their princes to conduct
  Themselves by virtue's rule,
And all their senators instruct
  In wisdom's godly school.

And Israel drove his herds and flocks
  Where he was Pharaoh's guest,
And Jacob with his silver locks
  The Egyptian monarch blessed.

And by his grace his people rose
  To be a mighty host;
And they were stronger than their foes
  In their wide-peopled coast.

Whose heart was changed to black deceit
  From friendship and good will;
The men with cruelty to treat,
  And put in chains and kill.

Then Moses his command appoints
  To succor their complaint,
And by the holy ghost anoints
  Great Aaron for his saint.

And these applied his vengeful rod
  Against their hate and guile,
And showed the miracles of God
  In all the coasts of Nile.

He sent the dark till it was felt,
  And grievous was the gloom;
Nor yet their hearts with pity melt,
  But stiffly still presume.

He turned their waters into blood
  As they rebelled the more;
And fishes choked in such a flood
  Were thrown upon the shore.

The pools o'erflowed with frogs unclean
  Which on the land were heaped,
And were in royal chambers seen,
  And on the couches leaped.

He spake—and of a thousand forms
  Came flies of deadly sting,
And filthy lice in swarms on swarms
  On pompous garments cling.

The hail in massy stones he shot
  The trees and herbs to wound;
And 'midst the shower the lightnings hot
  Came flashing to the ground.

He smote their vines and fig-trees void
  Of blossom, leaf, and fruit;
And all their woods and groves destroyed,
  By breaking branch and root.

He spoke—the caterpillars came,
  And locust with his powers,
A numerous troop, to mar and maim
  The tender grass and flowers.

The first-born of the land he smote,
  And caused a general grief,
Their youths of most especial note,
  And of their strength the chief.

He brought them forth with gems and gold,
  And led himself the van;
Nor could they in their tribes behold
  One feeble child or man.

Egypt was glad when all their force
  From their domains decamped,
Such terror added to remorse
  Had their oppressors damped.

A cloud its milder light reflects
  Their route by day to guide;
And fire their nightly march directs
  From heaven itself supplied.

While to his name with cries they sought
  As life had been at stake,
Innumerable quails he brought,
  The bread of heaven he brake.

He called forth water from the veins
  Of marble to their thirst,
So much, that on the desart plains
  A new-formed river burst.

For wherefore? he remembered well
  His covenant of grace,
When faithful Abraham meekly fell
  Before him on his face.

Thus he his people to release
  Kept angels in employ,
And led his heritage in peace,
  His chosen flock with joy.

And he transferred into their hands
  The heathen's vine to dress;
And all their labors and their lands
  To people and possess;

That they might worship him, and serve
  For more abundant cause,
And with fidelity observe
  The dictates of his laws.

THE HUNDRED-SIXTH PSALM

~ George Sandys

With grateful hearts Jehovah's praise resound,
In goodness great, whose mercy hath no bound.
What language can express his mighty deeds,
Or utter his due praise which words exceeds?
Thrice blessed they who his commands observe,
Nor ever from the track of justice swerve.
Great God! O with benevolent aspect
(Even with the love thou bearest to thine elect)
Behold and succor; that my ravished eyes
May see a period of their miseries,
Who thee adore; that I may give a voice
To thy great acts, and in their joy rejoice.
We, as our fathers, have thy grace exiled,
Revolted, and our souls with sin defiled.
They, of thy miracles in Egypt wrought,
So full of fear and wonder, never thought;
Thy mercies, than their hairs in number more;
But murmured on the Erythræan shore.
Yet for his honor saved them from the foe,
That all the world his wondrous power might know.
There the commanded sea asunder rent,
While Israel through his dusty channel went.
Whom he from Pharaoh and his army saves,
The swift-returning floods their fatal graves.

Then they his word believed, and sung his praise;
Yet soon forgot, and wandered from his ways.
Who long for flesh to pamper their excess,
And tempt him in the barren wilderness.
He grants their wish, and, with a flight of fowls,
Sent meagre death into their hungry souls.
They Moses' gentle government oppose,
And envy Aaron whom the Lord had chose.
The yawning earth then in her silent womb
Did Dathan and Abiram's troops entomb.
A swiftly spreading fire among them burns,
And those conspirators to ashes turns.
Yet they, the slaves of sin, in Horeb made
A calf of gold, and to an idol prayed.
The Lord, their glory, thus exchanged they
For the image of a beast that feeds on hay;
For their saviour, all his wonders shown

In Zoan, and the plains by Nile o'erflown;
The wonders acted by his powerful hand,
Where the Red Sea obeyed his stern command.
God had pronounced their ruin: Moses then,
His servant Moses, and the best of men,
Stood in the breach which their rebellions made,
And by his prayer the hand of vengeance stayed.

Yea they this fruitful paradise despised,
Nor his so-oft confirmed promise prized,
But mutinied against their faithful guide,
And basely wished they had in Egypt died.
For this the Lord advanced his dreadful hand,
To overthrow them on the Arabian sand;
To scatter their rebellious seed among
Their foes, exposed to poverty and wrong.
Besides, Baal-Peor they adored, and fed
On sacrifices offered to the dead.
Thus their impieties the Lord incense,
Who smote them with devouring pestilence.
But when with noble anger Phinehas slew
The bold offenders, he his plagues withdrew.
This was reputed for a righteous deed,
Which should forever consecrate his seed.
So they at Meribah his anger moved,
The sacred prophet for their sakes reproved.
Their cries his saint-like sufferance provoke,
Who rashly in his soul's distemper spoke,
Nor ever entered the affected land.
They, still rebellious to divine command,
Preserved those nations by his wrath subdued,
Mixed with the heathen, and their sins pursued;
Their cursed idols serve with rites profane,
(Snares to their soul) and from no crime abstain:

Their sons and virgin-daughters sacrifice
To devils, and look on with tearless eyes;
Defiled the land with innocent blood, which sprung
From their own loins on flaming altars flung.
Unto adulterate deities they prayed,
And worshipped those gods their hands had made.
These crying sins exasperate the Lord,
Who now his own inheritance abhorred:
Given up unto the heathen for a prey;
Slaves to their foes, who hate them most, obey;

Delivered oft, as oft his wrath provoke,
And with increasing sins renew their yoke.
Yet he compassionates their miseries,
And with soft pity hears their mournful cries.
His former promise calls to mind, relents,
And in his mercy of his wrath repents.
In savage hearts unknown compassion bred,
By whom but lately into thralldom led.
Great God of gods, thy votaries protect,
And from among the barbarous recollect!
That we to thee may dedicate our days,
And jointly triumph in thy glorious praise.
Blessed, O for ever blessed, be Israel's king:
All you his people, Hallelujah sing.
Amen, Amen.

BOOK FIVE

Returning to the Promise

THE HUNDRED-SEVENTH PSALM

~ Laurance Wieder

Always returning to the promise, I remember
Some few kept in mind what they had seen
Of parted sea, of wasteland nurture, law.
Wandering the wilderness, they cried out
To God, to their confusion, and were heard.
Their children founded places, and were fed.

So later generations fill their mouths with praises:
Proud minds humbled clang on dentless shells
Of greed, of grief, of gorgeous meditations
In the captive darkness, until, light gone
They thought that death was freedom.

So later generations fill their mouths with praises:
Prisoners of self, good taste, they found no food
To like, and did not eat, and would have died
Had they not eased the grip on their own throats
And let slip bread and water past their lips.

So later generations fill their mouths with praises:
A sailor's business is the ocean. On his watch
He peered into the abyss: wind twisted masts
Like paper, breakers boiled yellow, rigging
Crackled with drowned souls. The compass spun.

So later generations fill their mouths with praises:
It's possible to die from too much skill,
And possible to live not knowing how
The storm blew, how merchant port was found.
It's possible to live and never once be calm.

So later generations fill their mouths with praises:
They sing in public and before their teachers,
How water turned the salt flats into orchards,
How people settled cities, planted vineyards,
Sowed grain in fields, covered grazing lands.

So the story keeps returning, of great armies
Lost in deserts, of the small made splendid
Blessed with family and flocks, of the wicked
Choking on their empty language, hands clapping
Shut the mouth. Some parts return to mind.
A wise one sees things, and may understand them.

THE HUNDRED-EIGHTH PSALM

A Song or Psalm of David.

~ Mary Sidney Herbert

To sing and play my heart is bent,
Is bent God's name to solemnize,
Thy service O my tongue, present:
Arise my lute, my harp arise.
My self will up with dawning skies,
And so in song report thy praise,
No ear but shall conceive my lays
As far as earth extended lies.

For, Lord, the heavens however high,
Are lower far than thy sweet grace:
Thy truth on steadfast wings doth fly,
Aspiring up to cloudy space.
O then thy self in highest place
Above the heavens, Jehovah, show:
And thence on all this earth below
Display the sunbeams of thy face,

To set thy dearly loved free,
To help and hear me when I pray.
Hark, hark, so shall, so shall it be,
Himself doth from his temple say.
Then make we here a merry stay,
And let me part out Sichem's fields:
The land that Succoth's valley yields,
By perch and pole divided lay.

Mine Gilead is, Manasseh mine:
Ephraim's arms shall guard the king:
My law shall Judah right define,
While I my shoe at Edom fling.
Thee, Moab, I will humbled bring
To wash my feet in servile place:
Thou Palestine, my late disgrace,
Triumphed, shalt my triumph sing.

But who shall cause us Edom take,
And enter Edom's strongest town;
Who; but thou God, used to forsake
Our troops, and at our suits to frown?
Then help us ere distressed we drown:

Who trusts in man doth vainly trust.
In only God prevail we must,
He, he, shall tread our haters down.

THE HUNDRED-NINTH PSALM

To the chief Musician, A Psalm of David.

~ Laurance Wieder

A pack of liars, spitting adders, sometime
Friends accused me of my prayers,
Hauled me to court, and thought
Because their purchased justice heard
The case, that I was caught.
Orchestrated charges clamor could not drown
The oath I muttered in God's ear.
God is not deaf to truth, can tell
Good judgment from a smear.
I said: Lord,
Is truth auctioned to the highest
Bidder? Make the devil court's attorney
For this kangaroo judge when he comes
Before you. String his bartered sentences
Through nose-rings. Hale him living
Out of office. Let his life be short,
His widow laugh, then turn a hag,
A char, his orphan children cruise
City streets for bread. Let tax men
Reappraise him, creditors foreclose.
Hold his father's greed against him.
Gratify his mother's lust with strangers,
By an open window in full view of neighbors.
Crush his name to powder, rub away
His chalk. This man brought innocence
To market, has earned hatred.
He wears lies as his robe of justice,
As a tiger skin, so cinch the sash,
Turn blood to water, bone to wax.
Pay back my loveless friends
One hundredfold in coin struck
By themselves, and loaned, and spent.
Not for my sake but because
Your name can slow the reaching

Shadows of an afternoon, make
The full sun halt and blaze for me,
My enemies' near bygone watchword
Hardly worth a taunt.
                    Show your hand,
Lord, make them fear you
    And an old man's verse.

WADDELL
Psalm 110

THE HUNDRED-TENTH PSALM

A Psalm of David.

~ P. Hately Waddell

Quo' the Lord till that Lord o' mine,
    Sit ye on my ain right han';
Till I mak ill-willers o' thine,
    A brod for yer feet till stan':
The rod o' yer might frae Zioun,
    The Lord, he sal rax't himsel;
In midds o' a' yer ill-willers,
    Haud ye the gree fu' snell.
Folk wi' a will, sal be thine,
    I' the day o' yer might an' a';
        Wi' braws sae meet,
        The dewy weet,
        O' yer bairn-time sweet,
    Frae the lap o' the light sal fa'.

The Lord's taen a tryst,
    An' he winna gae frae 't;
Yersel sal be priest
    On Melchizedek's gate, lang eneugh:
The Lord, on yer ain right han',
    Sal ding kings in the day o' his wuth:
He sal redd amang hethen folk;
    Wi' the dead, he sal pang the sheugh:
        He sal clour the crown,
        Owre lan' out o' boun':
        Frae the burn he gaes by,
        He sal drink whan he's dry;
    An' syne rax his head fu' heigh.

THE HUNDRED-ELEVENTH PSALM

~ Mary Sidney Herbert

At home, abroad most willingly I will
Bestow on God my praise's utmost skill:
Chanting his works, works of unmatched might,
Deemed so by them, who in their search delight.
Endless the honor to his power pertains:
From end as far his justice eke remains,
Gracious and good and working wonders so,
His wonders never can forgotten go.
In hungry waste he fed his faithful crew,
Keeping his league, and still in promise true.
Lastly his strength he caused them understand,
Making them lords of all the heathen's land.
Now what could more each promise, doom, decree,
Of him confirm sure, just, unmoved to be!
Preserved his folk, his league eternal framed:
Quake then with fear when holy he is named.
Reverence of him is perfect wisdom's well:
Stand in his law, so understand you well.
The praise of him (though wicked hearts repine)
Unbounded bides, no time can it define.

THE HUNDRED-TWELFTH PSALM

~ George Wither

All they that fear the Lord, attain to bliss;
Because, that such delight God's will to do.
Conferred on them, shall honors be, for this
Deriving to their seed, great blessings too.
Increasing wealth, their houses, full shall fill.
For aye, the just man's righteousness remains.
Great light, on him, in darkness beameth still.
He righteous is, and kind, and mercy deigns.
If need require he lends, and gives besides.
Kept straight are all his ways, by prudent care.
Laid fast his groundworks are; and firm he bides.
Made endless, his memorials (likewise) are.
No fears he feels, though evil news there be.
On God with fixed heart he doth rely:
Puts trust in him; not shrinking, till that he
Quite overthrown doth all his foes espy.

Relief among the poor bestoweth he;
So keeping still his dealings all upright
That, him advanced, ungodly men shall see,
Vex, gnash their teeth, and loose their longings quite.

THE HUNDRED-THIRTEENTH PSALM

~ Thomas Carew

Ye children of the Lord, that wait
Upon his will, sing hymns divine
From henceforth, to time's endless date
To his name praised, from the first shine
Of the early sun, till it decline.

The hosts of heaven or earth have none
May to his height of glory rise:
For who like him hath fixed his throne
So high, yet bends down to the skies
And lower earth his humble eyes?

The poor from loathed dust he draws,
And makes them regal state invest
'Mongst kings, that gives his people laws:
He makes the barren mother rest
Under her roof with children blessed.

THE HUNDRED-FOURTEENTH PSALM

~ Thomas Carew

When the seed of Jacob fled
From the cruel Pharaoh's land,
Judah was in safety led
By the Lord, whose powerful hand
Guided all the Hebrew band.

This the sea saw, and dismayed
Flies, swift Jordan backward makes,
Mountains skipped like rams afraid,
And the lower hillocks shakes
Like a tender lamb that quakes.

What, O sea, hath thee dismayed?
Why did Jordan backwards make?
Mountains, why like rams afraid

Skipped ye, wherefore did ye shake
Hillocks, like the lambs that quake?

Tremble O thou steadfast Earth
At the presence of the Lord
That makes rocks give rivers birth,
And by virtue of whose word
Flints shall flowing springs afford.

THE HUNDRED-FIFTEENTH PSALM

Christopher Smart

Not to ourselves the praise we take,
O Lord, but to thy name
Ascribe for truth and mercy's sake
The merit of the claim.

Why should the heathen, who this hour
Have felt thy chastening rod,
Make impious question of thy power
With "Where is now their God?"

Our God, which has the battle won,
O'er heaven and mortals reigns,
Whatever his wisdom wills is done,
And what is done remains.

The stocks to which the pagan fools
Their sighs and incense waft,
Are gold and silver formed by tools
Of mean mechanic craft.

Their mouths are fashioned, but from thence,
Nor voice nor accent falls;
Their eyes are graved, but have no sense
Of vision in their balls;

Their ears are hollowed, which to hear
No clamor can compel;
The noses of their busts appear
With which they cannot smell.

Their hands are formed, but not to feel
Their feet, but not to move;
Nor through their throats, while madmen kneel,
Comes breath their life to prove.

The stupid maker's like the bust,
   And so are all degrees
Of impious slaves that put their trust,
   And bow to gods like these.

But thou, Jeshurun, in the Lord
   Alone your trust repose:
He is their saving health to ward
   The swords of all their foes.

And you, ye priests of Aaron's stock,
   With faithfulness devout,
Trust in the Lord, he is their rock,
   And unapproached redoubt.

And ye whose heart through fear repents,
   Who meek obeisance yield,
Trust in the Lord—in all events
   He is their help and shield.

The Lord regards us in success,
   And in our day of need;
And Israel's children he shall bless,
   And bless all Aaron's seed.

He blesses all that fear, and thank
   Their saviour for his grace;
As well the men of meaner rank
   As those of wealth and place.

The Lord shall bless you more and more
   In all you take in hand,
And prosper your increase and store
   Your children and your land.

Ye are through grace the Lord's elect,
   And he can keep you free,
Which could the ethereal vault erect
   O'er continent and sea.

The heavens are God's imperial throne
   Beyond all mortal ken;
Earth to be traversed, tilled and sown
   He has bestowed on men.

The barren grave affords no fruit,
   O God, to praise or prayer;
And mirth and melody are mute
   In darkness and despair.

But we with all our zeal and force
Will in thy praises rise,
Praise ye the Lord through nature's course,
And for the immortal prize.

THE HUNDRED-SIXTEENTH PSALM

George Wither

I love the Lord; for he an ear
To my complaints doth give:
And, since he pleaseth me to hear,
I'll seek him whilst I live.
The fears of death enclosed me round;
Hell torments me enthralled.
But still, when pained myself I found,
On God's great name I called.

Preserve my soul, O Lord, I said;
For thou art full of grace.
Just, kind, and every poor man's aid.
My help, when grieved I was.
My soul, to this thy refuge fly,
For God is thy large meed.
From death my soul, from tears mine eye,
From falls my feet he freed.

I shall, with God, enjoy my life
Where living men abide.
This I profess with firm belief
Though I was terrified.
Yea, though in rashness I did say,
That all men liars were;
What for thy gifts I should repay
Now, Lord, my questions are.

Thy cup of saving health I'll take.
Upon thy name I'll call,
And of my vows I'll payment make
Before thy servants all.
Thy faints, their deaths, and sufferings be
Right precious in thine eye.
O Lord, thy servant serving thee,
Thy handmaid's child, am I.

My fetters all thou breakst away,
And I, O Lord, therefore,
The sacrifice of thanks will pay
And thy great name adore.
To thee, O Lord, I'll pay my vows,
Where thy assemblies be:
Even in the courts of God's own house,
Jerusalem, in thee. Hallelujah.

THE HUNDRED-SEVENTEENTH PSALM

Mary Sidney Herbert

Praise him that aye
R emains the same:
A ll tongues display
I ehovah's fame.
S ing all that share
T his earthly ball:
H is mercies are
E xposed to all:
L ike as the word
O nce he doth give,
R olled in record,
D oth time outlive.

THE HUNDRED-EIGHTEENTH PSALM

Laurance Wieder

Thank goodness just one god always returning.
Let children learn to say, "Always returning."
Let those who lead thought say, "Always returning."
Let those who've seen fear say, "Always returning."

I called from my narrow self:
The great expanse answered,
Said: If God is for you, what matter
Who hates you. Far better to trust
Found disorder than tugs
Of war, others: give up
To the sky, not mean men.

Surrounded, I cut off
Their shouts in mid-sentence, shaved

Fringes off whatever small point
They boasted: bee swarms and smoke
    Crackling fired thorns, pinky rings,
Squid-sucker foreskins in heaps on the floor.

    A hip-slapper.
Winners' tents pitch, but the fortunate
Dancer chose pebbles, more killing
Than coping stones dropped from a temple wall.
    Shelter's how things fall out;
    Hope is tomorrow's door.

Happy for good from the name I can't say aloud,
Blue hazes wind through the horns of the altar.
Praise for the ornament, heart plays the instrument:
Thank goodness just one god always returning.

THE HUNDRED-NINETEENTH PSALM

~ Mary Sidney Herbert

A

An undefiled course who leadeth,
And in Jehovah's doctrine treadeth,
    How blessed he!
    How blessed they be
Who still his testimonies keeping,
Do seek him still with hearty seeking!

For whom in walk God's way directeth,
Sure them no sinful blot infecteth
    Of deed or word:
    For thou, O Lord,
Hast to be done thy laws commanded,
Not only to be understanded.

O were my steps so stayed from swerving,
That I me to thy hests observing
    Might wholly give:
    Then would I live
With constant cheer all chances brooking,
To all thy precepts ever looking.

Then would I worship thee sincerely,
When what thy justice bids severely
    Thou shouldst me teach:

I would no breach
Make of thy law to me betaken:
O leave me not in whole forsaken.

B

By what correcting line
May a young man make straight his crooked way
By level of thy lore divine?
Sith then with so good cause
My heart thee seeks, O Lord, I seeking pray
Let me not wander from thy laws.

Thy speeches have I hid
Close locked up in casket of my heart:
Fearing to do what they forbid.
But this cannot suffice
Thou wisest Lord, who ever blessed art,
Yet make me in thy statutes wise.

Then shall my lips declare
The sacred laws that from thy mouth proceed:
And teach all nations what they are;
For what thou dost decree,
To my conceit, far more delight doth breed,
Than worlds of wealth, if worlds might be.

Thy precepts, therefore, I
Will my continual meditation make:
And to thy paths will have good eye;
The orders of thee set
Shall cause me in them greatest pleasure take,
Nor once will I thy words forget.

C

Confer, O Lord
This benefit on me,
That I may live, and keep thy word.
Open mine eyes,
They may the riches see,
Which in thy law enfolded lies.

A pilgrim right
On earth I wandering live,
O bar me not thy statutes' light.
I waste and spill,
While still I longing grieve,
Grieve, longing for thy judgments still.

Thou proud and high
Dost low and lowly make:
Cursed from thy rule who bend awry.
What shame they lay
On me, then from me take:
For I have kept thy will allway.

Let princes talk,
And talk their worst of me:
In thy decrees my thoughts shall walk.
All my delight
Thy witness will shall be:
My counsel to advise me right.

D

Dead as if I were,
My soul to dust doth cleave:
Lord keep thy word, and do not leave
Me here:
But quicken me anew.
When I did confess
My sinful ways to thee,
As then thy ear thou didst to me
Address:
So teach me now, thy statutes true.

Make that I may know
And thoroughly understand
What way to walk thou dost command,
Then show
Will I thy wonders all.
Very woe and grief
My soul do melt and fry;
Revive me Lord, and send me thy
Relief;
And let on me thy comfort fall.

From the liars' trace,
From falsehood's wreathed way,
O save me Lord, and grant I may
Embrace
The law thou dost commend.
For the path aye right,
Where truth unfeigned goes,
My tongue to tread hath gladly chose:
My sight
Thy judgments doth, as guides, attend.

Since therefore, O Lord,
Still did I, still I do
So nearly, dearly cleave unto
Thy word:
All shame from me avert.
Then lo, lo then I
Will tread, yea running tread
The trace which thy commandments lead:
When thy
Free grace hath fully freed my heart.

E

Explain, O Lord, the way to me,
That thy divine edicts enfold:
And I to end will run it right.
O make my blinded eyes to see,
And I thy law will hold: yea hold
Thy law with all my heart's delight.

O be my guide, O guide me so,
I thy commandments' path may pace:
Wherein to walk my heart is fain.
O bend it then to things that show
True witness of thy might and grace,
And not to hungry thirst of gain.

Avert mine eye, it may not view
Of vanity the falsed face:
And strength my treadings in thy trade.
Let doings prove thy sayings true
To him that holds thy servant's place,
And thee his awe, his fear hath made.

Thou then my fear, remove the fear
Of coming blame from careful me,
For gracious are thy judgments still:
Behold, to me thy precepts dear,
Most dear, and most delightful be:
O let thy justice aid my will.

F

Frankly pour O Lord on me
Saving grace to set me free:
That, supported, I may see
Promise truly kept by thee.

That to them who me defame,
Roundly I may answer frame:
Who because thy word and name
Are my trust, thus seek my shame.

Thy true word O do not make
Utterly my mouth forsake:
Since I thus still waiting wake,
When thou wilt just vengeance take.

Then lo I thy doctrine pure,
Sure I hold, will hold more sure:
Nought from it shall me allure,
All the time my time shall dure.

Then as brought to widest way
From restraint of straitest stay,
All their thinking night and day:
On thy law my thoughts shall lay.

Yea then unto any king
Witness will I any thing,
That from thee can witness bring:
In my face no blush shall spring.

Then will I set forth to sight
With what pleasure, what delight,
I embrace thy precepts right,
Whereunto all love I plight.

Then will I, with either hand
Clasp the rules of thy command:
There my study still shall stand,
Striving them to understand.

G

Grave deeply in remembering mind
   My trust, thy promise true:
This only joy in grief I find,
   Thy words my life renew.
Though proudly scorned, yet from thy lore
   I no way have declined:
I hold for comfort what of yore
   Thy dooms, O Lord, defined.

I quake to view how people vile,
   Do from thy doctrine swerve:

Thy just edicts even in exile
   Did me for music serve.
I keep thy learning and in night
   Record Jehovah's style:
Observing still thy precepts right,
   Lo this I have the while.

H

High Jehovah once I say,
   For my choice and lot I take,
I will sure his words obey.
   Hot and hearty suit I make,
Praying thus even to thy face:
   Pity me for thy word's sake.
Every path, and every pace
   Taught by thee, observing well,
To thy rule I frame my race.
   Lest upon delays I dwell
But to keep, contend with speed
   What to me thy precepts tell.
By lewd robbers brought to need,
   From my losses, of thy laws
Never did neglect proceed.
   Midnights watch thy praises cause,
While that me from bed and rest
   Thought of thy just judgments draws.
Fellowship and friendship's hest,
   With thy fearers all I hold,
Such as hold thy biddings best.
   Lord the earth can scarce enfold,
What thou dost benignly give:
   Let me then by thee be told
In thy learning how to live.

I

In all kindness, thou, O Lord,
Hast to me performed thy word:
   This now resteth that I learn
From thy skill a skillful taste,
   Good from evil to discern,
On thy laws whose trust is placed.

Yet unhumbled I did stray:
Now I will thy words obey.
   Thou that art so highly good

Nothing can thy goodness reach,
 Thou where floweth bounties flood
Willing me thy statutes teach.

What if proud men on me lie?
I will on thy laws rely.
 Wallow they in their delights,
Fat in body, fat in mind:
 I the pleasures of my sprites
Will unto thy doctrine bind.

Now I find the good of woe,
How thy hests it makes me know:
 Of whose mouth the lectures true,
Are alone all wealth to me:
 Millions then, and mines adieu,
Gold and silver dross you be.

K

Knit and conformed by thy hand
 Hath been every part of me:
Then make me well to understand,
Conceiving all thou dost command:
 That when me thy fearers see,
 They for me may justly joy:
 Seeing what I looked from thee
 In thy word I now enjoy.

O Lord, thy judgments just I know;
 When thy scourges scourged me,
Thou, in that doing, nought didst show
That might thy promise overthrow.
 Let me then thy comfort see
 Kindly sent as thou hast said:
 Bring thy mercies life from thee:
 On thy laws my joys are laid.

Let blame and shame the proud betide
 Falsely who subverted me:
Whose meditations shall not slide,
But fast in thy commandments bide.
 So shall I thy fearers see
 On my part who know thy will:
 While I purely worship thee,
 Blot nor blush my face shall fill.

L

Looking and longing for deliverance
Upon thy promise, mightless is my mind,
Sightless mine eyes, which often I advance
Unto thy word,
Thus praying: when, O Lord,
When will it be I shall thy comfort find?

I like a smoked bottle am become:
And yet the wine of thy commandments hold.
Aye me! when shall I see the total sum
Of all my woes?
When wilt thou on my foes
Make wronged me thy just revenge behold?

Their pride hath digged pits me to ensnare,
Which with thy teachings, how doth it agree?
True or more truly, truth thy precepts are:
By falsehood they
Would make of me their prey:
Let truth, O Lord, from falsehood rescue me.

Nigh quite consumed by them on earth I lie:
Yet from thy statutes never did I swerve.
Lord, of thy goodness quicken me, and I
Will still pursue
Thy testimonies true,
And all the biddings of thy lips observe.

M

Most plainly, Lord, the frame of sky
Doth show thy word decayeth never;
And constant stay of earth descry
Thy word, that stayed it, stayeth ever.
For by thy laws they hold their standings,
Yea all things do thy service try:
But that I joyed in thy commandings,
I had myself been sure to die.

Thy word that hath revived me
I will retain, forgetting never:
Let me, thine own, be saved by thee
Whose statutes are my studies ever.
I mark thy will the while their standings
The wicked take, my bane to be:
For I no close of thy commandings,
Of best things else, an end, I see.

N

Nought can enough declare
How I thy learning love:
Whereon all day my meditation lies;
By whose edicts I prove
Far than my foes more wise,
For they a wisdom never-failing are.

My teachers all of old
May now come learn of me,
Whose studies tend but to thy witnessed will:
Nay who most aged be,
Thought therefore most of skill,
In skill I pass, for I thy precepts hold.

I did refrain my feet
From every wicked way,
That they might firmly in thy statutes stand.
Nor ever did I stray
From what thy laws command,
For I of thee have learned what is meet.

How pleasing to my taste!
How sweet thy speeches be!
No touch of honey so affects my tongue.
From whose edicts in me
Hath such true wisdom sprung,
That all false ways quite out of love I cast.

O

O what a lantern, what a lamp of light
Is thy pure word to me!
To clear my paths, and guide my goings right.
I swear and swear again,
I of the statutes will observer be,
Thou justly dost ordain.

The heavy weights of grief oppress me sore:
Lord, raise me by thy word,
As thou to me didst promise heretofore.
And this unforced praise,
I for an offering bring, accept O Lord,
And show to me thy ways.

What if my life lie naked in my hand,
To every chance exposed!
Should I forget what thou dost me command?

No, no, I will not stray
From thy edicts though round about enclosed
With snares the wicked lay.

Thy testimonies, as mine heritage,
I have retained still:
And unto them my heart's delight engage;
My heart which still doth bend,
And only bend, to do what thou dost will,
And do it, to the end.

P

People that inconstant be,
Constant hatred have from me:
But thy doctrine changeless ever
Holds my love that changeth never.
For thou, the closet where I hide
The shield whereby I safe abide:
My confidence expects thy promise just.
Hence, away you cursed crew,
Get you gone, that rid from you
I at better ease and leisure,
May perform my God's good pleasure:
O Lord, as thou thy word didst give,
Sustain me so that I may live,
Nor make me blush, as frustrate of my trust.

Be my pillar, be my stay,
Safe then I shall swerve no way:
All my wit and understanding
Shall then work on thy commanding,
For under foot thou treadst them all,
Who swerving from thy precepts fall:
And vainly in their guile and treason trust.
Yea the wicked sort by thee
All as dross abjected be:
Therefore what thy proof approveth,
That my love entirely loveth.
And such regard of thee I make,
For fear of thee my flesh doth quake:
And of thy laws, thy laws severely just.

Q

Quit and clear from doing wrong,
O let me not betrayed be
Unto them, who ever strong

Do wrongly seek to ruin me.
Nay, my Lord,
Bail thy servant on thy word:
And let not these that soar too high
By my low stoop yet higher fly.

Eye doth fail while I not fail
With eye thy safety to pursue:
Looking when will once prevail,
And take effect, thy promise true.
All I crave,
I at mercy's hand would have:
And from thy wisdom, which I pray
May cause me know thy law and way.

Since thy servant still I stay,
My understanding, Lord, enlight:
So enlight it that I may
Thy ordinances know aright.
Now, O now
Time requires, O Lord, that thou
Thy law's defence shouldst undertake:
For now thy law they sorely shake.

Hope whereof makes that more dear
I thy edicts and statutes hold,
Than if gold to me they were,
Yea than they were the purest gold;
Makes that right
Are thy precepts in my sight:
Makes that I hate each lying way,
That from their truth, may cause me stray.

R

Right wonderful thy testimonies be;
My heart to keep them I, therefore, bend.
Their very threshold gives men light,
And gives men sight,
That light to see:
Yea even to babes doth understanding lend.

Opening my mouth: I drank a greedy draught,
And did on them my whole pleasure place.
Look then, O Lord, and pity me
As erst I see
Ordained and taught
By thee, for them whose hearts thy name embrace.

Of all my goings make thy word the guide,
Nor let injustice upon me reign:
From them that false accusers be
Lord, set me free:
So never slide
Shall I from what thy statutes do ordain.

Shine on thy servant with thy face's beams,
And thoroughly me thy commandments teach;
From fountains of whose watery eyes
Do welling rise
Of tears huge streams,
Viewing each where thy doctrines daily breach.

S

Sure, Lord, thy self art just,
Thy laws as rightful be:
What rightly bid thou dost,
Is firmly bound by thee.
I flame with zeal to see
My foes thy word forget:
Pure words, whereon by me
A servant's love is set.

Though bare, and though debased
I yet thy rules retain:
Whose dooms do endless last,
And doctrine true remain.
In pleasure, and in pain
My joys thy precepts give:
No date thy judgments deign;
O make me wise to live.

T

To thee my hearty plaint I send,
Lord turn thine ear
My plaint to hear,
For to thy law my life I bend
Since I have invoked thee;
Let me, Lord, thy succor see:
And what thy ordinances will
I will persist observing still.

My cry more early than the day
Doth daily rise:
Because mine eyes

Upon thy promise waiting stay;
  Eyes, I say, which still prevent
  Watches best to watching bent:
Esteeming it but pleasing pains
To muse on that thy word contains.

O in thy mercy hear my voice,
  And as thy laws
  Afford the cause
So make me, Lord, revived rejoice.
  Lord, thou seest the graceless crew
  Press me near, who me pursue.
As for the doctrine of thy law
They far from it themselves withdraw.

That Lord, thou seest, and this I see:
  Thou every where
  To me art near,
For true, nay, truth thy precepts be.
  Now, though not now first, I know,
  For I knew it long ago:
That firmly founded once by thee
Thy ordinance no end can see.

V

  View how I am distressed,
  And let me be released:
For look what me thy word hath bidden
Out of my mind hath never slidden.

  Then be my cause's deemer:
  Be thou my soul's redeemer:
And as good hope thy word doth give me,
Let with good help thy work relieve me.

  Where wickedness is loved,
  There health is far removed.
For since thy sole edicts contain it,
Who search not them, how can they gain it?

  Thy mercies are so many,
  Their number is not any:
Then as thou usest, Lord, to use me,
Revive me now, and not refuse me.

  Exceeding is their number
  That me pursue and cumber:

Yet what thy witness hath defined,
From that my steps have not declined.

I saw, and grieved seeing
Their ways, who wayward being,
With guileful stubbornness withstanded
What by thy speeches was commanded.

Since therefore plain is proved
That I thy laws have loved:
Look Lord, and here thy bounty showing
Restore my life now feeble growing.

This in thy doctrine reigneth
It nought but truth containeth:
This in thy justice brightly shineth,
Thy just edicts no date defineth.

W

Wronged I was by men of might,
Hotly chased and hard assailed:
Little they my heart to fright,
But, O much, thy words prevailed:
Words to me of more delight,
Than rich booty won by fight.

Fraud do I with hate detest,
But with love embrace thy learnings,
Seven times daily ere I rest,
Sing thy dooms and right discernings.
Whom who love, with peace are blessed,
Plenteous peace without unrest.

Doing what thy precepts will
I thy help have long expected:
My soul by thy doctrine still,
Loved most, is most directed.
Thy edicts my deeds fulfill
Who surveyst my good and ill.

Y

Yield me this favor, Lord,
My plaint may press into thy sight,
And make me understand aright
According to thy word.

Admit to sight I say
The prayer that to thee I send,

And unto me thy help extend,
Who on thy promise stay.

Then from my lips shall flow
A holy hymn of praise to thee:
When I, thy scholar, taught shall be
By thee thy laws to know.

Then shall my tongue declare
And teach again what thou hast taught:
All whose decrees to trial brought
Most just, nay justice are.

O then reach out thy hand,
And yield me aid I justly crave,
Since all things I forsaken have,
And chosen thy command.

I look, I long, O Lord,
To see at length thy saving grace:
And only do my gladness place,
In thy glad-making word.

I know my soul shall live,
And, living, thee due honor yield:
I know thy law shall be my shield,
And me all succor give.

As sheep from shepherd gone
So wander I: O seek thy sheep,
Who so in mind thy precepts keep,
That I forget not one.

THE HUNDRED-TWENTIETH PSALM

A Song of Degrees.

~ *Laurance Wieder*

I called out to the one and he heard me say,
Save me from the plausible liars.
What can be said to a twister of truth, someone
Who preys upon trust, who mints coin from desire?
Bludgeon the bastards with bricks and bats, fire
Them, forbid them to sit on a bench in the sun.
No matter what I say, they contradict it. I say,
Peace, my soul wants peace. But they say, War.

THE HUNDRED-TWENTY-FIRST PSALM

A Song of Degrees.

~ Henry Vaughan

Up to those bright, and gladsome hills
Whence flows my weal, and mirth,
I look, and sigh for him, who fills
(Unseen) both heaven and earth.

The glorious God is my sole stay,
He is my sun, and shade,
The cold by night, the heat by day,
Neither shall me invade.

He keeps me from the spite of foes,
Doth all their plots control,
And is a shield (not reckoning those)
Unto my very soul.

Whether abroad, amidst the crowd,
Or else within my door,
He is my pillar and my cloud,
Now, and for evermore.

THE HUNDRED-TWENTY-SECOND PSALM

A Song of Degrees.

~ Mary Sidney Herbert

O fame most joyful! O joy most lovely delightful!
Lo, I do hear God's temple, as erst, so again be frequented,
And we within thy porches again glad-wonted abiding,
Lovely Salem shall find: thou city rebuilt as a city,
Late dispersed, but now united in absolute order.
Now there shall be the place for God's holy people appointed
First to behold his pledge, then sing almighty Jehovah.
Now there shall be the seat, where not to be justiced only
All shall freely resort whom strife, hate, injury vexeth:
But where David's house and offspring, heavenly beloved,
Shall both judges sit and reign kings throned in honor.
Pray then peace to Salem: to her friends all happy proceeding,
Wish to her walls all rest, to her forts all blessed abundance.
This with cause I do pray, since from these blisses a blessing
My brother and kinsman, my friend and country deriveth;
This I do wish and more, if more good rest to be wished,
Since our God here builds him an house, almighty Jehovah.

THE HUNDRED-TWENTY-THIRD PSALM

A Song of Degrees.

Christopher Smart

To thee from thy temple I lift up mine eyes,
And breathe from my heart-strings the passionate sighs,
O thou that with goodness and glory replete,
Hast fixed in the holiest of holies thy seat!

The looks of a servant his master revere,
The damsel her mistress with meekness and fear,
Thus elder and matron, and all our whole race
Attend at thy footstool for strength and for grace.

O Lord, let thine angel of comfort descend,
With blessed compassion our woes to befriend,
For in this dejection and wretched estate
They make us their object of scorn and of hate.

Our souls are disgusted and loaded with care,
Whilst hardly the taunts of the wealthy we bear,
And stand all abashed at the spiteful disdain
We daily receive from the pompous and vain.

THE HUNDRED-TWENTY-FOURTH PSALM

A Song of Degrees.

Miles Coverdale

Except the Lord had been with us—
Now may Israel say boldly—
Except the Lord had been with us,
When men rose up against us fiercely,
    They had devoured us quick doubtless,
    And had overwon us comfortless,
They were so wroth at us truly.

The waves of waters had wrapped us in;
Our soul had gone under the flood;
The deep waters of these proud men
Had run our souls over where they stood.
    The Lord be praised every hour,
    That would not suffer them us to devour,
Nor in their teeth to suck our blood!

Our soul is delivered from their power,
They can not have that they have sought.

As the bird from the snare of the fowler,
So are we from their dangers brought.
   The snare is broken, and we are free;
   Our help is in the Lord's name truly,
Which hath made heaven and earth of nought.

THE HUNDRED-TWENTY-FIFTH PSALM

A Song of Degrees.

George Wither

Mount Sion-like, forever fixed are those
Whose hopeful trust upon the Lord is founded,
For he his faithful people will enclose
(Even as with hills Jerusalem is rounded)
   As long as time's perpetual motion goes.
The rod of wicked men shall not alight
Where God the lot of righteousness bestoweth,
Lest righteous men partake in evil might.
For, to the good, the Lord his mercy showeth
   And favors all that are in heart upright.
But sliders-back, and such as wander wide
In their own crooked paths and ways uneven,
Shall by the Lord be thither led aside,
Where portions due to hypocrites are given:
   But Israel shall in endless peace abide.

THE HUNDRED-TWENTY-SIXTH PSALM

A Song of Degrees.

Francis Bacon

When God returned us graciously
   Unto our native land,
We seemed as in a dream to be,
   And in a maze to stand.

The heathen likewise they could say,
   The God that these men serve
Hath done great things for them this day,
   Their nation to preserve.

'Tis true; God hath poured out his grace
   On us abundantly,
For which we yield him psalms and praise,
   And thanks with jubilee.

O Lord, turn our captivity
As winds that blow at south
Do pour the tides with violence
Back to the river's mouth.

Who sows in tears shall reap in joy,
The Lord doth so ordain;
So that his seed be pure and good,
His harvest shall be gain.

THE HUNDRED-TWENTY-SEVENTH PSALM

A Song of degrees for Solomon.

Christopher Smart

If the work be not direct,
And the Lord the fabric build,
All the plans that men project
Are but labor idly spilled.

If the Lord be not the guard,
And the forts and towers sustain,
All the city gates are barred,
And the watchman wakes in vain.

Vainly for the bread of care
Late and early hours ye keep,
For 'tis thus by fervent prayer
That he lays the blessed asleep.

Lo! thy children are not thine,
Nor the fruits of female love,
But an heritage divine,
And a blessing from above.

Like as arrows in the grasp
Of a valiant man of might,
Are the children that you clasp
In some future hour of fight.

Blessed! who in his quiver stows
Darts like these, a goodly freight,
Nor shall blush when with his foes
He shall parley in the gate.

THE HUNDRED-TWENTY-EIGHTH PSALM

A Song of Degrees.

~ Miles Coverdale

Blessed are all they that fear the Lord and walk in his ways.
For thou shalt eat the labors of thine hands.
O well is thee, and happy shalt thou be.
Thy wife shall be as the fruit full vine upon the walls of thine house.
Thy children like the olive branches round about thy table.
Lo, thus shall the man be blessed that feareth the Lord.
The Lord from out of you shall so bless thee, that thou shalt see Jerusalem in prosperity all thy life long.
Yea, that thou shalt see thy children's children, and peace upon Israel.

THE HUNDRED-TWENTY-NINTH PSALM

A Song of Degrees.

~ Mary Sidney Herbert

Oft and ever from my youth,
So now, Israel may say:
Israel may say for truth,
Oft and ever my decay
From my youth their force hath sought:
Yet effect it never wrought.

Unto them my back did yield
Place and pain (O height of woe)
Where as in a plowed field,
Long and deep did furrows go.
But O just Jehovah, who
Hast their plow-ropes cut in two!

Tell me you that Sion hate,
What you think shall be your end?
Terror shall your minds amate:
Blush and shame your faces shend.
Mark the wheat on house's top:
Such your harvest, such your crop.

Wither shall you where you stand;
Gathered? no: but, wanting sap,
Filling neither reaper's hand,
Nor the binder's inbowed lap.
Nay who you shall reap or bind
Common kindness shall not find.

Such as travail by the way,
    Where as they their pains employ,
Shall not once saluting say,
    God speed friends, God give you joy:
He in whom all blessing reigns,
Bless your selves, and bless your pains.

THE HUNDRED-THIRTIETH PSALM

A Song of Degrees.

~ Thomas Wyatt

From depth of sin, and from a deep despair,
    From depth of death, from depth of heart's sorrow,
    From this deep cave, of darkness deep repair,
Thee have I called, O Lord, to be my borrow;
    Thou in my voice, O Lord, perceive and hear
    My heart, my hope, my plaint, my overthrow,
My will to rise, and let by grant appear
    That to my voice thine ears do well intend.
    No place so far that to thee is not near,
No depth so deep that thou ne mayst extend
    Thine ear thereto: hear then my woeful plaint.
    For, Lord, if thou do observe what men offend
And put thy native mercy in restraint,
    If just exaction demand recompense,
    Who may endure, O Lord? Who shall not faint
At such account? Dread, and not reverence,
    Should so reign large. But thou seeks rather love,
    For in thy hand is mercy's residence,
By hope whereof thou dost our hearts move.
    I in thee, Lord, have set my confidence,
    My soul such trust doth evermore approve.
Thy holy word of eterne excellence,
    Thy mercy's promise, that is always just,
    Have been my stay, my pillar, and pretence.
My soul in God hath more desirous trust
    Than hath the watchman looking for the day
    By the relief to quench of sleep the thrust.
Let Israel trust unto the Lord alway,
    For grace and favor are his property:
    Plenteous ransom shall come with him I say,
And shall redeem all our iniquity.

THE HUNDRED-THIRTY-FIRST PSALM

A Song of degrees of David.

~ P. Hately Waddell

My heart, O Lord, was-na haughty; nor my een, they hae-na been heigh:
Nor no, wi' sic ferlies afore me, hae I gaen govan skeigh.
O gin I hae-na been quaiet! an gin I hae-na whush'd my thought;
Like a wean, that's been spean'd fare his mither, my life on mylane it's been wrought.
Till Jehovah, lat Israel lippen; frae the now, till o' time thar's nought.

THE HUNDRED-THIRTY-SECOND PSALM

A Song of Degrees.

~ George Wither

Remember Lord what David's troubles be,
And what to Jacob's mighty God he swore.
In house or bed I will not rest, said he,
Nor shall mine eyes, or sleep, or slumber more,
Until a place be found, of my providing,
For Jacob's God, the mighty Lord's abiding.

Lo, Ephrata, we heard, the place should be,
And in the forest-fields we found the same.
Thy house therefore to enter purpose we,
And at thy footstool will adore thy name.
Arise, O Lord, ascend thy resting bower;
Thou, and the ark of thy almighty power.

Let righteousness thy sacred priests array,
And let thy saints a joyful triumph make:
O turn not thy messiah's face away,
For thy beloved servant David's sake,
To whom thou swearst thy promise, unrecalled,
That on his throne his seed should be installed.

If they, saidst thou, my league and word respect,
Thy children on thy throne shall ever sit:
For I the Lord did Sion hill elect;
And for my dwelling I have chosen it.
My settled rest is there, and I'll possess it;
I love it, and with plenties I will bless it.

The poor thereof, with bread I will sustain,
Her priests I'll clothe with health, her saints shall sing,
A lamp for mine anointed I'll ordain,
And I will make the horn of David spring:
I those will shame, that for his harm endeavor;
But on himself, his crown shall flourish ever.

THE HUNDRED-THIRTY-THIRD PSALM

A Song of degrees of David.

David Rosenberg

It's so good, the turn of a season
people living for a moment as equals
secure in the human family

as sweet as spring rain
making the beard silky
Aaron's beard

his robes sparkle
rich with heaven's simple jewels
like the crown of dew

on Lebanon's Mt. Hermon
shared equally on the hills
of Israel

where the Lord graces our eyes
fresh from reborn wonder
as if we'd live forever.

THE HUNDRED-THIRTY-FOURTH PSALM

A Song of Degrees.

Mary Sidney Herbert

You that Jehovah's servants are,
Whose careful watch, whose watchful care,
Within his house are spent;
Say thus with one assent:
Jehovah's name be praised.
Then let your hands be raised
To holiest place,
Where holiest grace
Doth aye

Remain:
And say
Again,
Jehovah's name be praised.
Say last unto the company,
Who tarrying make
Their leave to take:
All blessings you accompany,
From him in plenty showered,
Whom Sion holds embowered,
Who heaven and earth of nought hath raised.

THE HUNDRED-THIRTY-FIFTH PSALM

~ Christopher Smart

O praise the Lord, and bless his name,
Ye servants of the Lord,
To God your anthems frame
With swelling voice and chord.

You unto whom are stated posts
Within God's hallowed fane,
Who serve the Lord of hosts,
And in his courts remain,

O to the Lord address your praise,
Which is with grace replete,
His fair perfections blaze,
For they are passing sweet.

For Jacob claims his saviour's care
As God's peculiar plant,
And Israel is his heir
Assigned by special grant.

I know the Lord our God is great
And infinite, above
The measure or the weight
Of other power or love.

Whatever is the Lord's command
Beyond, beneath the sun,
In ocean or by land,
Or in the depth, is done.

He from the world's remotest ends
The pregnant cloud explores;
With rain he lightning sends,
The wind is from his stores.

His plagues the Egyptian race consume
From greatest to the least,
The firstlings from the womb
Of man as well as beast.

Then institutes his paschal lamb,
And triumphs o'er the waves,
And thee, O land of Ham,
With Pharaoh and his slaves.

He smote with his Mosaic rod
The realms of divers climes;
And he, the almighty God,
Slew tyrants for their crimes.

Sihon, who dwelt at Heshbon, fell,
And Og, the world's disgrace,
And all the tools of hell,
In Canaan's boundless space;

And gave their regions far and wide
Of vineyards, fruits and flowers,
For Israel to divide,
Proud domes and fragrant bowers.

O God, thy name and word endure
In infinite renown;
From race to race secure
Thy fame is handed down.

For God, in our behalf aroused,
Will strict reprisals make;
His people thus espoused,
His special grace partake.

As for the gods the heathen serves
And true religion mocks,
They're moved by fictitious nerves,
Cast gold and silver blocks.

Their mouths are framed, from whence there comes
Not even the breath of lies;
Ecstatic death benumbs
Their glass-constructed eyes.

Their ears are fashioned by the mold,
Nor can they hear a sound;
Their molten lips are cold,
In breathless fetters bound.

The founders of such gods as these
Resemble their own dross,
And so do all whose knees
Are bowed to form and gloss.

Praise ye the Lord, each branch and bud
Of Jacob's chosen root,
And you of Aaron's blood
The praise to God impute.

Praise ye the Lord of Levi's line
That in the temple keep;
In fear and praises join
Ye congregated sheep.

The Lord be praised from Zion's brow
Which dwells in Salem's dome,
And gives his people now
The promised milk and comb.

THE HUNDRED-THIRTY-SIXTH PSALM

~ John Milton

Let us with a gladsome mind
Praise the Lord, for he is kind,
For his mercies aye endure,
Ever faithful, ever sure.
Let us blaze his name abroad,
For of gods he is the God;
For his mercies aye endure,
Ever faithful, ever sure.
O let us his praises tell,
That doth the wrathful tyrants quell.
For his mercies aye endure,
Ever faithful, ever sure.
That with his miracles doth make
Amazed heaven and earth to shake.
For his mercies aye endure,
Ever faithful, ever sure.
That by his wisdom did create

The painted heavens so full of state.
For his mercies aye endure,
Ever faithful, ever sure.
That did the solid earth ordain
To rise above the watery plain.
For his mercies aye endure,
Ever faithful, ever sure.
That by his all-commanding might,
Did fill the new-made world with light.
For his mercies aye endure,
Ever faithful, ever sure.
And caused the golden-tressed sun,
All the day long his course to run.
For his mercies aye endure,
Ever faithful, ever sure.
The horned moon to shine by night,
Amongst her spangled sisters bright.
For his mercies aye endure,
Ever faithful, ever sure.
He with his thunder-clasping hand,
Smote the first-born of Egypt land.
For his mercies aye endure,
Ever faithful, ever sure.
And in despite of Pharaoh fell,
He brought from thence his Israel.
For his mercies aye endure,
Ever faithful, ever sure.
The ruddy waves he cleft in twain,
Of the Erythraean main.
For his mercies aye endure,
Ever faithful, ever sure.
The floods stood still like walls of glass,
While the Hebrew bands did pass.
For his mercies aye endure,
Ever faithful, ever sure.
But full soon they did devour
The tawny king with all his power.
For his mercies aye endure,
Ever faithful, ever sure.
His chosen people he did bless
In the wasteful wilderness.
For his mercies aye endure,
Ever faithful, ever sure.
In bloody battle he brought down

Kings of prowess and renown.
For his mercies aye endure,
Ever faithful, ever sure.
He foiled bold Sihon and his host,
That ruled the Amorrean coast.
For his mercies aye endure,
Ever faithful, ever sure.
And large-limbed Og he did subdue,
With all his over-hardy crew.
For his mercies aye endure,
Ever faithful, ever sure.
And to his servant Israel
He gave their land therein to dwell.
For his mercies aye endure,
Ever faithful, ever sure.
He hath with a piteous eye
Beheld us in our misery.
For his mercies aye endure,
Ever faithful, ever sure.
And freed us from the slavery
Of the invading enemy.
For his mercies aye endure,
Ever faithful, ever sure.
All living creatures he doth feed,
And with full hand supplies their need.
For his mercies aye endure,
Ever faithful, ever sure.
Let us therefore warble forth
His mighty majesty and worth.
For his mercies aye endure,
Ever faithful, ever sure.
That his mansion hath on high
Above the reach of mortal eye.
For his mercies aye endure.
Ever faithful, ever sure.

THE HUNDRED-THIRTY-SEVENTH PSALM

~ Thomas Carew

Sitting by the streams that glide
Down by Babel's towering wall,
With our tears we filled the tide
Whilst our mindful thoughts recall
Thee O Sion, and thy fall.

Our neglected harps unstrung,
  Not acquainted with the hand
Of the skillful tuner, hung
  On the willow trees that stand
  Planted in the neighbor land.

Yet the spiteful foe commands
  Songs of mirth, and bids us lay
To dumb harps, our captive hands,
  And, (to scoff our sorrows) say
  Sing us some sweet Hebrew lay.

But say we, our holy strain
  Is too pure for heathen land,
Nor may we God's hymns profane,
  Or move either voice or hand
  To delight a savage band.

Holy Salem, if thy love
  Fall from my forgetful heart,
May the skill by which I move
  Strings of music tuned with art,
  From my withered hand depart!

May my speechless tongue give sound
  To no accents, but remain
To my prison roof fast bound,
  If my sad soul entertain
  Mirth, till thou rejoice again!

In that day remember, Lord
  Edom's brood, that in our groans
They triumph; with fire and sword
  Burn their city, hew their bones
  And make all one heap of stones.

Cruel Babel, thou shalt feel
  The revenger of our groans,
When the happy victors' steel
  As thine, ours, shall hew thy bones,
  And make thee one heap of stones.

Men shall bless the hand that tears
  From the mother's soft embraces
Sucking infants, and besmears
  With their brains the rugged faces
  Of the rocks and stony places.

THE HUNDRED-THIRTY-EIGHTH PSALM

A Psalm of David.

~ *Mary Sidney Herbert*

Even before kings by thee as gods commended,
And angels all, by whom thou art attended,
In hearty tunes I will thy honor tell.
The palace where thy holiness doth dwell
Shall be the place, where falling down before thee,
With reverence meet I prostrate will adore thee.

There will I sing how thou thy mercy sendest,
And to thy promise due performance lendest,
Whereby thy name above all names doth fly.
There will I sing, how when my careful cry
Mounted to thee, my care was straight released,
My courage by thee mightily increased.

Sure Lord, all kings that understand the story
Of thy contract with me, nought but thy glory
And means shall sing whereby that glory grew;
Whose highly seated eye yet well doth view
With humbled look the soul that lowly lieth,
And, far aloof, aspiring things espieth.

On every side, though tribulation grieve me,
Yet shalt thou aid, yet shalt thou still relieve me,
From angry foe thy succor shall me save.
Thou Lord shalt finish what in hand I have:
Thou Lord, I say, whose mercy lasteth ever,
Thy work begun, shall leave unended never.

THE HUNDRED-THIRTY-NINTH PSALM

To the chief Musician, A Psalm of David.

~ *Mary Sidney Herbert*

O Lord in me there lieth nought
But to thy search revealed lies:
For when I sit
Thou markest it;
No less thou notest when I rise.
Yea, closest closet of my thought
Hath open windows to thine eyes.

Thou walkest with me when I walk;
When to my bed for rest I go,
I find thee there,
And everywhere;
Not youngest thought in me doth grow,
No, not one word I cast to talk,
But yet unuttered thou dost know.

If forth I march, thou goest before,
If back I turn, thou comest behind;
So forth nor back
Thy guard I lack,
Nay on me too thy hand I find.
Well I thy wisdom may adore,
But never reach with earthy mind.

To shun thy notice, leave thine eye,
O whither might I take my way?
To starry sphere?
Thy throne is there.
To dead men's undelightsome stay?
There is thy walk, and there to lie
Unknown in vain I should assay.

O sun, whom light nor flight can match,
Suppose thy lightful, flightful wings
Thou lend to me,
And I could flee
As far as thee the evening brings,
Even led to west he would me catch
Nor should I lurk with western things.

Do thou thy best, O secret night,
In sable veil to cover me,
Thy sable veil
Shall vainly fail;
With day unmasked my night shall be,
For night is day, and darkness light,
O father of all lights, to thee.

Each inmost piece in me is thine:
While yet I in my mother dwelt,
All that me clad
From thee I had.
Thou in my frame hast strangely dealt;
Needs in my praise thy works must shine,
So inly them my thoughts have felt.

Thou, how my back was beam-wise laid
    And raftering of my ribs, dost know;
        Knowst every point
        Of bone and joint,
    How to this whole these parts did grow,
In brave embroidery fair arrayed
    Though wrought in shop both dark and low.

Nay, fashionless, ere form I took,
    Thy all-and-more-beholding eye
        My shapeless shape
        Could not escape;
    All these, time-framed successively
Ere one had being, in the book
    Of thy foresight enrolled did lie.

My God, how I these studies prize
    That do thy hidden workings show!
        Whose sum is such
        No sum so much,
    Nay, summed as sand, they sumless grow.
I lie to sleep, from sleep I rise,
    Yet still in thought with thee I go.

My God, if thou but one wouldst kill,
    Then straight would leave my further chase
        This cursed brood
        Inured to blood
    Whose graceless taunts at thy disgrace
Have aimed oft, and, hating still,
    Would with proud lies thy truth outface.

Hate not I them, who thee do hate?
    Thine, Lord, I will the censure be.
        Detest I not
        The cankered knot
    Whom I against thee banded see?
O Lord, thou knowst in highest rate
    I hate them all as foes to me.

Search me, my God, and prove my heart,
    Examine me, and try my thought:
        And mark in me
        If aught there be
    That hath with cause their anger wrought.
If not (as not) my life's each part,
    Lord, safely guide from danger brought.

THE HUNDRED-FORTIETH PSALM

To the chief Musician, A Psalm of David.

~ John Hall

Deliver me, O Lord,
According to thy word,
Lord let me not be shent.
On me some pity have,
From subtle wights me save,
Of enemies violent.

In heart they think mischief
And seek to do me grief.
Their tongues they whet so sharp
As adders' venom vile:
That they may us beguile,
Full wicked wiles they warp.

Keep me, O Lord, therefore
From enemies ever more,
Which wicked be and ill:
Thy help let me not want,
For they would me supplant
From doing of thy will.

These proud men they have set
For me a privy net,
Where I should out and in:
Yea and in my pathway
My soul for to betray,
They lay both snare and gin.

Lord, therefore have I said,
Thou art mine only aid.
Lord, hear my deep desire:
O Lord thou art my wealth,
O God my saving health,
Grant me that I require.

Let not these men unpure
On me take their pleasure,
Destroy their ill intent:
They are so proud and haute,
That they themselves exalt,
Therefore let them be shent.

I mean such men as be
Of their great subtlety,
At no time unprepared:
Lord, in their own deceit,
Wherewith they laid such weight.
Let their own feet be snared.

Let coals of fire fall down
And cast them on their crown
And throw them into hell,
From whence how for to rise
There is no tongue so wise,
That can them rede or tell.

Let nothing prosper well
On earth where such men dwell,
Reprove their rich renown:
To mischief they be wont;
With plagues therefore them hunt
And headlong throw them down.

I know the Lord will wound
And utterly confound
All men to pride addict:
And will avenge in deed
The poor that stand in need,
And are thus sore afflict.

The righteous verily
Shall praise and magnify
Thy holy name therefore:
The hearts of pure pretence
Shall dwell in thy presence,
Good Lord, for ever more.

THE HUNDRED-FORTY-FIRST PSALM

A Psalm of David.

~ Christopher Smart

Lord, I thy present help implore,
Respect my voice, and meet
My breathings as they soar
Towards thy holy seat.

The prayer which I set forth receive
As frankincense and nard,
And as a gift at eve
My lifted hands regard.

Set thou a watch my youth to ward
From inadvertent slips,
And lock, O gracious Lord,
The portal of my lips.

O let my heart be clean and chaste,
Nor let my members share
In wicked works, nor taste
Of Mammon's tempting fare.

No, let the righteous rather thwart
And friendly smite my cheek,
I would not then retort,
But be resigned and meek.

But let not what they give for balm
Increase my raging smart;
Nay, I will pray my psalm
Against their hand and heart.

Let such false judges as commend
Their harsh precarious prose,
To this my song attend,
Which in sweet measure flows.

Our bones beside the grave are strewed
From life's extinguished spark,
Like timber cast abroad,
Which woodmen fell and bark.

But, holy Lord, and God most just,
To thee mine eyes I turn;
In thee I put my trust,
Nor thou my spirit spurn.

Preserve me from the covered mines
That impious men have made
And from the dark designs
Which traitors have assayed.

Let thy deceivers be confused
As they their bounds infringe;
But let my soul be loosed
From every net and springe.

THE HUNDRED-FORTY-SECOND PSALM

A Maschil of David; A Prayer when he was in the cave.

George Wither

My voice to thee, O God, I rear,
  To thee, O Lord, I sue;
To thee my troubles I declare,
  My griefs to thee I show.
For when o'erwhelmed my spirit was,
  My path was known to thee:
Even when they hid, where I should pass,
  A secret snare for me.

I looked on my right-hand side,
  But no man knew me there.
All succors failed; not one I spied
  That of my soul had care.
Then, Lord, thou art my hope, said I,
  My lot, whilst life I have.
In my distress, observe my cry;
  From spoil thy servant save.

Yea, since for me they are too strong,
  To praise thee, set me free:
So righteous men to me shall throng,
  When thy great love they see.

THE HUNDRED-FORTY-THIRD PSALM

A Psalm of David.

Thomas Wyatt

Hear my prayer, O Lord, hear my request,
  'Complish my boon, answer to my desire,
  Not by desert, but for thine own behest,
In whose firm truth thou promised mine empire
  To stand stable. And after thy justice
  Perform, O Lord, the thing that I require,
But not of law after the form and guise
  To enter judgment with thy thrall bondslave
  To plead his right, for in such manner wise
Before thy sight no man his right shall save.
  For of myself lo this my righteousness
  By scourge and whip and pricking spurs I have
Scant risen up, such is my beastliness;

For that my enemy hath pursued my life
And in the dust hath foiled my lustiness;
For that in hate, to flee his rage so rife,
He hath me forced as dead to hide my head;
And for because within myself at strife
My heart and sprite with all my force were fled.
I had recourse to times that have been past,
And did remember thy deeds in all my dread,
And did peruse thy works that ever last,
Whereby I knew above those wonders all
Thy mercies were. Then lift I up in haste
My hands to thee, my soul to thee did call
Like barren soil for moisture of thy grace.
Haste to my help, O Lord, afore I fall,
For sure I feel my sprite doth faint apace.
Turn not thy face from me, that I be laid
In count of them that headlong down do pass
Into the pit. Show me betimes thine aid,
For on thy grace I wholly do depend
And in thy hand since all my health is stayed.
Do me to know what way thou wilt I bend,
For unto thee I have raised up my mind.
Rid me, O Lord, from that that do intend
My foes to me, for I have me assigned
Always within thy secret protection.
Teach me thy will, that I by thee may find
The way to work the same in affection.
For thou, my God, thy blessed upright sprite,
In land of truth shall be my direction.
Thou for thy name, Lord, shalt revive my sprite
Within the right that I receive by thee,
Whereby my life of danger shall be quite.
Thou hast fordone their great iniquity
That vexed my soul, thou shalt also confound
My foes, O Lord, for thy benignity:
For thine am I, thy servant aye most bound.

THE HUNDRED-FORTY-FOURTH PSALM

A Psalm of David.

~ *Mary Sidney Herbert*

Praised be the Lord of might,
   My rock in all alarms,
By whom my hands do fight,
   My fingers manage arms;
My grace, my guard, my fort,
   On whom my safety stays:
To whom my hopes resort
   By whom my realm obeys.

Lord, what is man that thou
   Shouldst tender so his fare?
What hath his child to bow
   Thy thoughts unto his care?
Whose nearest kin is nought,
   No image of whose days
More lively can be thought,
   Than shade that never stays.

Lord bend thy arched skies
   With ease to let thee down;
And make the storms arise
   From mountains fuming crown.
Let follow flames from sky,
   To back their stoutest hand:
Let fast thy arrows fly,
   Dispersing thickest band.

Thy heavenly help extend
   And lift me from this flood:
Let me thy hand defend
   From hand of foreign brood,
Whose mouth no mouth at all,
   But forge of false intent,
Whereto their hand doth fall
   As aptest instrument.

Then in new song to thee
   Will I exalt my voice:
Then shall, O God, with me
   My ten-stringed lute rejoice.
Rejoice in him, I say,
   Who royal right preserves

And saves from sword's decay
   His David that him serves.

O Lord, thy help extend,
   And lift me from this flood:
Let me thy hand defend
   From hand of foreign brood
Whose mouth no mouth at all
   But forge of false intent,
Whereto their hand doth fall
   As aptest instrument.

So then our sons shall grow
   As plants of timely spring:
Whom soon to fairest show
   Their happy growth doth bring.
As pillars both do bear
   And garnish kingly hall:
Our daughters straight and fair,
   Each house embellish shall.

Our store shall aye be full,
   Yea shall such fullness find
Though all from thence we pull,
   Yet more shall rest behind.
The millions of increase
   Shall break the wonted fold:
Yea such the sheepy press,
   The streets shall scantly hold.

Our herds shall brave the best:
   Abroad no foes alarm:
At home to break our rest,
   No cry, the voice of harm.
If blessed term I may
   On whom such blessings fall:
Then blessed blessed they
   Their God Jehovah call.

THE HUNDRED-FORTY-FIFTH PSALM

David's Psalm of praise.

~ *Christopher Smart*

O God, my king, I will adore
And magnify thy name,
To thee the praise I will restore,
And blazon ever more and more
Thy glory, of eternal fame.

I will acknowledge day by day
Thy grace with thankful heart;
And to thy name the praise repay,
And thine immortal worth display,
Nor ever from the theme depart.

The Lord is infinitely great,
And of amazing might;
His endless being knows no date,
His greatness is above all height,
And should our utmost laud excite.

One generation shall declare
To all succeeding times
Thy works and providential care,
Thy power, which high o'er earth and air,
And topmost heaven itself sublimes.

As for my part, I will converse
Upon religious themes,
Thy glory and thy praise rehearse,
And psalms upon thy word disperse,
Which with perpetual wonder teems:

So that the language of mankind
Upon thine acts shall dwell;
Thy works in matchless skill designed,
And in such harmony combined,
I likewise will the chorus swell.

The justly memorable tale
Of thine abounding love,
Shall o'er malevolence prevail,
And men with songs thy truth shall hail,
Connecting earth with heaven above.

The Lord is of exceeding grace
In pardon to our sin,

Long-suffering to the human race,
And great our follies to efface,
   And good our contrite hearts to win.

The Lord his tenderness extends
   To every man and beast;
His pity with his bounty blends,
To all their sustenance he sends,
   From greatest to the last and least.

Lord, all thy works thy laud include,
   The vocal and the mute;
And all thy saints elect, endued,
With never-failing gratitude,
   To their glad harps their numbers suit.

The glories of thine endless reign
   In hymns of praise they show;
And sing of thy supreme domain,
Which thou transcendest to maintain
   By marvels various, great and new,

That thine uncontroverted power,
   The lustre of thy throne,
And might exerted day and hour,
Which can o'er all resistance tower,
   Should to all human kind be known.

Thou art an everlasting king,
   In endless glory crowned;
Truth is the signet of thy ring,
And thy dominion takes a swing
   From alpha—from omega—round.

The Lord, the grand support of all,
   From heaven where he resides,
Recovers such as faint or fall,
And kindly listens to the call
   Of those that sink, or him that slides.

The eyes of all, O Lord, appeal,
   And heavenwards look to thee;
And in due season thou shalt deal
For every beak and mouth its meal,
   By fixed and regular decree.

Thine hand, omnipotent to save,
   Thou openest from on high,

And to it all things living crave,
From air, from earth, and from the wave,
And have a plentiful supply.

The Lord has all his word fulfilled
In measure passing thought;
And whatsoe'er his wisdom willed,
His matchless art has aptly skilled,
And to the last perfection brought.

The Lord to those is ever near
Whose lips his aid invoke;
Yea, such as hearty faith endear
By holy meekness, and by fear,
And yield them to his easy yoke.

He will complete the fervent vows
Of them that fear his laws,
He likewise will their part espouse,
And for their help his might arouse,
And patronize their righteous cause.

The Lord is gracious to uphold
All those that love his word;
But severs from his special fold,
And will not such a race behold,
As have nor praise nor prayer preferred.

My mouth shall to the Lord confess
His meritorious praise;
Let all mankind his fear caress,
And as with holy thanks they bless
His name for ever, ever blaze.

THE HUNDRED-FORTY-SIXTH PSALM

Anne Finch

O! praise the Lord, and let his fame be told,
O! now my soul, thy best affections raise
To him, who gave, and does thy being hold,
Return thy grateful hymns, and thy loud songs of praise.

In man, in princes, who the scepters sway,
Can there be faith reposed, can there be trust?
Their promises, alas, are vain as they,
Their promises are air, and they, alas, are dust.

The breath of man shall certainly expire,
His soul forsake him, and his thoughts shall die,
His body to the lowly grave retire:
Who then can trust on man, who can on man rely?

He only can be safe, he only blessed,
Above the reach of falsehood or decay,
His hopes at anchor, and his fears at rest,
Whose trust is in the Lord, whose God is all his stay.

He who the heavens, and air, and earth, the deep
With all therein, created by his word,
His word to all eternity shall keep;
His will is sacred truth, and power is with the Lord.

Mercy and justice still with him remain:
That feeds the hungry, this the oppressed relieves;
Mercy dissolves the afflicted prisoner's chain;
To long benighted eyes, mercy the light retrieves.

The righteous are the Lord's peculiar care,
To him, for refuge, the poor widows come;
The fatherless is God's adopted heir;
The stranger, too, in God is sure to find an home.

Those that are fallen, he again erects.
The wicked, that pursue ungodly ways,
He searches out, he frustrates, and detects;
He ruins their designs, and on them builds his praise.

Thy Lord, O Sion! this, thy Lord, is king;
Throughout all ages, shall his reign endure,
Thou everlasting praise mayst to him sing,
And ever mayst thou rest, beneath his love, secure.

THE HUNDRED-FORTY-SEVENTH PSALM

Mary Sidney Herbert

Sing to the Lord, for what can better be
Than of our God that we the honor sing?
With seemly pleasure what can more agree
Than praiseful voice, and touch of tuned string?
For lo, the Lord again to form doth bring
Jerusalem's long ruinated walls;
And Jacob's house, which all the earth did see
Dispersed erst, to union now recalls;

And now by him their broken hearts made sound,
And now by him their bleeding wounds are bound.

For what could not, who can the number tell
Of stars, the torches of his heavenly hall;
And tell so readily, he knoweth well
How every star by proper name to call?
What great to him, whose greatness doth not fall
Within precincts? whose power no limits stay?
Whose knowledges all number so excel,
Not numbering number can their number lay?
Easy to him, to lift the lowly just;
Easy, to down proud wicked to the dust.

O then Jehovah's causeful honor sing,
His, whom our God we by his goodness find!
O make harmonious mix of voice and string
To him by whom the skies with clouds are lined;
By whom the rain, from clouds to drop assigned,
Supples the clods of summer-scorched fields,
Fresheth the mountains with such needful spring,
Fuel of life to mountain cattle yields
From whom young ravens careless old forsake,
Croaking to him of alms, their diet take.

The stately shape, the force of bravest steed,
Is far too weak to work in him delight;
No more in him can any pleasure breed
In flying footman, foot of nimblest flight.
Nay, which is more, his fearers in his sight
Can well of nothing but his bounty brave;
Which, never failing, never lets them need
Who fixed their hopes upon his mercies have.
O then, Jerusalem, Jehovah praise,
With honor due thy God, O Sion, raise.

His strength it is thy gates doth surely bar;
His grace in thee thy children multiplies;
By him thy borders lie secure from wars,
And finest flour thy hunger satisfies.
Nor means he needs; for fast his pleasure flies,
Borne by his word, when aught him list to bid.
Snow's woolly locks by him wide scattered are,
And hoary plains with frost, as ashes, hid;
Gross icy gobbets from his hand he flings,
And blows a cold too strong for strongest things.

He bids again, and ice in water flows,
As water erst in ice congealed lay;
Abroad the southern wind, his melter, goes;
The streams relenting take their wonted way.
O much is this, but more I come to say:
The words of life he hath to Jacob told;
Taught Israel, who by his teaching knows
What laws in life, what rules he wills to hold.
No nation else hath found him half so kind,
For to his light, what other is not blind?

THE HUNDRED-FORTY-EIGHTH PSALM

Thomas Stanley

Angeli

You blessed spirits that bestow,
For every good or bad intent
Throughout our universe below,
Either reward, or punishment;
You that instruct the industrious spheres
(Your scholars) in a harmony
Which doth as far exceed the ears
Of man, as they transcend the eye—
Teach them to praise the power to whom all sue,
By the same lesson that they learn of you.

Sol

Thou universal paint, whose light
Alone all beauty doth dispose,
Who on the lily spreadst the white,
And the carnation on the rose:
Great painter of this solid frame,
Whose luminous pencils gild the earth
And water; to whose radiant flame
All shape and color owe their birth—
In a new hymn the world's great author praise,
Of which thou drawst the picture by thy rays.

Luna

Thou that amidst the darkest night
Dost entertain a lesser day,
Expecting till the King of light
Drive the obscurer shades away;
Bright regent of one half of the year,

Whose secret influence doth cause
The oceans' flux, which learns to bear
The weight of thy uncertain laws—
Praise him who gives thy weakness strength to guide
By hidden power, the sea's obsequious tide.

Stellae

Roses of gold on azure sown,
You sparkling jewels of the night,
Who silently encamp unknown,
Your squadrons in their tents of light;
Whom the militia of the skies
In several factions doth bestow,
To kindle war, which spreading, flies
Throughout our lesser world below—
Praise him by whom you shall at last be thrown
To earth, and forced to lay your bright arms down.

Lumen

Soul of the sun, and life of sight,
That dost the 'namelled heavens adorn,
Though sensibly, yet subtly bright,
Smile of the early rising morn;
Whose soft impression far all art
Exceeds, or strongest violence;
Esteemed of a corporeal part
An incorporeal effluence—
Praise him to whom thou dost thy being owe,
And from whose light, thy fountain, thou dost flow.

Caeli caelorum

Great palace of the empyree,
Of which the spheres are the foundation,
The walls of glass, a fluid sea,
Eternity thy long duration:
Which with harmonious airs dost ring,
Composed by thy most sacred choir,
Whose life is music, and to sing,
The only being they desire—
Praise him, and if spirits can vanquished be
By bodies, let those angels yield to thee.

Aquae super caelos

Waters that by mysterious skill
Are placed above this arch of pleasure,
Whose careful concave doth not spill

One drop of this their liquid treasure;
Conservatory beyond art,
Waves which above your bridge do flow,
And to your neighbor flames impart
No cold, nor from them heat do know—
In his just praise, with all his works conspire,
Whose power can water reconcile to fire.

Dracones

Dragons who nature's soldiers are,
Furnished as soon as born, with arms,
Whose martial industry our care
Resists, and counterchecks your harms;
Feared monsters both of earth and air,
Dwelling in either element,
Who such a deadly poison bear,
As but it self nought can prevent—
That great physician praise, who doth reveal
An art, which teacheth the disease to heal.

Abyssi

You dark abysses of the main,
Whose soundless depths the fuel hide,
That earth doth in her womb retain,
Mixed with the waves in yours reside,
Who treacherously the wealth devour,
Which fools commit unto your care,
And in whose caverns, made by power
Of winds, your dead waves buried are—
Praise that profounder skill, which by strong chains,
You in the prison of your selves restrains.

Ignis

Fire, which above the air hast seat,
And dost both light, and lightness wear;
So placed, as if thy subtle heat
Did purify pale Cynthia's sphere:
Thou sea, whose bright waves ebb and flow,
Swift as the spheres by which they move,
Whilst the small fires that dwell below,
Direct their flames to you above—
Praise his diviner power, who placed your throne
Of light so near the glory of his own.

Grando

Unwelcome tempests, that annoy
The hopeful treasure of the year,

And often ravish, or destroy
The virgin pride our flowers do wear,
Who first as messengers, convey
The just displeasure of the skies,
Then melting into tears, away,
Weep for the crimes which you chastise—
Praise that great God, who can the tempest veil
Of his displeasure, in a storm of hail.

Nix

Wool, which celestial art hath made,
And knit into one ornament,
And like rich tapestry displayed
Upon the smoother plane's extent;
Ivory, whose hardness, unknown skill
Doth render tractable as silk;
A flood, whose solid streams distill
From melted pearls, or frozen milk—
Praise that diviner power, who of so light
A vapor, hath a body made so bright.

Glacies

Thou child of water, whose brow wears
The image of our vanity,
And melting back again in tears,
Thy mother is new born of thee:
Thou crystal signet that dost seal
The folds which on the waves do lie,
And rivers as away they steal,
Dost stop, and with cold fetters tie—
That chemist praise, who doth all tempers mix,
And can the fluid state of water fix.

Spiritus procellarum

You mutinous causes of those wars
That wrinkle the smooth face of the deep,
Greedy, or curious passengers
Betraying to eternal sleep:
Sighs, which the winds to those bequeath,
Are tossed upon these watery graves;
You, who by power of your rough breath,
Level the earth, and plough the waves—
Praise him who doth your forces disunite,
The God of peace, who forceth you to fight.

Montes et Colles

You mountains, whose proud heads defy
The fury of the troubled air,
Whose bases still unshaken lie,
Nor winds can move, nor storms impair:
And lesser hills, whose smooth tops yield
Pastimes to swains, who there resort,
Striving in beauty with the field,
Where wanton flocks both feed and sport—
Join in this hymn, that his great power may be
Praised equally, in inequality.

Ligna fructifera Cedri

Pleasant and fertile trees that bear
What may both sight and taste invite,
And with the riches of the year,
All senses equally delight,
Exalt your humble tops, and join
With the proud cedars in this praise,
To celebrate that power divine,
Who from the earth you both did raise—
That in this pious strife, both win the field,
Cedars to shrubs, shrubs may to cedars yield.

Bestiæ Pecora

Beasts, who your humble being owe
To a material form alone,
Whose hidden natures neither know
Reason, nor are to reason known;
You that are circumscribed by laws,
Tied to the fetters of your sense,
And ranked beneath the freer cause
That can with those dull chains dispense—
In a new hymn, praise those diviner powers,
And act men's parts, who act so often yours.

Serpentes

Serpents, who can the shapes you wear
Into a living labyrinth wind,
Retiring to dark dwellings, where
None but yourselves the way can find:
Who by the poison you distilled
Into your first fore-father's breast
The souls of our whole species killed,
And did of innocence divest—

Praise him who can your subtle curls unwind,
And your deserted mansions track and find.

Volucres

You winged choristers, that dwell
In woods, and there maintain a choir,
Whose music doth all art excel;
Nor can we emulate, but admire,
You living galleys of the air,
That through the strongest tempest slide,
And by your wanton flight, who dare
The fury of the winds divide—
Praise him, and in this harmony and love,
Let your soft choir contend with that above.

Reges et Populi

Kings, whose just power the heavens dispense,
Not by less power to be controlled,
Praise that celestial influence,
Which of your glories is the mold;
And you who seated are below,
Taught even by nature to obey,
His praise in your obedience show,
To their divinely ordered sway;
And as his name shall celebrated be,
Let high and low compose one harmony.

Judices

You oracles of heaven's decrees,
Who by the curb, and scourge of law,
Which to your trust committed lies,
Keep the inferior world in awe,
Who with impartial justice weigh
The crime and punishment of vice,
And by an unresisted sway,
Reward the good, the bad chastise—
Praise that great judge, to whom all knees must bow,
And him that duty pay, which we to you.

Juvenes

You buds of human nature, who,
By the progression of your years,
Disclose those glories, which in you
(By your great master hid) appears;
You the first copies of mankind,
To whom that hand's exacter art

By which you were at first designed
Doth still new light and shade impart—
Praise that great power, who the mysterious ways
Of nature thus from day to day displays.

Virgines

You happy virgins, that retain
The image of divinity,
And carefully preserve from stain
That sacred first impression free:
You who the easy breasts inflame,
Of all that subject are to sense,
And do a double pureness claim,
Of beauty, and of innocence—
Praise that great deity, whom all implore,
And those bright glories we in you adore.

Senes

Old men, whose weak decaying frames
The spoils and ruins are of time,
Whose near-expiring lease he claims,
And will ere long be due to him:
You drooping swans by age dyed white,
Bowed with its weight; who shortly must
To a new dwelling take your flight,
Resolved into forgotten dust—
Praise that great God, who gave, and takes your breath,
And like true swans, go singing to your death.

THE HUNDRED-FORTY-NINTH PSALM

Laurance Wieder

New song? Nearly. Better
Hums through a kazoo than fancy fretwork
Strums to dazzle children.
Echoes in the shower, muffled bedroom
Cries: a two-edged sword:
It cuts the mute and those who should know better.
Writers without spirit
Cannot even praise the letter truly.

THE HUNDRED-FIFTIETH PSALM

~ John Davies

To him with trumpets and with flutes,
With cornets, clarions, and with lutes,
With harps, with organs, and with shawms,
With holy anthems and with psalms,
With voice of angels and of men,
Sing Alleluia: amen, amen.

THE BOOK *of* PSALMS

King James Version

PSALM 1

BLESSED is the man that walketh not in the counsel of the ungodly, nor standeth in the way of sinners, nor sitteth in the seat of the scornful.

2 But his delight is in the law of the Lord; and in his law doth he meditate day and night.

3 And he shall be like a tree planted by the rivers of water, that bringeth forth his fruit in his season; his leaf also shall not wither; and whatsoever he doeth shall prosper.

4 The ungodly are not so: but are like the chaff which the wind driveth away.

5 Therefore the ungodly shall not stand in the judgment, nor sinners in the congregation of the righteous.

6 For the Lord knoweth the way of the righteous: but the way of the ungodly shall perish.

PSALM 2

WHY DO the heathen rage, and the people imagine a vain thing?

2 The kings of the earth set themselves, and the rulers take counsel together, against the Lord, and against his anointed, saying,

3 Let us break their bands asunder, and cast away their cords from us.

4 He that sitteth in the heavens shall laugh: the Lord shall have them in derision.

5 Then shall he speak unto them in his wrath, and vex them in his sore displeasure.

6 Yet have I set my king upon my holy hill of Zion.

7 I will declare the decree: the Lord hath said unto me, Thou art my Son; this day have I begotten thee.

8 Ask of me, and I shall give thee the heathen for thine inheritance, and the uttermost parts of the earth for thy possession.

9 Thou shalt break them with a rod of iron; thou shalt dash them in pieces like a potter's vessel.

10 Be wise now therefore, O ye kings: be instructed, ye judges of the earth.

11 Serve the Lord with fear, and rejoice with trembling.

12 Kiss the Son, lest he be angry, and ye perish from the way, when his wrath is kindled but a little. Blessed are all they that put their trust in him.

PSALM 3

A Psalm of David, when he fled from Absalom his son.

LORD, how are they increased that trouble me! many are they that rise up against me.

2 Many there be which say of my soul, There is no help for him in God. Selah.

3 But thou, O Lord, art a shield for me; my glory, and the lifter up of mine head.

4 I cried unto the Lord with my voice, and he heard me out of his holy hill. Selah.

5 I laid me down and slept; I awaked; for the Lord sustained me.

6 I will not be afraid of ten thousands of people, that have set themselves against me round about.

7 Arise, O Lord; save me, O my God: for thou hast smitten all mine enemies upon the cheek bone; thou hast broken the teeth of the ungodly.

8 Salvation belongeth unto the Lord: thy blessing is upon thy people. Selah.

PSALM 4

To the chief Musician on Neginoth, A Psalm of David.

HEAR me when I call, O God of my righteousness: thou hast enlarged me when I was in distress; have mercy upon me, and hear my prayer.

2 O ye sons of men, how long will ye turn my glory into shame? how long will ye love vanity, and seek after leasing? Selah.

3 But know that the Lord hath set apart him that is godly for himself:

the Lord will hear when I call unto him.
4 Stand in awe, and sin not: commune with your own heart upon your bed, and be still. Selah.
5 Offer the sacrifices of righteousness, and put your trust in the Lord.
6 There be many that say, Who will show us any good? Lord, lift thou up the light of thy countenance upon us.
7 Thou hast put gladness in my heart, more than in the time that their corn and their wine increased.
8 I will both lay me down in peace, and sleep: for thou, Lord, only makest me dwell in safety.

PSALM 5

To the chief Musician upon Nehiloth, A Psalm of David.

GIVE ear to my words, O Lord, consider my meditation.
2 Hearken unto the voice of my cry, my King, and my God: for unto thee will I pray.
3 My voice shalt thou hear in the morning, O Lord; in the morning will I direct my prayer unto thee, and will look up.
4 For thou art not a God that hath pleasure in wickedness: neither shall evil dwell with thee.
5 The foolish shall not stand in thy sight: thou hatest all workers of iniquity.
6 Thou shalt destroy them that speak leasing: the Lord will abhor the bloody and deceitful man.
7 But as for me, I will come into thy house in the multitude of thy mercy: and in thy fear will I worship toward thy holy temple.
8 Lead me, O Lord, in thy righteousness because of mine enemies; make thy way straight before my face.
9 For there is no faithfulness in their mouth; their inward part is very wickedness; their throat is an open sepulchre; they flatter with their tongue.
10 Destroy thou them, O God; let them fall by their own counsels; cast them out in the multitude of their transgressions; for they have rebelled against thee.
11 But let all those that put their trust in thee rejoice: let them ever shout for joy, because thou defendest them: let them also that love thy name be joyful in thee.
12 For thou, Lord, wilt bless the righteous; with favour wilt thou compass him as with a shield.

PSALM 6

To the chief Musician on Neginoth upon Sheminith, A Psalm of David.

O LORD, rebuke me not in thine anger, neither chasten me in thy hot displeasure.
2 Have mercy upon me, O Lord; for I am weak: O Lord, heal me; for my bones are vexed.
3 My soul is also sore vexed: but thou, O Lord, how long?
4 Return, O Lord, deliver my soul: oh save me for thy mercies' sake.
5 For in death there is no remembrance of thee: in the grave who shall give thee thanks?
6 I am weary with my groaning; all the night make I my bed to swim; I water my couch with my tears.
7 Mine eye is consumed because of grief; it waxeth old because of all mine enemies.
8 Depart from me, all ye workers of iniquity; for the Lord hath heard the voice of my weeping.
9 The Lord hath heard my supplication; the Lord will receive my prayer.
10 Let all mine enemies be ashamed and sore vexed: let them return and be ashamed suddenly.

PSALM 7

Shiggaion of David, which he sang unto the Lord, concerning the words of Cush the Benjamite.

O LORD my God, in thee do I put my trust: save me from all them that persecute me, and deliver me:
2 Lest he tear my soul like a lion,

rending it in pieces, while there is
none to deliver.
3 O Lord my God, if I have done
this; if there be iniquity in my
hands;
4 If I have rewarded evil unto him
that was at peace with me; (yea, I
have delivered him that without
cause is mine enemy:)
5 Let the enemy persecute my soul,
and take it; yea, let him tread down
my life upon the earth, and lay mine
honour in the dust. Selah.
6 Arise, O Lord, in thine anger, lift
up thyself because of the rage of
mine enemies: and awake for me to
the judgment that thou hast commanded.
7 So shall the congregation of the
people compass thee about: for their
sakes therefore return thou on high.
8 The Lord shall judge the people:
judge me, O Lord, according to my
righteousness, and according to
mine integrity that is in me.
9 Oh let the wickedness of the
wicked come to an end; but establish the just: for the righteous God
trieth the hearts and reins.
10 My defence is of God, which
saveth the upright in heart.
11 God judgeth the righteous, and
God is angry with the wicked every
day.
12 If he turn not, he will whet his
sword; he hath bent his bow, and
made it ready.
13 He hath also prepared for him
the instruments of death; he or-
daineth his arrows against the persecutors.
14 Behold, he travaileth with iniquity, and hath conceived mischief,
and brought forth falsehood.
15 He made a pit, and digged it,
and is fallen into the ditch which he
made.
16 His mischief shall return upon
his own head, and his violent dealing shall come down upon his own
pate.
17 I will praise the Lord according
to his righteousness: and will sing
praise to the name of the Lord most
high.

PSALM 8

*To the chief Musician upon Gittith,
A Psalm of David.*

O LORD our Lord, how excellent
is thy name in all the earth!
who hast set thy glory above the
heavens.
2 Out of the mouth of babes
and sucklings hast thou ordained
strength because of thine enemies,
that thou mightest still the enemy
and the avenger.
3 When I consider thy heavens, the
work of thy fingers, the moon and
the stars, which thou hast ordained;
4 What is man, that thou art mindful of him? and the son of man, that
thou visitest him?
5 For thou hast made him a little
lower than the angels, and hast
crowned him with glory and honour.
6 Thou madest him to have dominion over the works of thy hands;
thou hast put all things under his
feet:
7 All sheep and oxen, yea, and the
beasts of the field;
8 The fowl of the air, and the fish
of the sea, and whatsoever passeth
through the paths of the seas.
9 O Lord our Lord, how excellent
is thy name in all the earth!

PSALM 9

*To the chief Musician upon Muthlabben,
A Psalm of David.*

I WILL praise thee, O Lord, with my
whole heart; I will show forth all
thy marvellous works.
2 I will be glad and rejoice in thee:
I will sing praise to thy name, O
thou most High.
3 When mine enemies are turned
back, they shall fall and perish at thy
presence.
4 For thou hast maintained my
right and my cause; thou satest in
the throne judging right.
5 Thou hast rebuked the heathen,
thou hast destroyed the wicked,

thou hast put out their name for ever and ever.

6 O thou enemy, destructions are come to a perpetual end: and thou hast destroyed cities; their memorial is perished with them.

7 But the Lord shall endure for ever: he hath prepared his throne for judgment.

8 And he shall judge the world in righteousness, he shall minister judgment to the people in uprightness.

9 The Lord also will be a refuge for the oppressed, a refuge in times of trouble.

10 And they that know thy name will put their trust in thee: for thou, Lord, hast not forsaken them that seek thee.

11 Sing praises to the Lord, which dwelleth in Zion: declare among the people his doings.

12 When he maketh inquisition for blood, he remembereth them: he forgetteth not the cry of the humble.

13 Have mercy upon me, O Lord; consider my trouble which I suffer of them that hate me, thou that liftest me up from the gates of death:

14 That I may show forth all thy praise in the gates of the daughter of Zion: I will rejoice in thy salvation.

15 The heathen are sunk down in the pit that they made: in the net which they hid is their own foot taken.

16 The Lord is known by the judgment which he executeth: the wicked is snared in the work of his own hands. Higgaion. Selah.

17 The wicked shall be turned into hell, and all the nations that forget God.

18 For the needy shall not always be forgotten: the expectation of the poor shall not perish for ever.

19 Arise, O Lord; let not man prevail: let the heathen be judged in thy sight.

20 Put them in fear, O Lord: that the nations may know themselves to be but men. Selah.

PSALM 10

WHY STANDEST thou afar off, O Lord? why hidest thou thyself in times of trouble?

2 The wicked in his pride doth persecute the poor: let them be taken in the devices that they have imagined.

3 For the wicked boasteth of his heart's desire, and blesseth the covetous, whom the Lord abhorreth.

4 The wicked, through the pride of his countenance, will not seek after God: God is not in all his thoughts.

5 His ways are always grievous; thy judgments are far above out of his sight: as for all his enemies, he puffeth at them.

6 He hath said in his heart, I shall not be moved: for I shall never be in adversity.

7 His mouth is full of cursing and deceit and fraud: under his tongue is mischief and vanity.

8 He sitteth in the lurking places of the villages: in the secret places doth he murder the innocent: his eyes are privily set against the poor.

9 He lieth in wait secretly as a lion in his den: he lieth in wait to catch the poor: he doth catch the poor, when he draweth him into his net.

10 He croucheth, and humbleth himself, that the poor may fall by his strong ones.

11 He hath said in his heart, God hath forgotten: he hideth his face; he will never see it.

12 Arise, O Lord; O God, lift up thine hand: forget not the humble.

13 Wherefore doth the wicked contemn God? he hath said in his heart, Thou wilt not require it.

14 Thou hast seen it; for thou beholdest mischief and spite, to requite it with thy hand: the poor committeth himself unto thee; thou art the helper of the fatherless.

15 Break thou the arm of the wicked and the evil man: seek out his wickedness till thou find none.

16 The Lord is King for ever and ever: the heathen are perished out of his land.

17 Lord, thou hast heard the desire of the humble: thou wilt prepare their heart, thou wilt cause thine ear to hear:

18 To judge the fatherless and the oppressed, that the man of the earth may no more oppress.

PSALM 11

To the chief Musician, A Psalm of David.

IN THE Lord put I my trust: how say ye to my soul, Flee as a bird to your mountain?

2 For, lo, the wicked bend their bow, they make ready their arrow upon the string, that they may privily shoot at the upright in heart.

3 If the foundations be destroyed, what can the righteous do?

4 The Lord is in his holy temple, the Lord's throne is in heaven: his eyes behold, his eyelids try, the children of men.

5 The Lord trieth the righteous: but the wicked and him that loveth violence his soul hateth.

6 Upon the wicked he shall rain snares, fire and brimstone, and an horrible tempest: this shall be the portion of their cup.

7 For the righteous Lord loveth righteousness; his countenance doth behold the upright.

PSALM 12

To the chief Musician upon Sheminith, A Psalm of David.

HELP, Lord; for the godly man ceaseth; for the faithful fail from among the children of men.

2 They speak vanity every one with his neighbour: with flattering lips and with a double heart do they speak.

3 The Lord shall cut off all flattering lips, and the tongue that speaketh proud things:

4 Who have said, With our tongue will we prevail; our lips are our own: who is lord over us?

5 For the oppression of the poor, for the sighing of the needy, now will I arise, saith the Lord; I will set him in safety from him that puffeth at him.

6 The words of the Lord are pure words: as silver tried in a furnace of earth, purified seven times.

7 Thou shalt keep them, O Lord, thou shalt preserve them from this generation for ever.

8 The wicked walk on every side, when the vilest men are exalted.

PSALM 13

To the chief Musician, A Psalm of David.

HOW LONG wilt thou forget me, O Lord? for ever? how long wilt thou hide thy face from me?

2 How long shall I take counsel in my soul, having sorrow in my heart daily? how long shall mine enemy be exalted over me?

3 Consider and hear me, O Lord my God: lighten mine eyes, lest I sleep the sleep of death;

4 Lest mine enemy say, I have prevailed against him; and those that trouble me rejoice when I am moved.

5 But I have trusted in thy mercy; my heart shall rejoice in thy salvation.

6 I will sing unto the Lord, because he hath dealt bountifully with me.

PSALM 14

To the chief Musician, A Psalm of David.

THE FOOL hath said in his heart, There is no God. They are corrupt, they have done abominable works, there is none that doeth good.

2 The Lord looked down from heaven upon the children of men, to see if there were any that did understand, and seek God.

3 They are all gone aside, they are all together become filthy: there is none that doeth good, no, not one.

4 Have all the workers of iniquity no knowledge? who eat up my people as they eat bread, and call not upon the Lord.

5 There were they in great fear: for God is in the generation of the righteous.
6 Ye have shamed the counsel of the poor, because the Lord is his refuge.
7 Oh that the salvation of Israel were come out of Zion! when the Lord bringeth back the captivity of his people, Jacob shall rejoice, and Israel shall be glad.

PSALM 15

A Psalm of David.

LORD, who shall abide in thy tabernacle? who shall dwell in thy holy hill?
2 He that walketh uprightly, and worketh righteousness, and speaketh the truth in his heart.
3 He that backbiteth not with his tongue, nor doeth evil to his neighbour, nor taketh up a reproach against his neighbour.
4 In whose eyes a vile person is contemned; but he honoureth them that fear the Lord. He that sweareth to his own hurt, and changeth not.
5 He that putteth not out his money to usury, nor taketh reward against the innocent. He that doeth these things shall never be moved.

PSALM 16

Michtam of David.

PRESERVE me, O God: for in thee do I put my trust.
2 O my soul, thou hast said unto the Lord, Thou art my Lord: my goodness extendeth not to thee;
3 But to the saints that are in the earth, and to the excellent, in whom is all my delight.
4 Their sorrows shall be multiplied that hasten after another god: their drink offerings of blood will I not offer, nor take up their names into my lips.
5 The Lord is the portion of mine inheritance and of my cup: thou maintainest my lot.
6 The lines are fallen unto me in pleasant places; yea, I have a goodly heritage.
7 I will bless the Lord, who hath given me counsel: my reins also instruct me in the night seasons.
8 I have set the Lord always before me: because he is at my right hand, I shall not be moved.
9 Therefore my heart is glad, and my glory rejoiceth: my flesh also shall rest in hope.
10 For thou wilt not leave my soul in hell; neither wilt thou suffer thine Holy One to see corruption.
11 Thou wilt show me the path of life: in thy presence is fulness of joy; at thy right hand there are pleasures for evermore.

PSALM 17

A Prayer of David.

HEAR the right, O Lord, attend unto my cry, give ear unto my prayer, that goeth not out of feigned lips.
2 Let my sentence come forth from thy presence; let thine eyes behold the things that are equal.
3 Thou hast proved mine heart; thou hast visited me in the night; thou hast tried me, and shalt find nothing; I am purposed that my mouth shall not transgress.
4 Concerning the works of men, by the word of thy lips I have kept me from the paths of the destroyer.
5 Hold up my goings in thy paths, that my footsteps slip not.
6 I have called upon thee, for thou wilt hear me, O God: incline thine ear unto me, and hear my speech.
7 Show thy marvellous lovingkindness, O thou that savest by thy right hand them which put their trust in thee from those that rise up against them.
8 Keep me as the apple of the eye, hide me under the shadow of thy wings,
9 From the wicked that oppress me, from my deadly enemies, who compass me about.
10 They are inclosed in their own

fat: with their mouth they speak
proudly.
11 They have now compassed us in
our steps: they have set their eyes
bowing down to the earth;
12 Like as a lion that is greedy of
his prey, and as it were a young lion
lurking in secret places.
13 Arise, O Lord, disappoint him,
cast him down: deliver my soul from
the wicked, which is thy sword:
14 From men which are thy hand,
O Lord, from men of the world,
which have their portion in this life,
and whose belly thou fillest with thy
hid treasure: they are full of children, and leave the rest of their substance to their babes.
15 As for me, I will behold thy face
in righteousness: I shall be satisfied,
when I awake, with thy likeness.

PSALM 18

To the chief Musician, A Psalm of David, the servant of the Lord, who spake unto the Lord the words of this song in the day that the Lord delivered him from the hand of all his enemies, and from the hand of Saul: And he said,

I WILL love thee, O Lord, my
strength.
2 The Lord is my rock, and my
fortress, and my deliverer; my God,
my strength, in whom I will trust;
my buckler, and the horn of my salvation, and my high tower.
3 I will call upon the Lord, who is
worthy to be praised: so shall I be
saved from mine enemies.
4 The sorrows of death compassed
me, and the floods of ungodly men
made me afraid.
5 The sorrows of hell compassed
me about: the snares of death prevented me.
6 In my distress I called upon the
Lord, and cried unto my God: he
heard my voice out of his temple,
and my cry came before him, even
into his ears.
7 Then the earth shook and trembled; the foundations also of the
hills moved and were shaken, because he was wroth.
8 There went up a smoke out of his
nostrils, and fire out of his mouth
devoured: coals were kindled by it.
9 He bowed the heavens also, and
came down: and darkness was under
his feet.
10 And he rode upon a cherub, and
did fly: yea, he did fly upon the
wings of the wind.
11 He made darkness his secret
place; his pavilion round about him
were dark waters and thick clouds of
the skies.
12 At the brightness that was before
him his thick clouds passed, hail
stones and coals of fire.
13 The Lord also thundered in the
heavens, and the Highest gave his
voice; hail stones and coals of fire.
14 Yea, he sent out his arrows, and
scattered them; and he shot out
lightnings, and discomfited them.
15 Then the channels of waters
were seen, and the foundations of
the world were discovered at thy rebuke, O Lord, at the blast of the
breath of thy nostrils.
16 He sent from above, he took me,
he drew me out of many waters.
17 He delivered me from my strong
enemy, and from them which hated
me: for they were too strong for me.
18 They prevented me in the day of
my calamity: but the Lord was my
stay.
19 He brought me forth also into a
large place; he delivered me, because
he delighted in me.
20 The Lord rewarded me according to my righteousness; according
to the cleanness of my hands hath
he recompensed me.
21 For I have kept the ways of the
Lord, and have not wickedly departed from my God.
22 For all his judgments were before me, and I did not put away his
statutes from me.
23 I was also upright before him,
and I kept myself from mine iniquity.
24 Therefore hath the Lord recompensed me according to my righteousness, according to the cleanness
of my hands in his eyesight.

25 With the merciful thou wilt
show thyself merciful; with an upright man thou wilt show thyself
upright;
26 With the pure thou wilt show
thyself pure; and with the froward
thou wilt show thyself froward.
27 For thou wilt save the afflicted
people; but wilt bring down high
looks.
28 For thou wilt light my candle:
the Lord my God will enlighten my
darkness.
29 For by thee I have run through a
troop; and by my God have I leaped
over a wall.
30 As for God, his way is perfect:
the word of the Lord is tried: he is a
buckler to all those that trust in him.
31 For who is God save the Lord?
or who is a rock save our God?
32 It is God that girdeth me with
strength, and maketh my way perfect.
33 He maketh my feet like hinds'
feet, and setteth me upon my high
places.
34 He teacheth my hands to war, so
that a bow of steel is broken by
mine arms.
35 Thou hast also given me the
shield of thy salvation: and thy right
hand hath holden me up, and thy
gentleness hath made me great.
36 Thou hast enlarged my steps
under me, that my feet did not slip.
37 I have pursued mine enemies,
and overtaken them: neither did I
turn again till they were consumed.
38 I have wounded them that they
were not able to rise: they are fallen
under my feet.
39 For thou hast girded me with
strength unto the battle: thou hast
subdued under me those that rose
up against me.
40 Thou hast also given me the
necks of mine enemies; that I might
destroy them that hate me.
41 They cried, but there was none
to save them: even unto the Lord,
but he answered them not.
42 Then did I beat them small as
the dust before the wind: I did cast
them out as the dirt in the streets.
43 Thou hast delivered me from the
strivings of the people; and thou
hast made me the head of the heathen: a people whom I have not
known shall serve me.
44 As soon as they hear of me, they
shall obey me: the strangers shall
submit themselves unto me.
45 The strangers shall fade away,
and be afraid out of their close
places.
46 The Lord liveth; and blessed be
my rock; and let the God of my salvation be exalted.
47 It is God that avengeth me, and
subdueth the people under me.
48 He delivereth me from mine enemies: yea, thou liftest me up above
those that rise up against me: thou
hast delivered me from the violent
man.
49 Therefore will I give thanks
unto thee, O Lord, among the heathen, and sing praises unto thy
name.
50 Great deliverance giveth he to
his king; and showeth mercy to his
anointed, to David, and to his seed
for evermore.

PSALM 19

To the chief Musician, A Psalm of David.

THE HEAVENS declare the glory
of God; and the firmament
showeth his handiwork.
2 Day unto day uttereth speech,
and night unto night showeth
knowledge.
3 There is no speech nor language,
where their voice is not heard.
4 Their line is gone out through all
the earth, and their words to the end
of the world. In them hath he set a
tabernacle for the sun,
5 Which is as a bridegroom coming
out of his chamber, and rejoiceth as
a strong man to run a race.
6 His going forth is from the end of
the heaven, and his circuit unto the
ends of it: and there is nothing hid
from the heat thereof.
7 The law of the Lord is perfect,

converting the soul: the testimony
of the Lord is sure, making wise the
simple.
8 The statutes of the Lord are right,
rejoicing the heart: the commandment of the Lord is pure, enlighten-
ing the eyes.
9 The fear of the Lord is clean, en-
during for ever: the judgments of
the Lord are true and righteous altogether.
10 More to be desired are they than
gold, yea, than much fine gold:
sweeter also than honey and the
honeycomb.
11 Moreover by them is thy servant
warned: and in keeping of them
there is great reward.
12 Who can understand his errors?
cleanse thou me from secret faults.
13 Keep back thy servant also from
presumptuous sins; let them not
have dominion over me: then shall I
be upright, and I shall be innocent
from the great transgression.
14 Let the words of my mouth, and
the meditation of my heart, be acceptable in thy sight, O Lord, my
strength, and my redeemer.

PSALM 20

To the chief Musician, A Psalm of David.

THE LORD hear thee in the day of
trouble; the name of the God
of Jacob defend thee;
2 Send thee help from the sanctuary, and strengthen thee out of
Zion;
3 Remember all thy offerings, and
accept thy burnt sacrifice; Selah.
4 Grant thee according to thine
own heart, and fulfil all thy counsel.
5 We will rejoice in thy salvation,
and in the name of our God we will
set up our banners: the Lord fulfil all
thy petitions.
6 Now know I that the Lord saveth
his anointed; he will hear him from
his holy heaven with the saving
strength of his right hand.
7 Some trust in chariots, and some
in horses: but we will remember the
name of the Lord our God.
8 They are brought down and
fallen: but we are risen, and stand
upright.
9 Save, Lord: let the king hear us
when we call.

PSALM 21

To the chief Musician, A Psalm of David.

THE KING shall joy in thy
strength, O Lord; and in thy
salvation how greatly shall he rejoice!
2 Thou hast given him his heart's
desire, and hast not withholden the
request of his lips. Selah.
3 For thou preventest him with the
blessings of goodness: thou settest a
crown of pure gold on his head.
4 He asked life of thee, and thou
gavest it him, even length of days for
ever and ever.
5 His glory is great in thy salvation:
honour and majesty hast thou laid
upon him.
6 For thou hast made him most
blessed for ever: thou hast made him
exceeding glad with thy countenance.
7 For the king trusteth in the Lord,
and through the mercy of the most
High he shall not be moved.
8 Thine hand shall find out all thine
enemies: thy right hand shall find
out those that hate thee.
9 Thou shalt make them as a fiery
oven in the time of thine anger: the
Lord shall swallow them up in his
wrath, and the fire shall devour
them.
10 Their fruit shalt thou destroy
from the earth, and their seed from
among the children of men.
11 For they intended evil against
thee: they imagined a mischievous
device, which they are not able to
perform.
12 Therefore shalt thou make them
turn their back, when thou shalt
make ready thine arrows upon thy
strings against the face of them.
13 Be thou exalted, Lord, in thine
own strength: so will we sing and
praise thy power.

PSALM 22

To the chief Musician upon Aijeleth Shahar, A Psalm of David.

MY GOD, my God, why hast thou forsaken me? why art thou so far from helping me, and from the words of my roaring?

2 O my God, I cry in the daytime, but thou hearest not; and in the night season, and am not silent.

3 But thou art holy, O thou that inhabitest the praises of Israel.

4 Our fathers trusted in thee: they trusted, and thou didst deliver them.

5 They cried unto thee, and were delivered: they trusted in thee, and were not confounded.

6 But I am a worm, and no man; a reproach of men, and despised of the people.

7 All they that see me laugh me to scorn: they shoot out the lip, they shake the head, saying,

8 He trusted on the Lord that he would deliver him: let him deliver him, seeing he delighted in him.

9 But thou art he that took me out of the womb: thou didst make me hope when I was upon my mother's breasts.

10 I was cast upon thee from the womb: thou art my God from my mother's belly.

11 Be not far from me; for trouble is near; for there is none to help.

12 Many bulls have compassed me: strong bulls of Bashan have beset me round.

13 They gaped upon me with their mouths, as a ravening and a roaring lion.

14 I am poured out like water, and all my bones are out of joint: my heart is like wax; it is melted in the midst of my bowels.

15 My strength is dried up like a potsherd; and my tongue cleaveth to my jaws; and thou hast brought me into the dust of death.

16 For dogs have compassed me: the assembly of the wicked have inclosed me: they pierced my hands and my feet.

17 I may tell all my bones: they look and stare upon me.

18 They part my garments among them, and cast lots upon my vesture.

19 But be not thou far from me, O Lord: O my strength, haste thee to help me.

20 Deliver my soul from the sword; my darling from the power of the dog.

21 Save me from the lion's mouth: for thou hast heard me from the horns of the unicorns.

22 I will declare thy name unto my brethren: in the midst of the congregation will I praise thee.

23 Ye that fear the Lord, praise him; all ye the seed of Jacob, glorify him; and fear him, all ye the seed of Israel.

24 For he hath not despised nor abhorred the affliction of the afflicted; neither hath he hid his face from him; but when he cried unto him, he heard.

25 My praise shall be of thee in the great congregation: I will pay my vows before them that fear him.

26 The meek shall eat and be satisfied: they shall praise the Lord that seek him: your heart shall live for ever.

27 All the ends of the world shall remember and turn unto the Lord: and all the kindreds of the nations shall worship before thee.

28 For the kingdom is the Lord's: and he is the governor among the nations.

29 All they that be fat upon earth shall eat and worship: all they that go down to the dust shall bow before him: and none can keep alive his own soul.

30 A seed shall serve him; it shall be accounted to the Lord for a generation.

31 They shall come, and shall declare his righteousness unto a people

that shall be born, that he hath done this.

PSALM 23

A Psalm of David.

THE LORD is my shepherd; I shall not want.

2 He maketh me to lie down in green pastures: he leadeth me beside the still waters.

3 He restoreth my soul: he leadeth me in the paths of righteousness for his name's sake.

4 Yea, though I walk through the valley of the shadow of death, I will fear no evil: for thou art with me; thy rod and thy staff they comfort me.

5 Thou preparest a table before me in the presence of mine enemies: thou anointest my head with oil; my cup runneth over.

6 Surely goodness and mercy shall follow me all the days of my life: and I will dwell in the house of the Lord for ever.

PSALM 24

A Psalm of David.

THE EARTH is the Lord's, and the fulness thereof; the world, and they that dwell therein.

2 For he hath founded it upon the seas, and established it upon the floods.

3 Who shall ascend into the hill of the Lord? or who shall stand in his holy place?

4 He that hath clean hands, and a pure heart; who hath not lifted up his soul unto vanity, nor sworn deceitfully.

5 He shall receive the blessing from the Lord, and righteousness from the God of his salvation.

6 This is the generation of them that seek him, that seek thy face, O Jacob. Selah.

7 Lift up your heads, O ye gates; and be ye lift up, ye everlasting doors; and the King of glory shall come in.

8 Who is this King of glory? The Lord strong and mighty, the Lord mighty in battle.

9 Lift up your heads, O ye gates; even lift them up, ye everlasting doors; and the King of glory shall come in.

10 Who is this King of glory? The Lord of hosts, he is the King of glory. Selah.

PSALM 25

A Psalm of David.

UNTO thee, O Lord, do I lift up my soul.

2 O my God, I trust in thee: let me not be ashamed, let not mine enemies triumph over me.

3 Yea, let none that wait on thee be ashamed: let them be ashamed which transgress without cause.

4 Show me thy ways, O Lord; teach me thy paths.

5 Lead me in thy truth, and teach me: for thou art the God of my salvation; on thee do I wait all the day.

6 Remember, O Lord, thy tender mercies and thy lovingkindnesses; for they have been ever of old.

7 Remember not the sins of my youth, nor my transgressions: according to thy mercy remember thou me for thy goodness' sake, O Lord.

8 Good and upright is the Lord: therefore will he teach sinners in the way.

9 The meek will he guide in judgment: and the meek will he teach his way.

10 All the paths of the Lord are mercy and truth unto such as keep his covenant and his testimonies.

11 For thy name's sake, O Lord, pardon mine iniquity; for it is great.

12 What man is he that feareth the Lord? him shall he teach in the way that he shall choose.

13 His soul shall dwell at ease; and his seed shall inherit the earth.

14 The secret of the Lord is with

them that fear him; and he will show them his covenant.
15 Mine eyes are ever toward the Lord; for he shall pluck my feet out of the net.
16 Turn thee unto me, and have mercy upon me; for I am desolate and afflicted.
17 The troubles of my heart are enlarged: O bring thou me out of my distresses.
18 Look upon mine affliction and my pain; and forgive all my sins.
19 Consider mine enemies; for they are many; and they hate me with cruel hatred.
20 O keep my soul, and deliver me: let me not be ashamed; for I put my trust in thee.
21 Let integrity and uprightness preserve me; for I wait on thee.
22 Redeem Israel, O God, out of all his troubles.

PSALM 26

A Psalm of David.

JUDGE me, O Lord; for I have walked in mine integrity: I have trusted also in the Lord; therefore I shall not slide.
2 Examine me, O Lord, and prove me; try my reins and my heart.
3 For thy lovingkindness is before mine eyes: and I have walked in thy truth.
4 I have not sat with vain persons, neither will I go in with dissemblers.
5 I have hated the congregation of evil doers; and will not sit with the wicked.
6 I will wash mine hands in innocency: so will I compass thine altar, O Lord:
7 That I may publish with the voice of thanksgiving, and tell of all thy wondrous works.
8 Lord, I have loved the habitation of thy house, and the place where thine honour dwelleth.
9 Gather not my soul with sinners, nor my life with bloody men:
10 In whose hands is mischief, and their right hand is full of bribes.
11 But as for me, I will walk in mine integrity: redeem me, and be merciful unto me.
12 My foot standeth in an even place: in the congregations will I bless the Lord.

PSALM 27

A Psalm of David.

THE LORD is my light and my salvation; whom shall I fear? the Lord is the strength of my life; of whom shall I be afraid?
2 When the wicked, even mine enemies and my foes, came upon me to eat up my flesh, they stumbled and fell.
3 Though an host should encamp against me, my heart shall not fear: though war should rise against me, in this will I be confident.
4 One thing have I desired of the Lord, that will I seek after; that I may dwell in the house of the Lord all the days of my life, to behold the beauty of the Lord, and to inquire in his temple.
5 For in the time of trouble he shall hide me in his pavilion: in the secret of his tabernacle shall he hide me; he shall set me up upon a rock.
6 And now shall mine head be lifted up above mine enemies round about me: therefore will I offer in his tabernacle sacrifices of joy; I will sing, yea, I will sing praises unto the Lord.
7 Hear, O Lord, when I cry with my voice: have mercy also upon me, and answer me.
8 When thou saidst, Seek ye my face; my heart said unto thee, Thy face, Lord, will I seek.
9 Hide not thy face far from me; put not thy servant away in anger: thou hast been my help; leave me not, neither forsake me, O God of my salvation.
10 When my father and my mother forsake me, then the Lord will take me up.
11 Teach me thy way, O Lord, and lead me in a plain path, because of mine enemies.
12 Deliver me not over unto the

will of mine enemies: for false witnesses are risen up against me, and such as breathe out cruelty.
13 I had fainted, unless I had believed to see the goodness of the Lord in the land of the living.
14 Wait on the Lord: be of good courage, and he shall strengthen thine heart: wait, I say, on the Lord.

PSALM 28

A Psalm of David.

UNTO thee will I cry, O Lord my rock; be not silent to me: lest, if thou be silent to me, I become like them that go down into the pit.
2 Hear the voice of my supplications, when I cry unto thee, when I lift up my hands toward thy holy oracle.
3 Draw me not away with the wicked, and with the workers of iniquity, which speak peace to their neighbours, but mischief is in their hearts.
4 Give them according to their deeds, and according to the wickedness of their endeavours: give them after the work of their hands; render to them their desert.
5 Because they regard not the works of the Lord, nor the operation of his hands, he shall destroy them, and not build them up.
6 Blessed be the Lord, because he hath heard the voice of my supplications.
7 The Lord is my strength and my shield; my heart trusted in him, and I am helped: therefore my heart greatly rejoiceth; and with my song will I praise him.
8 The Lord is their strength, and he is the saving strength of his anointed.
9 Save thy people, and bless thine inheritance: feed them also, and lift them up for ever.

PSALM 29

A Psalm of David.

GIVE unto the Lord, O ye mighty, give unto the Lord glory and strength.
2 Give unto the Lord the glory due unto his name; worship the Lord in the beauty of holiness.
3 The voice of the Lord is upon the waters: the God of glory thundereth: the Lord is upon many waters.
4 The voice of the Lord is powerful; the voice of the Lord is full of majesty.
5 The voice of the Lord breaketh the cedars; yea, the Lord breaketh the cedars of Lebanon.
6 He maketh them also to skip like a calf; Lebanon and Sirion like a young unicorn.
7 The voice of the Lord divideth the flames of fire.
8 The voice of the Lord shaketh the wilderness; the Lord shaketh the wilderness of Kadesh.
9 The voice of the Lord maketh the hinds to calve, and discovereth the forests: and in his temple doth every one speak of his glory.
10 The Lord sitteth upon the flood; yea, the Lord sitteth King for ever.
11 The Lord will give strength unto his people; the Lord will bless his people with peace.

PSALM 30

A Psalm and Song at the dedication of the house of David.

I WILL extol thee, O Lord; for thou hast lifted me up, and hast not made my foes to rejoice over me.
2 O Lord my God, I cried unto thee, and thou hast healed me.
3 O Lord, thou hast brought up my soul from the grave: thou hast kept me alive, that I should not go down to the pit.
4 Sing unto the Lord, O ye saints of his, and give thanks at the remembrance of his holiness.
5 For his anger endureth but a moment; in his favour is life: weeping may endure for a night, but joy cometh in the morning.
6 And in my prosperity I said, I shall never be moved.
7 Lord, by thy favour thou hast made my mountain to stand strong:

thou didst hide thy face, and I was troubled.

8 I cried to thee, O Lord; and unto the Lord I made supplication.

9 What profit is there in my blood, when I go down to the pit? Shall the dust praise thee? shall it declare thy truth?

10 Hear, O Lord, and have mercy upon me: Lord, be thou my helper.

11 Thou hast turned for me my mourning into dancing: thou hast put off my sackcloth, and girded me with gladness;

12 To the end that my glory may sing praise to thee, and not be silent. O Lord my God, I will give thanks unto thee for ever.

PSALM 31

To the chief Musician, A Psalm of David.

IN THEE, O Lord, do I put my trust; let me never be ashamed: deliver me in thy righteousness.

2 Bow down thine ear to me; deliver me speedily: be thou my strong rock, for an house of defence to save me.

3 For thou art my rock and my fortress; therefore for thy name's sake lead me, and guide me.

4 Pull me out of the net that they have laid privily for me: for thou art my strength.

5 Into thine hand I commit my spirit: thou hast redeemed me, O Lord God of truth.

6 I have hated them that regard lying vanities: but I trust in the Lord.

7 I will be glad and rejoice in thy mercy: for thou hast considered my trouble; thou hast known my soul in adversities;

8 And hast not shut me up into the hand of the enemy: thou hast set my feet in a large room.

9 Have mercy upon me, O Lord, for I am in trouble: mine eye is consumed with grief, yea, my soul and my belly.

10 For my life is spent with grief, and my years with sighing: my strength faileth because of mine iniquity, and my bones are consumed.

11 I was a reproach among all mine enemies, but especially among my neighbours, and a fear to mine acquaintance: they that did see me without fled from me.

12 I am forgotten as a dead man out of mind: I am like a broken vessel.

13 For I have heard the slander of many: fear was on every side: while they took counsel together against me, they devised to take away my life.

14 But I trusted in thee, O Lord: I said, Thou art my God.

15 My times are in thy hand: deliver me from the hand of mine enemies, and from them that persecute me.

16 Make thy face to shine upon thy servant: save me for thy mercies' sake.

17 Let me not be ashamed, O Lord; for I have called upon thee: let the wicked be ashamed, and let them be silent in the grave.

18 Let the lying lips be put to silence; which speak grievous things proudly and contemptuously against the righteous.

19 Oh how great is thy goodness, which thou hast laid up for them that fear thee; which thou hast wrought for them that trust in thee before the sons of men!

20 Thou shalt hide them in the secret of thy presence from the pride of man: thou shalt keep them secretly in a pavilion from the strife of tongues.

21 Blessed be the Lord: for he hath shown me his marvellous kindness in a strong city.

22 For I said in my haste, I am cut off from before thine eyes: nevertheless thou heardest the voice of my supplications when I cried unto thee.

23 O love the Lord, all ye his saints: for the Lord preserveth the faithful, and plentifully rewardeth the proud doer.

24 Be of good courage, and he shall

strengthen your heart, all ye that
hope in the Lord.

PSALM 32

A Psalm of David, Maschil.

BLESSED is he whose transgression
is forgiven, whose sin is covered.
2 Blessed is the man unto whom
the Lord imputeth not iniquity, and
in whose spirit there is no guile.
3 When I kept silence, my bones
waxed old through my roaring all
the day long.
4 For day and night thy hand was
heavy upon me: my moisture is
turned into the drought of summer.
Selah.
5 I acknowledged my sin unto thee,
and mine iniquity have I not hid. I
said, I will confess my transgressions
unto the Lord; and thou forgavest
the iniquity of my sin. Selah.
6 For this shall every one that is
godly pray unto thee in a time when
thou mayest be found: surely in the
floods of great waters they shall not
come nigh unto him.
7 Thou art my hiding place; thou
shalt preserve me from trouble; thou
shalt compass me about with songs
of deliverance. Selah.
8 I will instruct thee and teach thee
in the way which thou shalt go: I
will guide thee with mine eye.
9 Be ye not as the horse, or as the
mule, which have no understanding:
whose mouth must be held in with
bit and bridle, lest they come near
unto thee.
10 Many sorrows shall be to the
wicked: but he that trusteth in the
Lord, mercy shall compass him
about.
11 Be glad in the Lord, and rejoice,
ye righteous: and shout for joy, all ye
that are upright in heart.

PSALM 33

REJOICE in the Lord, O ye righteous: for praise is comely for
the upright.
2 Praise the Lord with harp: sing
unto him with the psaltery and an
instrument of ten strings.
3 Sing unto him a new song; play
skilfully with a loud noise.
4 For the word of the Lord is right;
and all his works are done in truth.
5 He loveth righteousness and
judgment: the earth is full of the
goodness of the Lord.
6 By the word of the Lord were the
heavens made; and all the host of
them by the breath of his mouth.
7 He gathereth the waters of the
sea together as an heap: he layeth up
the depth in storehouses.
8 Let all the earth fear the Lord: let
all the inhabitants of the world stand
in awe of him.
9 For he spake, and it was done; he
commanded, and it stood fast.
10 The Lord bringeth the counsel
of the heathen to nought: he
maketh the devices of the people of
none effect.
11 The counsel of the Lord
standeth for ever, the thoughts of his
heart to all generations.
12 Blessed is the nation whose God
is the Lord; and the people whom
he hath chosen for his own inheritance.
13 The Lord looketh from heaven;
he beholdeth all the sons of men.
14 From the place of his habitation
he looketh upon all the inhabitants
of the earth.
15 He fashioneth their hearts alike;
he considereth all their works.
16 There is no king saved by the
multitude of an host: a mighty man
is not delivered by much strength.
17 An horse is a vain thing for
safety: neither shall he deliver any by
his great strength.
18 Behold, the eye of the Lord is
upon them that fear him, upon
them that hope in his mercy;
19 To deliver their soul from death,
and to keep them alive in famine.
20 Our soul waiteth for the Lord:
he is our help and our shield.
21 For our heart shall rejoice in
him, because we have trusted in his
holy name.

22 Let thy mercy, O Lord, be upon
us, according as we hope in thee.

PSALM 34

A Psalm of David, when he changed his behaviour before Abimelech; who drove him away, and he departed.

I WILL bless the Lord at all times: his
praise shall continually be in my
mouth.
2 My soul shall make her boast in
the Lord: the humble shall hear
thereof, and be glad.
3 O magnify the Lord with me, and
let us exalt his name together.
4 I sought the Lord, and he heard
me, and delivered me from all my
fears.
5 They looked unto him, and were
lightened: and their faces were not
ashamed.
6 This poor man cried, and the
Lord heard him, and saved him out
of all his troubles.
7 The angel of the Lord encampeth
round about them that fear him, and
delivereth them.
8 O taste and see that the Lord is
good: blessed is the man that
trusteth in him.
9 O fear the Lord, ye his saints: for
there is no want to them that fear
him.
10 The young lions do lack, and
suffer hunger: but they that seek the
Lord shall not want any good thing.
11 Come, ye children, hearken
unto me: I will teach you the fear of
the Lord.
12 What man is he that desireth life,
and loveth many days, that he may
see good?
13 Keep thy tongue from evil, and
thy lips from speaking guile.
14 Depart from evil, and do good;
seek peace, and pursue it.
15 The eyes of the Lord are upon
the righteous, and his ears are open
unto their cry.
16 The face of the Lord is against
them that do evil, to cut off the remembrance of them from the earth.
17 The righteous cry, and the Lord
heareth, and delivereth them out of
all their troubles.
18 The Lord is nigh unto them that
are of a broken heart; and saveth
such as be of a contrite spirit.
19 Many are the afflictions of the
righteous: but the Lord delivereth
him out of them all.
20 He keepeth all his bones: not
one of them is broken.
21 Evil shall slay the wicked: and
they that hate the righteous shall be
desolate.
22 The Lord redeemeth the soul of
his servants: and none of them that
trust in him shall be desolate.

PSALM 35

A Psalm of David.

PLEAD my cause, O Lord, with
them that strive with me: fight
against them that fight against me.
2 Take hold of shield and buckler,
and stand up for mine help.
3 Draw out also the spear, and stop
the way against them that persecute
me: say unto my soul, I am thy salvation.
4 Let them be confounded and put
to shame that seek after my soul: let
them be turned back and brought to
confusion that devise my hurt.
5 Let them be as chaff before the
wind: and let the angel of the Lord
chase them.
6 Let their way be dark and slippery: and let the angel of the Lord
persecute them.
7 For without cause have they hid
for me their net in a pit, which
without cause they have digged for
my soul.
8 Let destruction come upon him
at unawares; and let his net that he
hath hid catch himself: into that
very destruction let him fall.
9 And my soul shall be joyful in the
Lord: it shall rejoice in his salvation.
10 All my bones shall say, Lord,
who is like unto thee, which de-
liverest the poor from him that is
too strong for him, yea, the poor

and the needy from him that spoil-
eth him?
11 False witnesses did rise up; they
laid to my charge things that I knew
not.
12 They rewarded me evil for good
to the spoiling of my soul.
13 But as for me, when they were
sick, my clothing was sackcloth: I
humbled my soul with fasting; and
my prayer returned into mine own
bosom.
14 I behaved myself as though he
had been my friend or brother: I
bowed down heavily, as one that
mourneth for his mother.
15 But in mine adversity they rejoiced, and gathered themselves together: yea, the abjects gathered
themselves together against me, and
I knew it not; they did tear me, and
ceased not:
16 With hypocritical mockers in
feasts, they gnashed upon me with
their teeth.
17 Lord, how long wilt thou look
on? rescue my soul from their destructions, my darling from the
lions.
18 I will give thee thanks in the
great congregation: I will praise thee
among much people.
19 Let not them that are mine enemies wrongfully rejoice over me:
neither let them wink with the eye
that hate me without a cause.
20 For they speak not peace: but
they devise deceitful matters against
them that are quiet in the land.
21 Yea, they opened their mouth
wide against me, and said, Aha, aha,
our eye hath seen it.
22 This thou hast seen, O Lord:
keep not silence: O Lord, be not far
from me.
23 Stir up thyself, and awake to my
judgment, even unto my cause, my
God and my Lord.
24 Judge me, O Lord my God, according to thy righteousness; and let
them not rejoice over me.
25 Let them not say in their hearts,
Ah, so would we have it: let them
not say, We have swallowed him up.
26 Let them be ashamed and
brought to confusion together that
rejoice at mine hurt: let them be
clothed with shame and dishonour
that magnify themselves against me.
27 Let them shout for joy, and be
glad, that favour my righteous cause:
yea, let them say continually, Let the
Lord be magnified, which hath
pleasure in the prosperity of his servant.
28 And my tongue shall speak of
thy righteousness and of thy praise
all the day long.

PSALM 36

To the chief Musician, A Psalm of David the servant of the Lord.

THE TRANSGRESSION of the
wicked saith within my heart,
that there is no fear of God before
his eyes.
2 For he flattereth himself in his
own eyes, until his iniquity be found
to be hateful.
3 The words of his mouth are iniquity and deceit: he hath left off to be
wise, and to do good.
4 He deviseth mischief upon his
bed; he setteth himself in a way that
is not good; he abhorreth not evil.
5 Thy mercy, O Lord, is in the
heavens; and thy faithfulness reacheth unto the clouds.
6 Thy righteousness is like the great
mountains; thy judgments are a
great deep: O Lord, thou preservest
man and beast.
7 How excellent is thy lovingkindness, O God! therefore the children
of men put their trust under the
shadow of thy wings.
8 They shall be abundantly satisfied
with the fatness of thy house; and
thou shalt make them drink of the
river of thy pleasures.
9 For with thee is the fountain of
life: in thy light shall we see light.
10 O continue thy lovingkindness
unto them that know thee; and thy
righteousness to the upright in
heart.
11 Let not the foot of pride come

against me, and let not the hand of
the wicked remove me.
12 There are the workers of iniquity fallen: they are cast down, and
shall not be able to rise.

PSALM 37

A Psalm of David.

FRET not thyself because of evildoers, neither be thou envious
against the workers of iniquity.
2 For they shall soon be cut down
like the grass, and wither as the
green herb.
3 Trust in the Lord, and do good;
so shalt thou dwell in the land, and
verily thou shalt be fed.
4 Delight thyself also in the Lord;
and he shall give thee the desires of
thine heart.
5 Commit thy way unto the Lord;
trust also in him; and he shall bring
it to pass.
6 And he shall bring forth thy righteousness as the light, and thy judgment as the noonday.
7 Rest in the Lord, and wait
patiently for him: fret not thyself
because of him who prospereth in
his way, because of the man who
bringeth wicked devices to pass.
8 Cease from anger, and forsake
wrath: fret not thyself in any wise to
do evil.
9 For evildoers shall be cut off: but
those that wait upon the Lord, they
shall inherit the earth.
10 For yet a little while, and the
wicked shall not be: yea, thou shalt
diligently consider his place, and it
shall not be.
11 But the meek shall inherit the
earth; and shall delight themselves in
the abundance of peace.
12 The wicked plotteth against the
just, and gnasheth upon him with
his teeth.
13 The Lord shall laugh at him: for
he seeth that his day is coming.
14 The wicked have drawn out the
sword, and have bent their bow, to
cast down the poor and needy, and
to slay such as be of upright conversation.
15 Their sword shall enter into their
own heart, and their bows shall be
broken.
16 A little that a righteous man hath
is better than the riches of many
wicked.
17 For the arms of the wicked shall
be broken: but the Lord upholdeth
the righteous.
18 The Lord knoweth the days of
the upright: and their inheritance
shall be for ever.
19 They shall not be ashamed in the
evil time: and in the days of famine
they shall be satisfied.
20 But the wicked shall perish, and
the enemies of the Lord shall be as
the fat of lambs: they shall consume;
into smoke shall they consume away.
21 The wicked borroweth, and
payeth not again: but the righteous
showeth mercy, and giveth.
22 For such as be blessed of him
shall inherit the earth; and they that
be cursed of him shall be cut off.
23 The steps of a good man are ordered by the Lord: and he delighteth
in his way.
24 Though he fall, he shall not be
utterly cast down: for the Lord upholdeth him with his hand.
25 I have been young, and now am
old; yet have I not seen the righteous forsaken, nor his seed begging
bread.
26 He is ever merciful, and lendeth;
and his seed is blessed.
27 Depart from evil, and do good;
and dwell for evermore.
28 For the Lord loveth judgment,
and forsaketh not his saints; they are
preserved for ever: but the seed of
the wicked shall be cut off.
29 The righteous shall inherit the
land, and dwell therein for ever.
30 The mouth of the righteous
speaketh wisdom, and his tongue
talketh of judgment.
31 The law of his God is in his
heart; none of his steps shall slide.
32 The wicked watcheth the righteous, and seeketh to slay him.
33 The Lord will not leave him in

his hand, nor condemn him when
he is judged.
34 Wait on the Lord, and keep his
way, and he shall exalt thee to inherit the land: when the wicked are
cut off, thou shalt see it.
35 I have seen the wicked in great
power, and spreading himself like a
green bay tree.
36 Yet he passed away, and, lo, he
was not: yea, I sought him, but he
could not be found.
37 Mark the perfect man, and behold the upright: for the end of that
man is peace.
38 But the transgressors shall be destroyed together: the end of the
wicked shall be cut off.
39 But the salvation of the righteous is of the Lord: he is their
strength in the time of trouble.
40 And the Lord shall help them,
and deliver them: he shall deliver
them from the wicked, and save
them, because they trust in him.

PSALM 38

A Psalm of David, to bring to remembrance.

O LORD, rebuke me not in thy
wrath: neither chasten me in
thy hot displeasure.
2 For thine arrows stick fast in me,
and thy hand presseth me sore.
3 There is no soundness in my flesh
because of thine anger; neither is
there any rest in my bones because
of my sin.
4 For mine iniquities are gone over
mine head: as an heavy burden they
are too heavy for me.
5 My wounds stink and are corrupt
because of my foolishness.
6 I am troubled; I am bowed down
greatly; I go mourning all the day
long.
7 For my loins are filled with a
loathsome disease: and there is no
soundness in my flesh.
8 I am feeble and sore broken: I
have roared by reason of the dis-
quietness of my heart.
9 Lord, all my desire is before thee;
and my groaning is not hid from
thee.
10 My heart panteth, my strength
faileth me: as for the light of mine
eyes, it also is gone from me.
11 My lovers and my friends stand
aloof from my sore; and my kins-
men stand afar off.
12 They also that seek after my life
lay snares for me: and they that seek
my hurt speak mischievous things,
and imagine deceits all the day long.
13 But I, as a deaf man, heard not;
and I was as a dumb man that
openeth not his mouth.
14 Thus I was as a man that heareth
not, and in whose mouth are no re-
proofs.
15 For in thee, O Lord, do I hope:
thou wilt hear, O Lord my God.
16 For I said, Hear me, lest otherwise they should rejoice over me:
when my foot slippeth, they magnify themselves against me.
17 For I am ready to halt, and my
sorrow is continually before me.
18 For I will declare mine iniquity;
I will be sorry for my sin.
19 But mine enemies are lively, and
they are strong: and they that hate
me wrongfully are multiplied.
20 They also that render evil for
good are mine adversaries; because I
follow the thing that good is.
21 Forsake me not, O Lord: O my
God, be not far from me.
22 Make haste to help me, O Lord
my salvation.

PSALM 39

To the chief Musician, even to Jeduthun, A Psalm of David.

I SAID, I will take heed to my ways,
that I sin not with my tongue: I
will keep my mouth with a bridle,
while the wicked is before me.
2 I was dumb with silence, I held
my peace, even from good; and my
sorrow was stirred.
3 My heart was hot within me,
while I was musing the fire burned:
then spake I with my tongue,
4 Lord, make me to know mine
end, and the measure of my days,

what it is; that I may know how frail I am.

5 Behold, thou hast made my days as an handbreadth; and mine age is as nothing before thee: verily every man at his best state is altogether vanity. Selah.

6 Surely every man walketh in a vain show: surely they are disquieted in vain: he heapeth up riches, and knoweth not who shall gather them.

7 And now, Lord, what wait I for? my hope is in thee.

8 Deliver me from all my transgressions: make me not the reproach of the foolish.

9 I was dumb, I opened not my mouth; because thou didst it.

10 Remove thy stroke away from me: I am consumed by the blow of thine hand.

11 When thou with rebukes dost correct man for iniquity, thou makest his beauty to consume away like a moth: surely every man is vanity. Selah.

12 Hear my prayer, O Lord, and give ear unto my cry; hold not thy peace at my tears: for I am a stranger with thee, and a sojourner, as all my fathers were.

13 O spare me, that I may recover strength, before I go hence, and be no more.

PSALM 40

To the chief Musician, A Psalm of David.

I WAITED patiently for the Lord; and he inclined unto me, and heard my cry.

2 He brought me up also out of an horrible pit, out of the miry clay, and set my feet upon a rock, and established my goings.

3 And he hath put a new song in my mouth, even praise unto our God: many shall see it, and fear, and shall trust in the Lord.

4 Blessed is that man that maketh the Lord his trust, and respecteth not the proud, nor such as turn aside to lies.

5 Many, O Lord my God, are thy wonderful works which thou hast done, and thy thoughts which are to us-ward: they cannot be reckoned up in order unto thee: if I would declare and speak of them, they are more than can be numbered.

6 Sacrifice and offering thou didst not desire; mine ears hast thou opened: burnt offering and sin offering hast thou not required.

7 Then said I, Lo, I come: in the volume of the book it is written of me,

8 I delight to do thy will, O my God: yea, thy law is within my heart.

9 I have preached righteousness in the great congregation: lo, I have not refrained my lips, O Lord, thou knowest.

10 I have not hid thy righteousness within my heart; I have declared thy faithfulness and thy salvation: I have not concealed thy lovingkindness and thy truth from the great congregation.

11 Withhold not thou thy tender mercies from me, O Lord: let thy lovingkindness and thy truth continually preserve me.

12 For innumerable evils have compassed me about: mine iniquities have taken hold upon me, so that I am not able to look up; they are more than the hairs of mine head: therefore my heart faileth me.

13 Be pleased, O Lord, to deliver me: O Lord, make haste to help me.

14 Let them be ashamed and confounded together that seek after my soul to destroy it; let them be driven backward and put to shame that wish me evil.

15 Let them be desolate for a reward of their shame that say unto me, Aha, aha.

16 Let all those that seek thee rejoice and be glad in thee: let such as love thy salvation say continually, The Lord be magnified.

17 But I am poor and needy; yet the Lord thinketh upon me: thou art my help and my deliverer; make no tarrying, O my God.

PSALM 41

To the chief Musician, A Psalm of David.

BLESSED is he that considereth the poor: the Lord will deliver him in time of trouble.
2 The Lord will preserve him, and keep him alive; and he shall be blessed upon the earth: and thou wilt not deliver him unto the will of his enemies.
3 The Lord will strengthen him upon the bed of languishing: thou wilt make all his bed in his sickness.
4 I said, Lord, be merciful unto me: heal my soul; for I have sinned against thee.
5 Mine enemies speak evil of me, When shall he die, and his name perish?
6 And if he come to see me, he speaketh vanity: his heart gathereth iniquity to itself; when he goeth abroad, he telleth it.
7 All that hate me whisper together against me: against me do they devise my hurt.
8 An evil disease, say they, cleaveth fast unto him: and now that he lieth he shall rise up no more.
9 Yea, mine own familiar friend, in whom I trusted, which did eat of my bread, hath lifted up his heel against me.
10 But thou, O Lord, be merciful unto me, and raise me up, that I may requite them.
11 By this I know that thou favourest me, because mine enemy doth not triumph over me.
12 And as for me, thou upholdest me in mine integrity, and settest me before thy face for ever.
13 Blessed be the Lord God of Israel from everlasting, and to everlasting. Amen, and Amen.

PSALM 42

To the chief Musician, Maschil, for the sons of Korah.

AS THE hart panteth after the water brooks, so panteth my soul after thee, O God.
2 My soul thirsteth for God, for the living God: when shall I come and appear before God?
3 My tears have been my meat day and night, while they continually say unto me, Where is thy God?
4 When I remember these things, I pour out my soul in me: for I had gone with the multitude, I went with them to the house of God, with the voice of joy and praise, with a multitude that kept holyday.
5 Why art thou cast down, O my soul? and why art thou disquieted in me? hope thou in God: for I shall yet praise him for the help of his countenance.
6 O my God, my soul is cast down within me: therefore will I remember thee from the land of Jordan, and of the Hermonites, from the hill Mizar.
7 Deep calleth unto deep at the noise of thy waterspouts: all thy waves and thy billows are gone over me.
8 Yet the Lord will command his lovingkindness in the daytime, and in the night his song shall be with me, and my prayer unto the God of my life.
9 I will say unto God my rock, Why hast thou forgotten me? why go I mourning because of the oppression of the enemy?
10 As with a sword in my bones, mine enemies reproach me; while they say daily unto me, Where is thy God?
11 Why art thou cast down, O my soul? and why art thou disquieted within me? hope thou in God: for I shall yet praise him, who is the health of my countenance, and my God.

PSALM 43

JUDGE me, O God, and plead my cause against an ungodly nation: O deliver me from the deceitful and unjust man.
2 For thou art the God of my strength: why dost thou cast me off? why go I mourning because of the oppression of the enemy?

3 O send out thy light and thy
truth: let them lead me; let them
bring me unto thy holy hill, and to
thy tabernacles.
4 Then will I go unto the altar of
God, unto God my exceeding joy:
yea, upon the harp will I praise thee,
O God my God.
5 Why art thou cast down, O my
soul? and why art thou disquieted
within me? hope in God: for I shall
yet praise him, who is the health of
my countenance, and my God.

PSALM 44

To the chief Musician for the sons of Korah, Maschil.

WE HAVE heard with our ears, O
God, our fathers have told us,
what work thou didst in their days,
in the times of old.
2 How thou didst drive out the
heathen with thy hand, and plant-
edst them; how thou didst afflict the
people, and cast them out.
3 For they got not the land in possession by their own sword, neither
did their own arm save them: but
thy right hand, and thine arm, and
the light of thy countenance, because thou hadst a favour unto
them.
4 Thou art my King, O God: command deliverances for Jacob.
5 Through thee will we push down
our enemies: through thy name will
we tread them under that rise up
against us.
6 For I will not trust in my bow,
neither shall my sword save me.
7 But thou hast saved us from our
enemies, and hast put them to
shame that hated us.
8 In God we boast all the day long,
and praise thy name for ever. Selah.
9 But thou hast cast off, and put us
to shame; and goest not forth with
our armies.
10 Thou makest us to turn back
from the enemy: and they which
hate us spoil for themselves.
11 Thou hast given us like sheep
appointed for meat; and hast scattered us among the heathen.
12 Thou sellest thy people for
nought, and dost not increase thy
wealth by their price.
13 Thou makest us a reproach to
our neighbours, a scorn and a derision to them that are round about
us.
14 Thou makest us a byword
among the heathen, a shaking of the
head among the people.
15 My confusion is continually before me, and the shame of my face
hath covered me,
16 For the voice of him that reproacheth and blasphemeth; by reason of the enemy and avenger.
17 All this is come upon us; yet
have we not forgotten thee, neither
have we dealt falsely in thy
covenant.
18 Our heart is not turned back,
neither have our steps declined from
thy way;
19 Though thou hast sore broken
us in the place of dragons, and covered us with the shadow of death.
20 If we have forgotten the name
of our God, or stretched out our
hands to a strange god;
21 Shall not God search this out?
for he knoweth the secrets of the
heart.
22 Yea, for thy sake are we killed all
the day long; we are counted as
sheep for the slaughter.
23 Awake, why sleepest thou, O
Lord? arise, cast us not off for ever.
24 Wherefore hidest thou thy face,
and forgettest our affliction and our
oppression?
25 For our soul is bowed down to
the dust: our belly cleaveth unto the
earth.
26 Arise for our help, and redeem
us for thy mercies' sake.

PSALM 45

To the chief Musician upon Shoshannim, for the sons of Korah, Maschil, A Song of loves.

MY HEART is inditing a good
matter: I speak of the things
which I have made touching the

king: my tongue is the pen of a
ready writer.
2 Thou art fairer than the children
of men: grace is poured into thy
lips: therefore God hath blessed thee
for ever.
3 Gird thy sword upon thy thigh, O
most mighty, with thy glory and thy
majesty.
4 And in thy majesty ride prosper-
ously because of truth and meekness
and righteousness; and thy right
hand shall teach thee terrible things.
5 Thine arrows are sharp in the
heart of the king's enemies;
whereby the people fall under thee.
6 Thy throne, O God, is for ever
and ever: the sceptre of thy kingdom is a right sceptre.
7 Thou lovest righteousness, and
hatest wickedness: therefore God,
thy God, hath anointed thee with
the oil of gladness above thy fellows.
8 All thy garments smell of myrrh,
and aloes, and cassia, out of the
ivory palaces, whereby they have
made thee glad.
9 Kings' daughters were among thy
honourable women: upon thy right
hand did stand the queen in gold of
Ophir.
10 Hearken, O daughter, and consider, and incline thine ear; forget
also thine own people, and thy father's house;
11 So shall the king greatly desire
thy beauty: for he is thy Lord; and
worship thou him.
12 And the daughter of Tyre shall
be there with a gift; even the rich
among the people shall entreat thy
favour.
13 The king's daughter is all glorious within: her clothing is of
wrought gold.
14 She shall be brought unto the
king in raiment of needlework: the
virgins her companions that follow
her shall be brought unto thee.
15 With gladness and rejoicing shall
they be brought: they shall enter
into the king's palace.
16 Instead of thy fathers shall be thy
children, whom thou mayest make
princes in all the earth.
17 I will make thy name to be remembered in all generations: therefore shall the people praise thee for
ever and ever.

PSALM 46

To the chief Musician for the sons of Korah, A Song upon Alamoth.

GOD IS our refuge and strength, a
very present help in trouble.
2 Therefore will not we fear,
though the earth be removed, and
though the mountains be carried
into the midst of the sea;
3 Though the waters thereof roar
and be troubled, though the mountains shake with the swelling
thereof. Selah.
4 There is a river, the streams
whereof shall make glad the city of
God, the holy place of the tabernacles of the most High.
5 God is in the midst of her; she
shall not be moved: God shall help
her, and that right early.
6 The heathen raged, the kingdoms
were moved: he uttered his voice,
the earth melted.
7 The Lord of hosts is with us; the
God of Jacob is our refuge. Selah.
8 Come, behold the works of the
Lord, what desolations he hath
made in the earth.
9 He maketh wars to cease unto the
end of the earth; he breaketh the
bow, and cutteth the spear in sunder; he burneth the chariot in the
fire.
10 Be still, and know that I am
God: I will be exalted among the
heathen, I will be exalted in the
earth.
11 The Lord of hosts is with us; the
God of Jacob is our refuge. Selah.

PSALM 47

To the chief Musician, A Psalm for the sons of Korah.

O CLAP your hands, all ye people;
shout unto God with the voice
of triumph.

2 For the Lord most high is terrible;
he is a great King over all the earth.
3 He shall subdue the people under
us, and the nations under our feet.
4 He shall choose our inheritance
for us, the excellency of Jacob
whom he loved. Selah.
5 God is gone up with a shout, the
Lord with the sound of a trumpet.
6 Sing praises to God, sing praises:
sing praises unto our King, sing
praises.
7 For God is the King of all the
earth: sing ye praises with understanding.
8 God reigneth over the heathen:
God sitteth upon the throne of his
holiness.
9 The princes of the people are
gathered together, even the people
of the God of Abraham: for the
shields of the earth belong unto
God: he is greatly exalted.

PSALM 48

A Song and Psalm for the sons of Korah.

GREAT is the Lord, and greatly to
be praised in the city of our
God, in the mountain of his holiness.
2 Beautiful for situation, the joy of
the whole earth, is mount Zion, on
the sides of the north, the city of
the great King.
3 God is known in her palaces for a
refuge.
4 For, lo, the kings were assembled,
they passed by together.
5 They saw it, and so they mar-
velled; they were troubled, and
hasted away.
6 Fear took hold upon them there,
and pain, as of a woman in travail.
7 Thou breakest the ships of
Tarshish with an east wind.
8 As we have heard, so have we
seen in the city of the Lord of hosts,
in the city of our God: God will establish it for ever. Selah.
9 We have thought of thy lovingkindness, O God, in the midst of
thy temple.
10 According to thy name, O God,
so is thy praise unto the ends of the
earth: thy right hand is full of righteousness.
11 Let mount Zion rejoice, let the
daughters of Judah be glad, because
of thy judgments.
12 Walk about Zion, and go round
about her: tell the towers thereof.
13 Mark ye well her bulwarks, consider her palaces; that ye may tell it
to the generation following.
14 For this God is our God for ever
and ever: he will be our guide even
unto death.

PSALM 49

To the chief Musician,
A Psalm for the sons of Korah.

HEAR this, all ye people; give ear,
all ye inhabitants of the world:
2 Both low and high, rich and
poor, together.
3 My mouth shall speak of wisdom;
and the meditation of my heart shall
be of understanding.
4 I will incline mine ear to a parable: I will open my dark saying upon
the harp.
5 Wherefore should I fear in the
days of evil, when the iniquity of
my heels shall compass me about?
6 They that trust in their wealth,
and boast themselves in the multitude of their riches;
7 None of them can by any means
redeem his brother, nor give to God
a ransom for him:
8 (For the redemption of their soul
is precious, and it ceaseth for ever:)
9 That he should still live for ever,
and not see corruption.
10 For he seeth that wise men die,
likewise the fool and the brutish
person perish, and leave their wealth
to others.
11 Their inward thought is, that
their houses shall continue for ever,
and their dwelling places to all generations; they call their lands after
their own names.
12 Nevertheless man being in hon-

our abideth not: he is like the beasts
that perish.
13 This their way is their folly: yet
their posterity approve their sayings.
Selah.
14 Like sheep they are laid in the
grave; death shall feed on them; and
the upright shall have dominion
over them in the morning; and their
beauty shall consume in the grave
from their dwelling.
15 But God will redeem my soul
from the power of the grave: for he
shall receive me. Selah.
16 Be not thou afraid when one is
made rich, when the glory of his
house is increased;
17 For when he dieth he shall carry
nothing away: his glory shall not descend after him.
18 Though while he lived he
blessed his soul: and men will praise
thee, when thou doest well to thyself.
19 He shall go to the generation of
his fathers; they shall never see light.
20 Man that is in honour, and un-
derstandeth not, is like the beasts
that perish.

PSALM 50

A Psalm of Asaph.

THE MIGHTY God, even the Lord,
hath spoken, and called the
earth from the rising of the sun
unto the going down thereof.
2 Out of Zion, the perfection of
beauty, God hath shined.
3 Our God shall come, and shall
not keep silence: a fire shall devour
before him, and it shall be very tempestuous round about him.
4 He shall call to the heavens from
above, and to the earth, that he may
judge his people.
5 Gather my saints together unto
me; those that have made a covenant
with me by sacrifice.
6 And the heavens shall declare his
righteousness: for God is judge himself. Selah.
7 Hear, O my people, and I will
speak; O Israel, and I will testify
against thee: I am God, even thy
God.
8 I will not reprove thee for thy sacrifices or thy burnt offerings, to
have been continually before me.
9 I will take no bullock out of thy
house, nor he goats out of thy folds.
10 For every beast of the forest is
mine, and the cattle upon a thousand hills.
11 I know all the fowls of the
mountains: and the wild beasts of
the field are mine.
12 If I were hungry, I would not
tell thee: for the world is mine, and
the fulness thereof.
13 Will I eat the flesh of bulls, or
drink the blood of goats?
14 Offer unto God thanksgiving;
and pay thy vows unto the most
High:
15 And call upon me in the day of
trouble: I will deliver thee, and thou
shalt glorify me.
16 But unto the wicked God saith,
What hast thou to do to declare my
statutes, or that thou shouldest take
my covenant in thy mouth?
17 Seeing thou hatest instruction,
and castest my words behind thee.
18 When thou sawest a thief, then
thou consentedst with him, and hast
been partaker with adulterers.
19 Thou givest thy mouth to evil,
and thy tongue frameth deceit.
20 Thou sittest and speakest against
thy brother; thou slanderest thine
own mother's son.
21 These things hast thou done,
and I kept silence; thou thoughtest
that I was altogether such an one as
thyself: but I will reprove thee, and
set them in order before thine eyes.
22 Now consider this, ye that forget
God, lest I tear you in pieces, and
there be none to deliver.
23 Whoso offereth praise glorifieth
me: and to him that ordereth his
conversation aright will I show the
salvation of God.

PSALM 51

To the chief Musician, A Psalm of David, when Nathan the prophet came unto him, after he had gone to Bath-sheba.

HAVE mercy upon me, O God, according to thy lovingkindness: according unto the multitude of thy tender mercies blot out my transgressions.

2 Wash me thoroughly from mine iniquity, and cleanse me from my sin.

3 For I acknowledge my transgressions: and my sin is ever before me.

4 Against thee, thee only, have I sinned, and done this evil in thy sight: that thou mightest be justified when thou speakest, and be clear when thou judgest.

5 Behold, I was shapen in iniquity; and in sin did my mother conceive me.

6 Behold, thou desirest truth in the inward parts: and in the hidden part thou shalt make me to know wisdom.

7 Purge me with hyssop, and I shall be clean: wash me, and I shall be whiter than snow.

8 Make me to hear joy and gladness; that the bones which thou hast broken may rejoice.

9 Hide thy face from my sins, and blot out all mine iniquities.

10 Create in me a clean heart, O God; and renew a right spirit within me.

11 Cast me not away from thy presence; and take not thy holy spirit from me.

12 Restore unto me the joy of thy salvation; and uphold me with thy free spirit.

13 Then will I teach transgressors thy ways; and sinners shall be converted unto thee.

14 Deliver me from bloodguiltiness, O God, thou God of my salvation: and my tongue shall sing aloud of thy righteousness.

15 O Lord, open thou my lips: and my mouth shall show forth thy praise.

16 For thou desirest not sacrifice; else would I give it: thou delightest not in burnt offering.

17 The sacrifices of God are a broken spirit: a broken and a contrite heart, O God, thou wilt not despise.

18 Do good in thy good pleasure unto Zion: build thou the walls of Jerusalem.

19 Then shalt thou be pleased with the sacrifices of righteousness, with burnt offering and whole burnt offering: then shall they offer bullocks upon thine altar.

PSALM 52

To the chief Musician, Maschil, A Psalm of David, when Doeg the Edomite came and told Saul, and said unto him, David is come to the house of Ahimelech.

WHY BOASTEST thou thyself in mischief, O mighty man? the goodness of God endureth continually.

2 Thy tongue deviseth mischiefs; like a sharp razor, working deceitfully.

3 Thou lovest evil more than good; and lying rather than to speak righteousness. Selah.

4 Thou lovest all devouring words, O thou deceitful tongue.

5 God shall likewise destroy thee for ever, he shall take thee away, and pluck thee out of thy dwelling place, and root thee out of the land of the living. Selah.

6 The righteous also shall see, and fear, and shall laugh at him:

7 Lo, this is the man that made not God his strength; but trusted in the abundance of his riches, and strengthened himself in his wickedness.

8 But I am like a green olive tree in the house of God: I trust in the mercy of God for ever and ever.

9 I will praise thee for ever, because thou hast done it: and I will wait on thy name; for it is good before thy saints.

PSALM 53

To the chief Musician upon Mahalath, Maschil, A Psalm of David.

THE FOOL hath said in his heart, There is no God. Corrupt are they, and have done abominable iniquity: there is none that doeth good.

2 God looked down from heaven upon the children of men, to see if there were any that did understand, that did seek God.

3 Every one of them is gone back: they are altogether become filthy; there is none that doeth good, no, not one.

4 Have the workers of iniquity no knowledge? who eat up my people as they eat bread: they have not called upon God.

5 There were they in great fear, where no fear was: for God hath scattered the bones of him that encampeth against thee: thou hast put them to shame, because God hath despised them.

6 Oh that the salvation of Israel were come out of Zion! When God bringeth back the captivity of his people, Jacob shall rejoice, and Israel shall be glad.

PSALM 54

To the chief Musician on Neginoth, Maschil, A Psalm of David, when the Ziphims came and said to Saul, Doth not David hide himself with us?

SAVE me, O God, by thy name, and judge me by thy strength.

2 Hear my prayer, O God; give ear to the words of my mouth.

3 For strangers are risen up against me, and oppressors seek after my soul: they have not set God before them. Selah.

4 Behold, God is mine helper: the Lord is with them that uphold my soul.

5 He shall reward evil unto mine enemies: cut them off in thy truth.

6 I will freely sacrifice unto thee: I will praise thy name, O Lord; for it is good.

7 For he hath delivered me out of all trouble: and mine eye hath seen his desire upon mine enemies.

PSALM 55

To the chief Musician on Neginoth, Maschil, A Psalm of David.

GIVE ear to my prayer, O God; and hide not thyself from my supplication.

2 Attend unto me, and hear me: I mourn in my complaint, and make a noise;

3 Because of the voice of the enemy, because of the oppression of the wicked: for they cast iniquity upon me, and in wrath they hate me.

4 My heart is sore pained within me: and the terrors of death are fallen upon me.

5 Fearfulness and trembling are come upon me, and horror hath overwhelmed me.

6 And I said, Oh that I had wings like a dove! for then would I fly away, and be at rest.

7 Lo, then would I wander far off, and remain in the wilderness. Selah.

8 I would hasten my escape from the windy storm and tempest.

9 Destroy, O Lord, and divide their tongues: for I have seen violence and strife in the city.

10 Day and night they go about it upon the walls thereof: mischief also and sorrow are in the midst of it.

11 Wickedness is in the midst thereof: deceit and guile depart not from her streets.

12 For it was not an enemy that reproached me; then I could have borne it: neither was it he that hated me that did magnify himself against me; then I would have hid myself from him:

13 But it was thou, a man mine equal, my guide, and mine acquaintance.

14 We took sweet counsel together,

and walked unto the house of God
in company.
15 Let death seize upon them, and
let them go down quick into hell:
for wickedness is in their dwellings,
and among them.
16 As for me, I will call upon God;
and the Lord shall save me.
17 Evening, and morning, and at
noon, will I pray, and cry aloud: and
he shall hear my voice.
18 He hath delivered my soul in
peace from the battle that was
against me: for there were many
with me.
19 God shall hear, and afflict them,
even he that abideth of old. Selah.
Because they have no changes,
therefore they fear not God.
20 He hath put forth his hands
against such as be at peace with him:
he hath broken his covenant.
21 The words of his mouth were
smoother than butter, but war was
in his heart: his words were softer
than oil, yet were they drawn
swords.
22 Cast thy burden upon the Lord,
and he shall sustain thee: he shall
never suffer the righteous to be
moved.
23 But thou, O God, shalt bring
them down into the pit of destruction: bloody and deceitful men shall
not live out half their days; but I will
trust in thee.

PSALM 56

To the chief Musician upon Jonath-elem-rechokim, Michtam of David, when the Philistines took him in Gath.

BE MERCIFUL unto me, O God:
for man would swallow me up;
he fighting daily oppresseth me.
2 Mine enemies would daily swallow me up: for they be many that
fight against me, O thou most High.
3 What time I am afraid, I will trust
in thee.
4 In God I will praise his word, in
God I have put my trust; I will not
fear what flesh can do unto me.
5 Every day they wrest my words:
all their thoughts are against me for
evil.
6 They gather themselves together,
they hide themselves, they mark my
steps, when they wait for my soul.
7 Shall they escape by iniquity? in
thine anger cast down the people, O
God.
8 Thou tellest my wanderings: put
thou my tears into thy bottle: are
they not in thy book?
9 When I cry unto thee, then shall
mine enemies turn back: this I
know; for God is for me.
10 In God will I praise his word: in
the Lord will I praise his word.
11 In God have I put my trust: I
will not be afraid what man can do
unto me.
12 Thy vows are upon me, O God:
I will render praises unto thee.
13 For thou hast delivered my soul
from death: wilt not thou deliver my
feet from falling, that I may walk before God in the light of the living?

PSALM 57

To the chief Musician, Al-taschith, Michtam of David, when he fled from Saul in the cave.

BE MERCIFUL unto me, O God, be
merciful unto me: for my soul
trusteth in thee: yea, in the shadow
of thy wings will I make my refuge,
until these calamities be overpast.
2 I will cry unto God most high;
unto God that performeth all things
for me.
3 He shall send from heaven, and
save me from the reproach of him
that would swallow me up. Selah.
God shall send forth his mercy and
his truth.
4 My soul is among lions: and I lie
even among them that are set on
fire, even the sons of men, whose
teeth are spears and arrows, and
their tongue a sharp sword.
5 Be thou exalted, O God, above
the heavens; let thy glory be above
all the earth.
6 They have prepared a net for my
steps; my soul is bowed down: they

have digged a pit before me, into the
midst whereof they are fallen themselves. Selah.
7 My heart is fixed, O God, my
heart is fixed: I will sing and give
praise.
8 Awake up, my glory; awake,
psaltery and harp: I myself will
awake early.
9 I will praise thee, O Lord, among
the people: I will sing unto thee
among the nations.
10 For thy mercy is great unto the
heavens, and thy truth unto the
clouds.
11 Be thou exalted, O God, above
the heavens: let thy glory be above
all the earth.

PSALM 58

*To the chief Musician, Al-taschith,
Michtam of David.*

DO YE indeed speak righteousness, O congregation? do ye
judge uprightly, O ye sons of men?
2 Yea, in heart ye work wickedness;
ye weigh the violence of your hands
in the earth.
3 The wicked are estranged from
the womb: they go astray as soon as
they be born, speaking lies.
4 Their poison is like the poison of
a serpent: they are like the deaf
adder that stoppeth her ear;
5 Which will not hearken to the
voice of charmers, charming never
so wisely.
6 Break their teeth, O God, in their
mouth: break out the great teeth of
the young lions, O Lord.
7 Let them melt away as waters
which run continually: when he
bendeth his bow to shoot his arrows, let them be as cut in pieces.
8 As a snail which melteth, let
every one of them pass away: like
the untimely birth of a woman, that
they may not see the sun.
9 Before your pots can feel the
thorns, he shall take them away as
with a whirlwind, both living, and
in his wrath.
10 The righteous shall rejoice when
he seeth the vengeance: he shall
wash his feet in the blood of the
wicked.
11 So that a man shall say, Verily
there is a reward for the righteous:
verily he is a God that judgeth in the
earth.

PSALM 59

*To the chief Musician, Al-taschith,
Michtam of David; when Saul sent, and
they watched the house to kill him.*

DELIVER me from mine enemies,
O my God: defend me from
them that rise up against me.
2 Deliver me from the workers of
iniquity, and save me from bloody
men.
3 For, lo, they lie in wait for my
soul: the mighty are gathered against
me; not for my transgression, nor
for my sin, O Lord.
4 They run and prepare themselves
without my fault: awake to help me,
and behold.
5 Thou therefore, O Lord God of
hosts, the God of Israel, awake to
visit all the heathen: be not merciful
to any wicked transgressors. Selah.
6 They return at evening: they
make a noise like a dog, and go
round about the city.
7 Behold, they belch out with their
mouth: swords are in their lips: for
who, say they, doth hear?
8 But thou, O Lord, shalt laugh at
them; thou shalt have all the heathen in derision.
9 Because of his strength will I wait
upon thee: for God is my defence.
10 The God of my mercy shall prevent me: God shall let me see my
desire upon mine enemies.
11 Slay them not, lest my people
forget: scatter them by thy power;
and bring them down, O Lord our
shield.
12 For the sin of their mouth and
the words of their lips let them even
be taken in their pride: and for cursing and lying which they speak.
13 Consume them in wrath, consume them, that they may not be:

and let them know that God ruleth
in Jacob unto the ends of the earth.
Selah.
14 And at evening let them return;
and let them make a noise like a
dog, and go round about the city.
15 Let them wander up and down
for meat, and grudge if they be not
satisfied.
16 But I will sing of thy power; yea,
I will sing aloud of thy mercy in the
morning: for thou hast been my defence and refuge in the day of my
trouble.
17 Unto thee, O my strength, will I
sing: for God is my defence, and the
God of my mercy.

PSALM 60

To the chief Musician upon Shushan-eduth, Michtam of David, to teach; when he strove with Aram-naharaim and with Aram-zobah, when Joab returned, and smote of Edom in the valley of salt twelve thousand.

O God, thou hast cast us off,
thou hast scattered us, thou
hast been displeased; O turn thyself
to us again.
2 Thou hast made the earth to
tremble; thou hast broken it: heal
the breaches thereof; for it shaketh.
3 Thou hast shown thy people hard
things: thou hast made us to drink
the wine of astonishment.
4 Thou hast given a banner to them
that fear thee, that it may be displayed because of the truth. Selah.
5 That thy beloved may be delivered; save with thy right hand, and
hear me.
6 God hath spoken in his holiness; I
will rejoice, I will divide Shechem,
and mete out the valley of Succoth.
7 Gilead is mine, and Manasseh is
mine; Ephraim also is the strength of
mine head; Judah is my lawgiver;
8 Moab is my washpot; over Edom
will I cast out my shoe: Philistia, triumph thou because of me.
9 Who will bring me into the
strong city? who will lead me into
Edom?
10 Wilt not thou, O God, which
hadst cast us off? and thou, O God,
which didst not go out with our
armies?
11 Give us help from trouble: for
vain is the help of man.
12 Through God we shall do
valiantly: for he it is that shall tread
down our enemies.

PSALM 61

To the chief Musician upon Neginah, A Psalm of David.

Hear my cry, O God; attend
unto my prayer.
2 From the end of the earth will I
cry unto thee, when my heart is
overwhelmed: lead me to the rock
that is higher than I.
3 For thou hast been a shelter for
me, and a strong tower from the
enemy.
4 I will abide in thy tabernacle for
ever: I will trust in the covert of thy
wings. Selah.
5 For thou, O God, hast heard my
vows: thou hast given me the heritage of those that fear thy name.
6 Thou wilt prolong the king's life:
and his years as many generations.
7 He shall abide before God for
ever: O prepare mercy and truth,
which may preserve him.
8 So will I sing praise unto thy
name for ever, that I may daily perform my vows.

PSALM 62

To the chief Musician, to Jeduthun, A Psalm of David.

Truly my soul waiteth upon
God: from him cometh my salvation.
2 He only is my rock and my salvation; he is my defence; I shall not be
greatly moved.
3 How long will ye imagine mischief against a man? ye shall be slain
all of you: as a bowing wall shall ye
be, and as a tottering fence.
4 They only consult to cast him
down from his excellency: they delight in lies: they bless with their

mouth, but they curse inwardly. Selah.

5 My soul, wait thou only upon God; for my expectation is from him.

6 He only is my rock and my salvation: he is my defence; I shall not be moved.

7 In God is my salvation and my glory: the rock of my strength, and my refuge, is in God.

8 Trust in him at all times; ye people, pour out your heart before him: God is a refuge for us. Selah.

9 Surely men of low degree are vanity, and men of high degree are a lie: to be laid in the balance, they are altogether lighter than vanity.

10 Trust not in oppression, and become not vain in robbery: if riches increase, set not your heart upon them.

11 God hath spoken once; twice have I heard this; that power belongeth unto God.

12 Also unto thee, O Lord, belongeth mercy: for thou renderest to every man according to his work.

PSALM 63

A Psalm of David,
when he was in the wilderness of Judah.

O God, thou art my God; early will I seek thee: my soul thirsteth for thee, my flesh longeth for thee in a dry and thirsty land, where no water is;

2 To see thy power and thy glory, so as I have seen thee in the sanctuary.

3 Because thy lovingkindness is better than life, my lips shall praise thee.

4 Thus will I bless thee while I live: I will lift up my hands in thy name.

5 My soul shall be satisfied as with marrow and fatness; and my mouth shall praise thee with joyful lips:

6 When I remember thee upon my bed, and meditate on thee in the night watches.

7 Because thou hast been my help, therefore in the shadow of thy wings will I rejoice.

8 My soul followeth hard after thee: thy right hand upholdeth me.

9 But those that seek my soul, to destroy it, shall go into the lower parts of the earth.

10 They shall fall by the sword: they shall be a portion for foxes.

11 But the king shall rejoice in God; every one that sweareth by him shall glory: but the mouth of them that speak lies shall be stopped.

PSALM 64

To the chief Musician, A Psalm of David.

Hear my voice, O God, in my prayer: preserve my life from fear of the enemy.

2 Hide me from the secret counsel of the wicked; from the insurrection of the workers of iniquity:

3 Who whet their tongue like a sword, and bend their bows to shoot their arrows, even bitter words:

4 That they may shoot in secret at the perfect: suddenly do they shoot at him, and fear not.

5 They encourage themselves in an evil matter: they commune of laying snares privily; they say, Who shall see them?

6 They search out iniquities; they accomplish a diligent search: both the inward thought of every one of them, and the heart, is deep.

7 But God shall shoot at them with an arrow; suddenly shall they be wounded.

8 So they shall make their own tongue to fall upon themselves: all that see them shall flee away.

9 And all men shall fear, and shall declare the work of God; for they shall wisely consider of his doing.

10 The righteous shall be glad in the Lord, and shall trust in him; and all the upright in heart shall glory.

PSALM 65

To the chief Musician,
A Psalm and Song of David.

Praise waiteth for thee, O God, in Sion: and unto thee shall the vow be performed.

2 O thou that hearest prayer, unto
thee shall all flesh come.
3 Iniquities prevail against me: as
for our transgressions, thou shalt
purge them away.
4 Blessed is the man whom thou
choosest, and causest to approach
unto thee, that he may dwell in thy
courts: we shall be satisfied with the
goodness of thy house, even of thy
holy temple.
5 By terrible things in righteousness
wilt thou answer us, O God of our
salvation; who art the confidence of
all the ends of the earth, and of
them that are afar off upon the sea:
6 Which by his strength setteth fast
the mountains; being girded with
power:
7 Which stilleth the noise of the
seas, the noise of their waves, and
the tumult of the people.
8 They also that dwell in the uttermost parts are afraid at thy tokens:
thou makest the outgoings of the
morning and evening to rejoice.
9 Thou visitest the earth, and waterest it: thou greatly enrichest it
with the river of God, which is full
of water: thou preparest them corn,
when thou hast so provided for it.
10 Thou waterest the ridges thereof
abundantly: thou settlest the furrows
thereof: thou makest it soft with
showers: thou blessest the springing
thereof.
11 Thou crownest the year with thy
goodness; and thy paths drop fatness.
12 They drop upon the pastures of
the wilderness: and the little hills rejoice on every side.
13 The pastures are clothed with
flocks; the valleys also are covered
over with corn; they shout for joy,
they also sing.

PSALM 66

To the chief Musician, A Song or Psalm.

MAKE a joyful noise unto God,
all ye lands:
2 Sing forth the honour of his
name: make his praise glorious.
3 Say unto God, How terrible art
thou in thy works! through the
greatness of thy power shall thine
enemies submit themselves unto
thee.
4 All the earth shall worship thee,
and shall sing unto thee; they shall
sing to thy name. Selah.
5 Come and see the works of God:
he is terrible in his doing toward the
children of men.
6 He turned the sea into dry land:
they went through the flood on
foot: there did we rejoice in him.
7 He ruleth by his power for ever;
his eyes behold the nations: let not
the rebellious exalt themselves.
Selah.
8 O bless our God, ye people, and
make the voice of his praise to be
heard:
9 Which holdeth our soul in life,
and suffereth not our feet to be
moved.
10 For thou, O God, hast proved
us: thou hast tried us, as silver is
tried.
11 Thou broughtest us into the net;
thou laidst affliction upon our loins.
12 Thou hast caused men to ride
over our heads; we went through
fire and through water: but thou
broughtest us out into a wealthy
place.
13 I will go into thy house with
burnt offerings: I will pay thee my
vows,
14 Which my lips have uttered, and
my mouth hath spoken, when I was
in trouble.
15 I will offer unto thee burnt sacrifices of fatlings, with the incense
of rams; I will offer bullocks with
goats. Selah.
16 Come and hear, all ye that fear
God, and I will declare what he hath
done for my soul.
17 I cried unto him with my
mouth, and he was extolled with my
tongue.
18 If I regard iniquity in my heart,
the Lord will not hear me:
19 But verily God hath heard me;
he hath attended to the voice of my
prayer.

20 Blessed be God, which hath not
turned away my prayer, nor his
mercy from me.

PSALM 67

To the chief Musician on Neginoth,
A Psalm or Song.

GOD BE merciful unto us, and
bless us; and cause his face to
shine upon us; Selah.
2 That thy way may be known
upon earth, thy saving health among
all nations.
3 Let the people praise thee, O
God; let all the people praise thee.
4 O let the nations be glad and sing
for joy: for thou shalt judge the people righteously, and govern the nations upon earth. Selah.
5 Let the people praise thee, O
God; let all the people praise thee.
6 Then shall the earth yield her increase; and God, even our own
God, shall bless us.
7 God shall bless us; and all the ends
of the earth shall fear him.

PSALM 68

To the chief Musician,
A Psalm or Song of David.

LET GOD arise, let his enemies be
scattered: let them also that hate
him flee before him.
2 As smoke is driven away, so drive
them away: as wax melteth before
the fire, so let the wicked perish at
the presence of God.
3 But let the righteous be glad; let
them rejoice before God: yea, let
them exceedingly rejoice.
4 Sing unto God, sing praises to his
name: extol him that rideth upon
the heavens by his name Jah, and rejoice before him.
5 A father of the fatherless, and a
judge of the widows, is God in his
holy habitation.
6 God setteth the solitary in families: he bringeth out those which are
bound with chains: but the rebellious dwell in a dry land.
7 O God, when thou wentest forth
before thy people, when thou didst
march through the wilderness;
Selah:
8 The earth shook, the heavens also
dropped at the presence of God:
even Sinai itself was moved at the
presence of God, the God of Israel.
9 Thou, O God, didst send a plentiful rain, whereby thou didst confirm thine inheritance, when it was
weary.
10 Thy congregation hath dwelt
therein: thou, O God, hast prepared
of thy goodness for the poor.
11 The Lord gave the word: great
was the company of those that published it.
12 Kings of armies did flee apace:
and she that tarried at home divided
the spoil.
13 Though ye have lain among the
pots, yet shall ye be as the wings of a
dove covered with silver, and her
feathers with yellow gold.
14 When the Almighty scattered
kings in it, it was white as snow in
Salmon.
15 The hill of God is as the hill of
Bashan; an high hill as the hill of
Bashan.
16 Why leap ye, ye high hills? this is
the hill which God desireth to dwell
in; yea, the Lord will dwell in it for
ever.
17 The chariots of God are twenty
thousand, even thousands of angels:
the Lord is among them, as in Sinai,
in the holy place.
18 Thou hast ascended on high,
thou hast led captivity captive: thou
hast received gifts for men; yea, for
the rebellious also, that the Lord
God might dwell among them.
19 Blessed be the Lord, who daily
loadeth us with benefits, even the
God of our salvation. Selah.
20 He that is our God is the God of
salvation; and unto God the Lord
belong the issues from death.
21 But God shall wound the head
of his enemies, and the hairy scalp
of such an one as goeth on still in
his trespasses.
22 The Lord said, I will bring again

from Bashan, I will bring my people
again from the depths of the sea:
23 That thy foot may be dipped in
the blood of thine enemies, and the
tongue of thy dogs in the same.
24 They have seen thy goings, O
God; even the goings of my God,
my King, in the sanctuary.
25 The singers went before, the
players on instruments followed
after; among them were the damsels
playing with timbrels.
26 Bless ye God in the congregations, even the Lord, from the fountain of Israel.
27 There is little Benjamin with
their ruler, the princes of Judah and
their council, the princes of Zebu-
lun, and the princes of Naphtali.
28 Thy God hath commanded thy
strength: strengthen, O God, that
which thou hast wrought for us.
29 Because of thy temple at
Jerusalem shall kings bring presents
unto thee.
30 Rebuke the company of spearmen, the multitude of the bulls,
with the calves of the people, till
every one submit himself with
pieces of silver: scatter thou the
people that delight in war.
31 Princes shall come out of Egypt;
Ethiopia shall soon stretch out her
hands unto God.
32 Sing unto God, ye kingdoms of
the earth; O sing praises unto the
Lord; Selah:
33 To him that rideth upon the
heavens of heavens, which were of
old; lo, he doth send out his voice,
and that a mighty voice.
34 Ascribe ye strength unto God:
his excellency is over Israel, and his
strength is in the clouds.
35 O God, thou art terrible out
of thy holy places: the God of
Israel is he that giveth strength and
power unto his people. Blessed be
God.

PSALM 69

To the chief Musician upon Shoshannim, A Psalm of David.

SAVE me, O God; for the waters
are come in unto my soul.
2 I sink in deep mire, where there is
no standing: I am come into deep
waters, where the floods overflow
me.
3 I am weary of my crying: my
throat is dried: mine eyes fail while I
wait for my God.
4 They that hate me without a
cause are more than the hairs of
mine head: they that would destroy
me, being mine enemies wrongfully,
are mighty: then I restored that
which I took not away.
5 O God, thou knowest my foolishness; and my sins are not hid from
thee.
6 Let not them that wait on thee, O
Lord God of hosts, be ashamed for
my sake: let not those that seek thee
be confounded for my sake, O God
of Israel.
7 Because for thy sake I have borne
reproach; shame hath covered my
face.
8 I am become a stranger unto my
brethren, and an alien unto my
mother's children.
9 For the zeal of thine house hath
eaten me up; and the reproaches of
them that reproached thee are fallen
upon me.
10 When I wept, and chastened my
soul with fasting, that was to my reproach.
11 I made sackcloth also my garment; and I became a proverb to
them.
12 They that sit in the gate speak
against me; and I was the song of
the drunkards.
13 But as for me, my prayer is unto
thee, O Lord, in an acceptable time:
O God, in the multitude of thy
mercy hear me, in the truth of thy
salvation.
14 Deliver me out of the mire, and
let me not sink: let me be delivered
from them that hate me, and out of
the deep waters.
15 Let not the waterflood overflow
me, neither let the deep swallow me
up, and let not the pit shut her
mouth upon me.
16 Hear me, O Lord; for thy lov-

ingkindness is good: turn unto me
according to the multitude of thy
tender mercies.
17 And hide not thy face from thy
servant; for I am in trouble: hear me
speedily.
18 Draw nigh unto my soul, and redeem it: deliver me because of mine
enemies.
19 Thou hast known my reproach,
and my shame, and my dishonour:
mine adversaries are all before thee.
20 Reproach hath broken my heart;
and I am full of heaviness: and I
looked for some to take pity, but
there was none; and for comforters,
but I found none.
21 They gave me also gall for my
meat; and in my thirst they gave me
vinegar to drink.
22 Let their table become a snare
before them: and that which should
have been for their welfare, let it become a trap.
23 Let their eyes be darkened, that
they see not; and make their loins
continually to shake.
24 Pour out thine indignation upon
them, and let thy wrathful anger
take hold of them.
25 Let their habitation be desolate;
and let none dwell in their tents.
26 For they persecute him whom
thou hast smitten; and they talk to
the grief of those whom thou hast
wounded.
27 Add iniquity unto their iniquity:
and let them not come into thy
righteousness.
28 Let them be blotted out of the
book of the living, and not be written with the righteous.
29 But I am poor and sorrowful: let
thy salvation, O God, set me up on
high.
30 I will praise the name of God
with a song, and will magnify him
with thanksgiving.
31 This also shall please the Lord
better than an ox or bullock that
hath horns and hoofs.
32 The humble shall see this, and
be glad: and your heart shall live that
seek God.
33 For the Lord heareth the poor,
and despiseth not his prisoners.
34 Let the heaven and earth praise
him, the seas, and every thing that
moveth therein.
35 For God will save Zion, and will
build the cities of Judah: that they
may dwell there, and have it in possession.
36 The seed also of his servants
shall inherit it: and they that love his
name shall dwell therein.

PSALM 70

To the chief Musician, A Psalm of David, to bring to remembrance.

MAKE haste, O God, to deliver
me; make haste to help me, O
Lord.
2 Let them be ashamed and confounded that seek after my soul: let
them be turned backward, and put
to confusion, that desire my hurt.
3 Let them be turned back for a reward of their shame that say, Aha,
aha.
4 Let all those that seek thee rejoice
and be glad in thee: and let such as
love thy salvation say continually,
Let God be magnified.
5 But I am poor and needy: make
haste unto me, O God: thou art my
help and my deliverer; O Lord,
make no tarrying.

PSALM 71

IN THEE, O Lord, do I put my
trust: let me never be put to confusion.
2 Deliver me in thy righteousness,
and cause me to escape: incline
thine ear unto me, and save me.
3 Be thou my strong habitation,
whereunto I may continually resort:
thou hast given commandment to
save me; for thou art my rock and
my fortress.
4 Deliver me, O my God, out of
the hand of the wicked, out of the
hand of the unrighteous and cruel
man.
5 For thou art my hope, O Lord
God: thou art my trust from my
youth.
6 By thee have I been holden up

from the womb: thou art he that
took me out of my mother's bowels:
my praise shall be continually of
thee.
7 I am as a wonder unto many; but
thou art my strong refuge.
8 Let my mouth be filled with thy
praise and with thy honour all the
day.
9 Cast me not off in the time of old
age; forsake me not when my
strength faileth.
10 For mine enemies speak against
me; and they that lay wait for my
soul take counsel together,
11 Saying, God hath forsaken him:
persecute and take him; for there is
none to deliver him.
12 O God, be not far from me: O
my God, make haste for my help.
13 Let them be confounded and
consumed that are adversaries to my
soul; let them be covered with reproach and dishonour that seek my
hurt.
14 But I will hope continually, and
will yet praise thee more and more.
15 My mouth shall show forth thy
righteousness and thy salvation all
the day; for I know not the numbers
thereof.
16 I will go in the strength of the
Lord God: I will make mention of
thy righteousness, even of thine
only.
17 O God, thou hast taught me
from my youth: and hitherto have I
declared thy wondrous works.
18 Now also when I am old and
grayheaded, O God, forsake me not;
until I have shown thy strength unto
this generation, and thy power to
every one that is to come.
19 Thy righteousness also, O God,
is very high, who hast done great
things: O God, who is like unto
thee!
20 Thou, which hast shown me
great and sore troubles, shalt
quicken me again, and shalt bring
me up again from the depths of the
earth.
21 Thou shalt increase my greatness, and comfort me on every side.
22 I will also praise thee with the
psaltery, even thy truth, O my God:
unto thee will I sing with the harp,
O thou Holy One of Israel.
23 My lips shall greatly rejoice
when I sing unto thee; and my soul,
which thou hast redeemed.
24 My tongue also shall talk of thy
righteousness all the day long: for
they are confounded, for they are
brought unto shame, that seek my
hurt.

PSALM 72

A Psalm for Solomon.

GIVE the king thy judgments, O
God, and thy righteousness
unto the king's son.
2 He shall judge thy people with
righteousness, and thy poor with
judgment.
3 The mountains shall bring peace
to the people, and the little hills, by
righteousness.
4 He shall judge the poor of the
people, he shall save the children of
the needy, and shall break in pieces
the oppressor.
5 They shall fear thee as long as the
sun and moon endure, throughout
all generations.
6 He shall come down like rain
upon the mown grass: as showers
that water the earth.
7 In his days shall the righteous
flourish; and abundance of peace so
long as the moon endureth.
8 He shall have dominion also from
sea to sea, and from the river unto
the ends of the earth.
9 They that dwell in the wilderness
shall bow before him; and his enemies shall lick the dust.
10 The kings of Tarshish and of the
isles shall bring presents: the kings of
Sheba and Seba shall offer gifts.
11 Yea, all kings shall fall down before him: all nations shall serve him.
12 For he shall deliver the needy
when he crieth; the poor also, and
him that hath no helper.
13 He shall spare the poor and

needy, and shall save the souls of the
needy.
14 He shall redeem their soul from
deceit and violence: and precious
shall their blood be in his sight.
15 And he shall live, and to him
shall be given of the gold of Sheba:
prayer also shall be made for him
continually; and daily shall he be
praised.
16 There shall be an handful of
corn in the earth upon the top of
the mountains; the fruit thereof
shall shake like Lebanon: and they of
the city shall flourish like grass of
the earth.
17 His name shall endure for ever:
his name shall be continued as long
as the sun: and men shall be blessed
in him: all nations shall call him
blessed.
18 Blessed be the Lord God, the
God of Israel, who only doeth wondrous things.
19 And blessed be his glorious
name for ever: and let the whole
earth be filled with his glory; Amen,
and Amen.
20 The prayers of David the son of
Jesse are ended.

PSALM 73

A Psalm of Asaph.

TRULY God is good to Israel, even
to such as are of a clean heart.
2 But as for me, my feet were almost gone; my steps had well nigh
slipped.
3 For I was envious at the foolish,
when I saw the prosperity of the
wicked.
4 For there are no bands in their
death: but their strength is firm.
5 They are not in trouble as other
men; neither are they plagued like
other men.
6 Therefore pride compasseth them
about as a chain; violence covereth
them as a garment.
7 Their eyes stand out with fatness:
they have more than heart could
wish.
8 They are corrupt, and speak
wickedly concerning oppression:
they speak loftily.
9 They set their mouth against the
heavens, and their tongue walketh
through the earth.
10 Therefore his people return
hither: and waters of a full cup are
wrung out to them.
11 And they say, How doth God
know? and is there knowledge in
the most High?
12 Behold, these are the ungodly,
who prosper in the world; they increase in riches.
13 Verily I have cleansed my heart
in vain, and washed my hands in innocency.
14 For all the day long have I been
plagued, and chastened every morning.
15 If I say, I will speak thus; behold,
I should offend against the generation of thy children.
16 When I thought to know this, it
was too painful for me;
17 Until I went into the sanctuary
of God; then understood I their
end.
18 Surely thou didst set them in
slippery places: thou castedst them
down into destruction.
19 How are they brought into des-
olation, as in a moment! they are utterly consumed with terrors.
20 As a dream when one awaketh;
so, O Lord, when thou awakest,
thou shalt despise their image.
21 Thus my heart was grieved, and
I was pricked in my reins.
22 So foolish was I, and ignorant: I
was as a beast before thee.
23 Nevertheless I am continually
with thee: thou hast holden me by
my right hand.
24 Thou shalt guide me with thy
counsel, and afterward receive me to
glory.
25 Whom have I in heaven but
thee? and there is none upon earth
that I desire beside thee.
26 My flesh and my heart faileth:
but God is the strength of my heart,
and my portion for ever.

27 For, lo, they that are far from thee shall perish: thou hast destroyed all them that go a-whoring from thee.

28 But it is good for me to draw near to God: I have put my trust in the Lord God, that I may declare all thy works.

PSALM 74

Maschil of Asaph.

O God, why hast thou cast us off for ever? why doth thine anger smoke against the sheep of thy pasture?

2 Remember thy congregation, which thou hast purchased of old; the rod of thine inheritance, which thou hast redeemed; this mount Zion, wherein thou hast dwelt.

3 Lift up thy feet unto the perpetual desolations; even all that the enemy hath done wickedly in the sanctuary.

4 Thine enemies roar in the midst of thy congregations; they set up their ensigns for signs.

5 A man was famous according as he had lifted up axes upon the thick trees.

6 But now they break down the carved work thereof at once with axes and hammers.

7 They have cast fire into thy sanctuary, they have defiled by casting down the dwelling place of thy name to the ground.

8 They said in their hearts, Let us destroy them together: they have burned up all the synagogues of God in the land.

9 We see not our signs: there is no more any prophet: neither is there among us any that knoweth how long.

10 O God, how long shall the adversary reproach? shall the enemy blaspheme thy name for ever?

11 Why withdrawest thou thy hand, even thy right hand? pluck it out of thy bosom.

12 For God is my King of old, working salvation in the midst of the earth.

13 Thou didst divide the sea by thy strength; thou brakest the heads of the dragons in the waters.

14 Thou brakest the heads of leviathan in pieces, and gavest him to be meat to the people inhabiting the wilderness.

15 Thou didst cleave the fountain and the flood: thou driedst up mighty rivers.

16 The day is thine, the night also is thine: thou hast prepared the light and the sun.

17 Thou hast set all the borders of the earth: thou hast made summer and winter.

18 Remember this, that the enemy hath reproached, O Lord, and that the foolish people have blasphemed thy name.

19 O deliver not the soul of thy turtledove unto the multitude of the wicked: forget not the congregation of thy poor for ever.

20 Have respect unto the covenant: for the dark places of the earth are full of the habitations of cruelty.

21 O let not the oppressed return ashamed: let the poor and needy praise thy name.

22 Arise, O God, plead thine own cause: remember how the foolish man reproacheth thee daily.

23 Forget not the voice of thine enemies: the tumult of those that rise up against thee increaseth continually.

PSALM 75

To the chief Musician, Al-taschith, A Psalm or Song of Asaph.

Unto thee, O God, do we give thanks, unto thee do we give thanks: for that thy name is near thy wondrous works declare.

2 When I shall receive the congregation I will judge uprightly.

3 The earth and all the inhabitants thereof are dissolved: I bear up the pillars of it. Selah.

4 I said unto the fools, Deal not foolishly: and to the wicked, Lift not up the horn:

5 Lift not up your horn on high:
speak not with a stiff neck.
6 For promotion cometh neither
from the east, nor from the west,
nor from the south.
7 But God is the judge: he putteth
down one, and setteth up another.
8 For in the hand of the Lord there
is a cup, and the wine is red; it is full
of mixture; and he poureth out of
the same: but the dregs thereof, all
the wicked of the earth shall wring
them out, and drink them.
9 But I will declare for ever; I will
sing praises to the God of Jacob.
10 All the horns of the wicked also
will I cut off; but the horns of the
righteous shall be exalted.

PSALM 76

To the chief Musician on Neginoth,
A Psalm or Song of Asaph.

IN JUDAH is God known: his name
is great in Israel.
2 In Salem also is his tabernacle,
and his dwelling place in Zion.
3 There brake he the arrows of the
bow, the shield, and the sword, and
the battle. Selah.
4 Thou art more glorious and excellent than the mountains of prey.
5 The stouthearted are spoiled, they
have slept their sleep: and none of
the men of might have found their
hands.
6 At thy rebuke, O God of Jacob,
both the chariot and horse are cast
into a dead sleep.
7 Thou, even thou, art to be feared:
and who may stand in thy sight
when once thou art angry?
8 Thou didst cause judgment to be
heard from heaven; the earth feared,
and was still,
9 When God arose to judgment, to
save all the meek of the earth. Selah.
10 Surely the wrath of man shall
praise thee: the remainder of wrath
shalt thou restrain.
11 Vow, and pay unto the Lord your
God: let all that be round about him
bring presents unto him that ought
to be feared.
12 He shall cut off the spirit of
princes: he is terrible to the kings of
the earth.

PSALM 77

To the chief Musician, to Jeduthun,
A Psalm of Asaph.

I CRIED unto God with my voice,
even unto God with my voice;
and he gave ear unto me.
2 In the day of my trouble I sought
the Lord: my sore ran in the night,
and ceased not: my soul refused to
be comforted.
3 I remembered God, and was
troubled: I complained, and my
spirit was overwhelmed. Selah.
4 Thou holdest mine eyes waking: I
am so troubled that I cannot speak.
5 I have considered the days of old,
the years of ancient times.
6 I call to remembrance my song in
the night: I commune with mine
own heart: and my spirit made diligent search.
7 Will the Lord cast off for ever?
and will he be favourable no more?
8 Is his mercy clean gone for ever?
doth his promise fail for evermore?
9 Hath God forgotten to be gracious? hath he in anger shut up his
tender mercies? Selah.
10 And I said, This is my infirmity:
but I will remember the years of the
right hand of the most High.
11 I will remember the works of
the Lord: surely I will remember thy
wonders of old.
12 I will meditate also of all thy
work, and talk of thy doings.
13 Thy way, O God, is in the sanctuary: who is so great a God as our
God?
14 Thou art the God that doest
wonders: thou hast declared thy
strength among the people.
15 Thou hast with thine arm redeemed thy people, the sons of
Jacob and Joseph. Selah.
16 The waters saw thee, O God,
the waters saw thee; they were
afraid: the depths also were troubled.
17 The clouds poured out water:

the skies sent out a sound: thine arrows also went abroad.
18 The voice of thy thunder was in the heaven: the lightnings lightened the world: the earth trembled and shook.
19 Thy way is in the sea, and thy path in the great waters, and thy footsteps are not known.
20 Thou leddest thy people like a flock by the hand of Moses and Aaron.

PSALM 78

Maschil of Asaph.

GIVE ear, O my people, to my law: incline your ears to the words of my mouth.
2 I will open my mouth in a parable: I will utter dark sayings of old:
3 Which we have heard and known, and our fathers have told us.
4 We will not hide them from their children, showing to the generation to come the praises of the Lord, and his strength, and his wonderful works that he hath done.
5 For he established a testimony in Jacob, and appointed a law in Israel, which he commanded our fathers, that they should make them known to their children:
6 That the generation to come might know them, even the children which should be born; who should arise and declare them to their children:
7 That they might set their hope in God, and not forget the works of God, but keep his commandments:
8 And might not be as their fathers, a stubborn and rebellious generation; a generation that set not their heart aright, and whose spirit was not stedfast with God.
9 The children of Ephraim, being armed, and carrying bows, turned back in the day of battle.
10 They kept not the covenant of God, and refused to walk in his law;
11 And forgat his works, and his wonders that he had shown them.
12 Marvellous things did he in the sight of their fathers, in the land of Egypt, in the field of Zoan.
13 He divided the sea, and caused them to pass through; and he made the waters to stand as an heap.
14 In the daytime also he led them with a cloud, and all the night with a light of fire.
15 He clave the rocks in the wilderness, and gave them drink as out of the great depths.
16 He brought streams also out of the rock, and caused waters to run down like rivers.
17 And they sinned yet more against him by provoking the most High in the wilderness.
18 And they tempted God in their heart by asking meat for their lust.
19 Yea, they spake against God; they said, Can God furnish a table in the wilderness?
20 Behold, he smote the rock, that the waters gushed out, and the streams overflowed; can he give bread also? can he provide flesh for his people?
21 Therefore the Lord heard this, and was wroth: so a fire was kindled against Jacob, and anger also came up against Israel;
22 Because they believed not in God, and trusted not in his salvation:
23 Though he had commanded the clouds from above, and opened the doors of heaven,
24 And had rained down manna upon them to eat, and had given them of the corn of heaven.
25 Man did eat angels' food: he sent them meat to the full.
26 He caused an east wind to blow in the heaven: and by his power he brought in the south wind.
27 He rained flesh also upon them as dust, and feathered fowls like as the sand of the sea:
28 And he let it fall in the midst of their camp, round about their habitations.
29 So they did eat, and were well filled: for he gave them their own desire;

30 They were not estranged from
their lust. But while their meat was
yet in their mouths,
31 The wrath of God came upon
them, and slew the fattest of them,
and smote down the chosen men of
Israel.
32 For all this they sinned still, and
believed not for his wondrous
works.
33 Therefore their days did he consume in vanity, and their years in
trouble.
34 When he slew them, then they
sought him: and they returned and
inquired early after God.
35 And they remembered that God
was their rock, and the high God
their redeemer.
36 Nevertheless they did flatter him
with their mouth, and they lied
unto him with their tongues.
37 For their heart was not right
with him, neither were they stedfast
in his covenant.
38 But he, being full of compassion, forgave their iniquity, and destroyed them not: yea, many a time
turned he his anger away, and did
not stir up all his wrath.
39 For he remembered that they
were but flesh; a wind that passeth
away, and cometh not again.
40 How oft did they provoke him
in the wilderness, and grieve him in
the desert!
41 Yea, they turned back and
tempted God, and limited the Holy
One of Israel.
42 They remembered not his hand,
nor the day when he delivered them
from the enemy.
43 How he had wrought his signs
in Egypt, and his wonders in the
field of Zoan:
44 And had turned their rivers into
blood; and their floods, that they
could not drink.
45 He sent divers sorts of flies
among them, which devoured
them; and frogs, which destroyed
them.
46 He gave also their increase unto
the caterpillar, and their labour unto
the locust.
47 He destroyed their vines with
hail, and their sycamore trees with
frost.
48 He gave up their cattle also to
the hail, and their flocks to hot
thunderbolts.
49 He cast upon them the fierceness of his anger, wrath, and indignation, and trouble, by sending evil
angels among them.
50 He made a way to his anger; he
spared not their soul from death, but
gave their life over to the pestilence;
51 And smote all the firstborn in
Egypt; the chief of their strength in
the tabernacles of Ham:
52 But made his own people to go
forth like sheep, and guided them in
the wilderness like a flock.
53 And he led them on safely, so
that they feared not: but the sea
overwhelmed their enemies.
54 And he brought them to the
border of his sanctuary, even to this
mountain, which his right hand had
purchased.
55 He cast out the heathen also before them, and divided them an inheritance by line, and made the
tribes of Israel to dwell in their
tents.
56 Yet they tempted and provoked
the most high God, and kept not his
testimonies:
57 But turned back, and dealt un-
faithfully like their fathers: they
were turned aside like a deceitful
bow.
58 For they provoked him to anger
with their high places, and moved
him to jealousy with their graven
images.
59 When God heard this, he was
wroth, and greatly abhorred Israel:
60 So that he forsook the tabernacle of Shiloh, the tent which he
placed among men;
61 And delivered his strength into
captivity, and his glory into the
enemy's hand.
62 He gave his people over also

unto the sword; and was wroth with
his inheritance.
63 The fire consumed their young
men; and their maidens were not
given to marriage.
64 Their priests fell by the sword;
and their widows made no lamentation.
65 Then the Lord awaked as one
out of sleep, and like a mighty man
that shouteth by reason of wine.
66 And he smote his enemies in the
hinder parts: he put them to a perpetual reproach.
67 Moreover he refused the tabernacle of Joseph, and chose not the
tribe of Ephraim:
68 But chose the tribe of Judah,
the mount Zion which he loved.
69 And he built his sanctuary like
high palaces, like the earth which he
hath established for ever.
70 He chose David also his servant,
and took him from the sheepfolds:
71 From following the ewes great
with young he brought him to feed
Jacob his people, and Israel his inheritance.
72 So he fed them according to the
integrity of his heart; and guided
them by the skilfulness of his hands.

PSALM 79

A Psalm of Asaph.

O GOD, the heathen are come
into thine inheritance; thy
holy temple have they defiled; they
have laid Jerusalem on heaps
2 The dead bodies of thy servants
have they given to be meat unto the
fowls of the heaven, the flesh of thy
saints unto the beasts of the earth.
3 Their blood have they shed like
water round about Jerusalem; and
there was none to bury them.
4 We are become a reproach to our
neighbours, a scorn and derision to
them that are round about us.
5 How long, Lord? wilt thou be
angry for ever? shall thy jealousy
burn like fire?
6 Pour out thy wrath upon the heathen that have not known thee, and
upon the kingdoms that have not
called upon thy name.
7 For they have devoured Jacob,
and laid waste his dwelling place.
8 O remember not against us former iniquities: let thy tender mercies
speedily prevent us: for we are
brought very low.
9 Help us, O God of our salvation,
for the glory of thy name: and deliver us, and purge away our sins, for
thy name's sake.
10 Wherefore should the heathen
say, Where is their God? let him be
known among the heathen in our
sight by the revenging of the blood
of thy servants which is shed.
11 Let the sighing of the prisoner
come before thee; according to the
greatness of thy power preserve
thou those that are appointed to die;
12 And render unto our neighbours
sevenfold into their bosom their reproach, wherewith they have reproached thee, O Lord.
13 So we thy people and sheep of
thy pasture will give thee thanks for
ever: we will show forth thy praise
to all generations.

PSALM 80

To the chief Musician upon Shoshannim-Eduth, A Psalm of Asaph.

GIVE ear, O Shepherd of Israel,
thou that leadest Joseph like a
flock; thou that dwellest between
the cherubims, shine forth.
2 Before Ephraim and Benjamin
and Manasseh stir up thy strength,
and come and save us.
3 Turn us again, O God, and cause
thy face to shine; and we shall be
saved.
4 O Lord God of hosts, how long
wilt thou be angry against the prayer
of thy people?
5 Thou feedest them with the
bread of tears; and givest them tears
to drink in great measure.
6 Thou makest us a strife unto our
neighbours: and our enemies laugh
among themselves.
7 Turn us again, O God of hosts,

and cause thy face to shine; and we
shall be saved.
8 Thou hast brought a vine out of
Egypt: thou hast cast out the heathen, and planted it.
9 Thou preparedst room before it,
and didst cause it to take deep root,
and it filled the land.
10 The hills were covered with the
shadow of it, and the boughs
thereof were like the goodly cedars.
11 She sent out her boughs unto
the sea, and her branches unto the
river.
12 Why hast thou then broken
down her hedges, so that all they
which pass by the way do pluck her?
13 The boar out of the wood doth
waste it, and the wild beast of the
field doth devour it.
14 Return, we beseech thee, O
God of hosts: look down from
heaven, and behold, and visit this
vine;
15 And the vineyard which thy
right hand hath planted, and the
branch that thou madest strong for
thyself.
16 It is burned with fire, it is cut
down: they perish at the rebuke of
thy countenance.
17 Let thy hand be upon the man of
thy right hand, upon the son of man
whom thou madest strong for thyself.
18 So will not we go back from
thee: quicken us, and we will call
upon thy name.
19 Turn us again, O Lord God of
hosts, cause thy face to shine; and
we shall be saved.

PSALM 81

To the chief Musician upon Gittith, A Psalm of Asaph.

SING aloud unto God our strength: make a joyful noise unto the God of Jacob.
2 Take a psalm, and bring hither the
timbrel, the pleasant harp with the
psaltery.
3 Blow up the trumpet in the new
moon, in the time appointed, on
our solemn feast day.
4 For this was a statute for Israel,
and a law of the God of Jacob.
5 This he ordained in Joseph for a
testimony, when he went out
through the land of Egypt: where I
heard a language that I understood
not.
6 I removed his shoulder from the
burden: his hands were delivered
from the pots.
7 Thou calledst in trouble, and I
delivered thee; I answered thee in
the secret place of thunder: I proved
thee at the waters of Meribah.
Selah.
8 Hear, O my people, and I will
testify unto thee: O Israel, if thou
wilt hearken unto me;
9 There shall no strange god be in
thee; neither shalt thou worship any
strange god.
10 I am the Lord thy God, which
brought thee out of the land of
Egypt: open thy mouth wide, and I
will fill it.
11 But my people would not hearken to my voice; and Israel would
none of me.
12 So I gave them up unto their
own hearts' lust: and they walked in
their own counsels.
13 Oh that my people had hearkened unto me, and Israel had
walked in my ways!
14 I should soon have subdued their
enemies, and turned my hand
against their adversaries.
15 The haters of the Lord should
have submitted themselves unto
him: but their time should have endured for ever.
16 He should have fed them also
with the finest of the wheat: and
with honey out of the rock should I
have satisfied thee.

PSALM 82

A Psalm of Asaph.

GOD STANDETH in the congregation of the mighty; he judgeth among the gods.

2 How long will ye judge unjustly,
and accept the persons of the
wicked? Selah.
3 Defend the poor and fatherless:
do justice to the afflicted and needy.
4 Deliver the poor and needy: rid
them out of the hand of the
wicked.
5 They know not, neither will they
understand; they walk on in darkness: all the foundations of the earth
are out of course.
6 I have said, Ye are gods; and all of
you are children of the most High.
7 But ye shall die like men, and fall
like one of the princes.
8 Arise, O God, judge the earth:
for thou shalt inherit all nations.

PSALM 83

A Song or Psalm of Asaph.

KEEP not thou silence, O God:
hold not thy peace, and be not
still, O God.
2 For, lo, thine enemies make a tumult: and they that hate thee have
lifted up the head.
3 They have taken crafty counsel
against thy people, and consulted
against thy hidden ones.
4 They have said, Come, and let us
cut them off from being a nation;
that the name of Israel may be no
more in remembrance.
5 For they have consulted together
with one consent: they are confed-
erate against thee:
6 The tabernacles of Edom, and
the Ishmaelites; of Moab, and the
Hagarenes;
7 Gebal, and Ammon, and Amalek;
the Philistines with the inhabitants
of Tyre;
8 Assur also is joined with them:
they have holpen the children of
Lot. Selah.
9 Do unto them as unto the
Midianites; as to Sisera, as to Jabin,
at the brook of Kison:
10 Which perished at En-dor: they
became as dung for the earth.
11 Make their nobles like Oreb, and
like Zeeb: yea, all their princes as
Zebah, and as Zalmunna:
12 Who said, Let us take to ourselves the houses of God in possession.
13 O my God, make them like a
wheel; as the stubble before the
wind.
14 As the fire burneth a wood, and
as the flame setteth the mountains
on fire;
15 So persecute them with thy
tempest, and make them afraid with
thy storm.
16 Fill their faces with shame; that
they may seek thy name, O Lord.
17 Let them be confounded and
troubled for ever; yea, let them be
put to shame, and perish:
18 That men may know that thou,
whose name alone is Jehovah, art
the most high over all the earth.

PSALM 84

To the chief Musician upon Gittith,
A Psalm for the sons of Korah.

HOW AMIABLE are thy tabernacles, O Lord of hosts!
2 My soul longeth, yea, even
fainteth for the courts of the Lord:
my heart and my flesh crieth out for
the living God.
3 Yea, the sparrow hath found an
house, and the swallow a nest for
herself, where she may lay her
young, even thine altars, O Lord of
hosts, my King, and my God.
4 Blessed are they that dwell in thy
house: they will be still praising
thee. Selah.
5 Blessed is the man whose strength
is in thee; in whose heart are the
ways of them.
6 Who passing through the valley
of Baca make it a well; the rain also
filleth the pools.
7 They go from strength to
strength, every one of them in Zion
appeareth before God.
8 O Lord God of hosts, hear my
prayer: give ear, O God of Jacob.
Selah.

9 Behold, O God our shield, and look upon the face of thine anointed.

10 For a day in thy courts is better than a thousand. I had rather be a doorkeeper in the house of my God, than to dwell in the tents of wickedness.

11 For the Lord God is a sun and shield: the Lord will give grace and glory: no good thing will he withhold from them that walk uprightly.

12 O Lord of hosts, blessed is the man that trusteth in thee.

PSALM 85

To the chief Musician,
A Psalm for the sons of Korah.

LORD, thou hast been favourable unto thy land: thou hast brought back the captivity of Jacob.

2 Thou hast forgiven the iniquity of thy people, thou hast covered all their sin. Selah.

3 Thou hast taken away all thy wrath: thou hast turned thyself from the fierceness of thine anger.

4 Turn us, O God of our salvation, and cause thine anger toward us to cease.

5 Wilt thou be angry with us for ever? wilt thou draw out thine anger to all generations?

6 Wilt thou not revive us again: that thy people may rejoice in thee?

7 Shew us thy mercy, O Lord, and grant us thy salvation.

8 I will hear what God the Lord will speak: for he will speak peace unto his people, and to his saints: but let them not turn again to folly.

9 Surely his salvation is nigh them that fear him; that glory may dwell in our land.

10 Mercy and truth are met together; righteousness and peace have kissed each other.

11 Truth shall spring out of the earth; and righteousness shall look down from heaven.

12 Yea, the Lord shall give that which is good; and our land shall yield her increase.

13 Righteousness shall go before him; and shall set us in the way of his steps.

PSALM 86

A Prayer of David.

BOW DOWN thine ear, O Lord, hear me: for I am poor and needy.

2 Preserve my soul; for I am holy: O thou my God, save thy servant that trusteth in thee.

3 Be merciful unto me, O Lord: for I cry unto thee daily.

4 Rejoice the soul of thy servant: for unto thee, O Lord, do I lift up my soul.

5 For thou, Lord, art good, and ready to forgive; and plenteous in mercy unto all them that call upon thee.

6 Give ear, O Lord, unto my prayer; and attend to the voice of my supplications.

7 In the day of my trouble I will call upon thee: for thou wilt answer me.

8 Among the gods there is none like unto thee, O Lord; neither are there any works like unto thy works.

9 All nations whom thou hast made shall come and worship before thee, O Lord; and shall glorify thy name.

10 For thou art great, and doest wondrous things: thou art God alone.

11 Teach me thy way, O Lord; I will walk in thy truth: unite my heart to fear thy name.

12 I will praise thee, O Lord my God, with all my heart: and I will glorify thy name for evermore.

13 For great is thy mercy toward me: and thou hast delivered my soul from the lowest hell.

14 O God, the proud are risen against me, and the assemblies of violent men have sought after my soul; and have not set thee before them.

15 But thou, O Lord, art a God full of compassion, and gracious, long-suffering, and plenteous in mercy and truth.

16 O turn unto me, and have mercy upon me; give thy strength unto thy servant, and save the son of thine handmaid.

17 Shew me a token for good; that they which hate me may see it, and be ashamed: because thou, Lord, hast holpen me, and comforted me.

PSALM 87

A Psalm or Song for the sons of Korah.

HIS FOUNDATION is in the holy mountains.

2 The Lord loveth the gates of Zion more than all the dwellings of Jacob.

3 Glorious things are spoken of thee, O city of God. Selah.

4 I will make mention of Rahab and Babylon to them that know me: behold Philistia, and Tyre, with Ethiopia; this man was born there.

5 And of Zion it shall be said, This and that man was born in her: and the highest himself shall establish her.

6 The Lord shall count, when he writeth up the people, that this man was born there. Selah.

7 As well the singers as the players on instruments shall be there: all my springs are in thee.

PSALM 88

A Song or Psalm for the sons of Korah, to the chief Musician upon Mahalath Leannoth, Maschil of Heman the Ezrahite.

O LORD God of my salvation, I have cried day and night before thee:

2 Let my prayer come before thee: incline thine ear unto my cry;

3 For my soul is full of troubles: and my life draweth nigh unto the grave.

4 I am counted with them that go down into the pit: I am as a man that hath no strength:

5 Free among the dead, like the slain that lie in the grave, whom thou rememberest no more: and they are cut off from thy hand.

6 Thou hast laid me in the lowest pit, in darkness, in the deeps.

7 Thy wrath lieth hard upon me, and thou hast afflicted me with all thy waves. Selah.

8 Thou hast put away mine acquaintance far from me; thou hast made me an abomination unto them: I am shut up, and I cannot come forth.

9 Mine eye mourneth by reason of affliction: Lord, I have called daily upon thee, I have stretched out my hands unto thee.

10 Wilt thou shew wonders to the dead? shall the dead arise and praise thee? Selah.

11 Shall thy lovingkindness be declared in the grave? or thy faithfulness in destruction?

12 Shall thy wonders be known in the dark? and thy righteousness in the land of forgetfulness?

13 But unto thee have I cried, O Lord; and in the morning shall my prayer prevent thee.

14 Lord, why castest thou off my soul? why hidest thou thy face from me?

15 I am afflicted and ready to die from my youth up: while I suffer thy terrors I am distracted.

16 Thy fierce wrath goeth over me; thy terrors have cut me off.

17 They came round about me daily like water; they compassed me about together.

18 Lover and friend hast thou put far from me, and mine acquaintance into darkness.

PSALM 89

Maschil of Ethan the Ezrahite.

I WILL sing of the mercies of the Lord for ever: with my mouth will I make known thy faithfulness to all generations.

2 For I have said, Mercy shall be built up for ever: thy faithfulness

shalt thou establish in the very heavens.
3 I have made a covenant with my
chosen, I have sworn unto David
my servant,
4 Thy seed will I establish for ever,
and build up thy throne to all generations. Selah.
5 And the heavens shall praise thy
wonders, O Lord: thy faithfulness
also in the congregation of the
saints.
6 For who in the heaven can be
compared unto the Lord? who
among the sons of the mighty can
be likened unto the Lord?
7 God is greatly to be feared in the
assembly of the saints, and to be had
in reverence of all them that are
about him.
8 O Lord God of hosts, who is a
strong Lord like unto thee? or to thy
faithfulness round about thee?
9 Thou rulest the raging of the sea:
when the waves thereof arise, thou
stillest them.
10 Thou hast broken Rahab in
pieces, as one that is slain; thou hast
scattered thine enemies with thy
strong arm.
11 The heavens are thine, the earth
also is thine: as for the world and the
fulness thereof, thou hast founded
them.
12 The north and the south thou
hast created them: Tabor and
Hermon shall rejoice in thy name.
13 Thou hast a mighty arm: strong
is thy hand, and high is thy right
hand.
14 Justice and judgment are the
habitation of thy throne: mercy and
truth shall go before thy face.
15 Blessed is the people that know
the joyful sound: they shall walk, O
Lord, in the light of thy countenance.
16 In thy name shall they rejoice all
the day: and in thy righteousness
shall they be exalted.
17 For thou art the glory of their
strength: and in thy favour our horn
shall be exalted.
18 For the Lord is our defence; and
the Holy One of Israel is our king.
19 Then thou spakest in vision to
thy holy one, and saidst, I have laid
help upon one that is mighty; I have
exalted one chosen out of the
people.
20 I have found David my servant;
with my holy oil have I anointed
him:
21 With whom my hand shall be
established: mine arm also shall
strengthen him.
22 The enemy shall not exact upon
him; nor the son of wickedness afflict him.
23 And I will beat down his foes
before his face, and plague them that
hate him.
24 But my faithfulness and my
mercy shall be with him: and in my
name shall his horn be exalted.
25 I will set his hand also in the sea,
and his right hand in the rivers.
26 He shall cry unto me, Thou art
my father, my God, and the rock of
my salvation.
27 Also I will make him my firstborn, higher than the kings of the
earth.
28 My mercy will I keep for him
for evermore, and my covenant shall
stand fast with him.
29 His seed also will I make to endure for ever, and his throne as the
days of heaven.
30 If his children forsake my law,
and walk not in my judgments;
31 If they break my statutes, and
keep not my commandments;
32 Then will I visit their transgression with the rod, and their iniquity
with stripes.
33 Nevertheless my lovingkindness
will I not utterly take from him, nor
suffer my faithfulness to fail.
34 My covenant will I not break,
nor alter the thing that is gone out
of my lips.
35 Once have I sworn by my holiness that I will not lie unto David.
36 His seed shall endure for ever,
and his throne as the sun before me.

37 It shall be established for ever as the moon, and as a faithful witness in heaven. Selah.

38 But thou hast cast off and abhorred, thou hast been wroth with thine anointed.

39 Thou hast made void the covenant of thy servant: thou hast profaned his crown by casting it to the ground.

40 Thou hast broken down all his hedges; thou hast brought his strong holds to ruin.

41 All that pass by the way spoil him: he is a reproach to his neighbours.

42 Thou hast set up the right hand of his adversaries; thou hast made all his enemies to rejoice.

43 Thou hast also turned the edge of his sword, and hast not made him to stand in the battle.

44 Thou hast made his glory to cease, and cast his throne down to the ground.

45 The days of his youth hast thou shortened: thou hast covered him with shame. Selah.

46 How long, Lord? wilt thou hide thyself for ever? shall thy wrath burn like fire?

47 Remember how short my time is: wherefore hast thou made all men in vain?

48 What man is he that liveth, and shall not see death? shall he deliver his soul from the hand of the grave? Selah.

49 Lord, where are thy former lovingkindnesses, which thou swarest unto David in thy truth?

50 Remember, Lord, the reproach of thy servants; how I do bear in my bosom the reproach of all the mighty people;

51 Wherewith thine enemies have reproached, O Lord; wherewith they have reproached the footsteps of thine anointed.

52 Blessed be the Lord for evermore. Amen, and Amen.

PSALM 90

A Prayer of Moses the man of God.

LORD, thou hast been our dwelling place in all generations.

2 Before the mountains were brought forth, or ever thou hadst formed the earth and the world, even from everlasting to everlasting, thou art God.

3 Thou turnest man to destruction; and sayest, Return, ye children of men.

4 For a thousand years in thy sight are but as yesterday when it is past, and as a watch in the night.

5 Thou carriest them away as with a flood; they are as a sleep: in the morning they are like grass which groweth up.

6 In the morning it flourisheth, and groweth up; in the evening it is cut down, and withereth.

7 For we are consumed by thine anger, and by thy wrath are we troubled.

8 Thou hast set our iniquities before thee, our secret sins in the light of thy countenance.

9 For all our days are passed away in thy wrath: we spend our years as a tale that is told.

10 The days of our years are threescore years and ten; and if by reason of strength they be fourscore years, yet is their strength labour and sorrow; for it is soon cut off, and we fly away.

11 Who knoweth the power of thine anger? even according to thy fear, so is thy wrath.

12 So teach us to number our days, that we may apply our hearts unto wisdom.

13 Return, O Lord, how long? and let it repent thee concerning thy servants.

14 O satisfy us early with thy mercy; that we may rejoice and be glad all our days.

15 Make us glad according to the days wherein thou hast afflicted us,

and the years wherein we have seen evil.
16 Let thy work appear unto thy servants, and thy glory unto their children.
17 And let the beauty of the Lord our God be upon us: and establish thou the work of our hands upon us; yea, the work of our hands establish thou it.

PSALM 91

He that dwelleth in the secret place of the most High shall abide under the shadow of the Almighty.
2 I will say of the Lord, He is my refuge and my fortress: my God; in him will I trust.
3 Surely he shall deliver thee from the snare of the fowler, and from the noisome pestilence.
4 He shall cover thee with his feathers, and under his wings shalt thou trust: his truth shall be thy shield and buckler.
5 Thou shalt not be afraid for the terror by night; nor for the arrow that flieth by day;
6 Nor for the pestilence that walketh in darkness; nor for the destruction that wasteth at noonday.
7 A thousand shall fall at thy side, and ten thousand at thy right hand; but it shall not come nigh thee.
8 Only with thine eyes shalt thou behold and see the reward of the wicked.
9 Because thou hast made the Lord, which is my refuge, even the most High, thy habitation;
10 There shall no evil befall thee, neither shall any plague come nigh thy dwelling.
11 For he shall give his angels charge over thee, to keep thee in all thy ways.
12 They shall bear thee up in their hands, lest thou dash thy foot against a stone.
13 Thou shalt tread upon the lion and adder: the young lion and the dragon shalt thou trample under feet.
14 Because he hath set his love upon me, therefore will I deliver him: I will set him on high, because he hath known my name.
15 He shall call upon me, and I will answer him: I will be with him in trouble; I will deliver him, and honour him.
16 With long life will I satisfy him, and shew him my salvation.

PSALM 92

A Psalm or Song for the sabbath day.

It is a good thing to give thanks unto the Lord, and to sing praises unto thy name, O most High:
2 To show forth thy lovingkindness in the morning, and thy faithfulness every night,
3 Upon an instrument of ten strings, and upon the psaltery; upon the harp with a solemn sound.
4 For thou, Lord, hast made me glad through thy work: I will triumph in the works of thy hands.
5 O Lord, how great are thy works! and thy thoughts are very deep.
6 A brutish man knoweth not; neither doth a fool understand this.
7 When the wicked spring as the grass, and when all the workers of iniquity do flourish; it is that they shall be destroyed for ever:
8 But thou, Lord, art most high for evermore.
9 For, lo, thine enemies, O Lord, for, lo, thine enemies shall perish; all the workers of iniquity shall be scattered.
10 But my horn shalt thou exalt like the horn of an unicorn: I shall be anointed with fresh oil.
11 Mine eye also shall see my desire on mine enemies, and mine ears shall hear my desire of the wicked that rise up against me.
12 The righteous shall flourish like the palm tree: he shall grow like a cedar in Lebanon.
13 Those that be planted in the

house of the Lord shall flourish in the courts of our God.

14 They shall still bring forth fruit in old age; they shall be fat and flourishing;

15 To shew that the Lord is upright: he is my rock, and there is no unrighteousness in him.

PSALM 93

THE LORD reigneth, he is clothed with majesty; the Lord is clothed with strength, wherewith he hath girded himself: the world also is stablished, that it cannot be moved.

2 Thy throne is established of old: thou art from everlasting.

3 The floods have lifted up, O Lord, the floods have lifted up their voice; the floods lift up their waves.

4 The Lord on high is mightier than the noise of many waters, yea, than the mighty waves of the sea.

5 Thy testimonies are very sure: holiness becometh thine house, O Lord, for ever.

PSALM 94

O LORD God, to whom vengeance belongeth; O God, to whom vengeance belongeth, show thyself.

2 Lift up thyself, thou judge of the earth: render a reward to the proud.

3 Lord, how long shall the wicked, how long shall the wicked triumph?

4 How long shall they utter and speak hard things? and all the workers of iniquity boast themselves?

5 They break in pieces thy people, O Lord, and afflict thine heritage.

6 They slay the widow and the stranger, and murder the fatherless.

7 Yet they say, The Lord shall not see, neither shall the God of Jacob regard it.

8 Understand, ye brutish among the people: and ye fools, when will ye be wise?

9 He that planted the ear, shall he not hear? he that formed the eye, shall he not see?

10 He that chastiseth the heathen, shall not he correct? he that teacheth man knowledge, shall not he know?

11 The Lord knoweth the thoughts of man, that they are vanity.

12 Blessed is the man whom thou chastenest, O Lord, and teachest him out of thy law;

13 That thou mayest give him rest from the days of adversity, until the pit be digged for the wicked.

14 For the Lord will not cast off his people, neither will he forsake his inheritance.

15 But judgment shall return unto righteousness: and all the upright in heart shall follow it.

16 Who will rise up for me against the evildoers? or who will stand up for me against the workers of iniquity?

17 Unless the Lord had been my help, my soul had almost dwelt in silence.

18 When I said, My foot slippeth; thy mercy, O Lord, held me up.

19 In the multitude of my thoughts within me thy comforts delight my soul.

20 Shall the throne of iniquity have fellowship with thee, which frameth mischief by a law?

21 They gather themselves together against the soul of the righteous, and condemn the innocent blood.

22 But the Lord is my defence; and my God is the rock of my refuge.

23 And he shall bring upon them their own iniquity, and shall cut them off in their own wickedness; yea, the Lord our God shall cut them off.

PSALM 95

O COME, let us sing unto the Lord: let us make a joyful noise to the rock of our salvation.

2 Let us come before his presence with thanksgiving, and make a joyful noise unto him with psalms.

3 For the Lord is a great God, and a great King above all gods.

4 In his hand are the deep places of

the earth: the strength of the hills is
his also.
5 The sea is his, and he made it: and
his hands formed the dry land.
6 O come, let us worship and bow
down: let us kneel before the Lord
our maker.
7 For he is our God; and we are the
people of his pasture, and the sheep
of his hand. To day if ye will hear
his voice,
8 Harden not your heart, as in the
provocation, and as in the day of
temptation in the wilderness:
9 When your fathers tempted me,
proved me, and saw my work.
10 Forty years long was I grieved
with this generation, and said, It is a
people that do err in their heart, and
they have not known my ways:
11 Unto whom I sware in my wrath
that they should not enter into my
rest.

PSALM 96

O SING unto the Lord a new
song: sing unto the Lord, all
the earth.
2 Sing unto the Lord, bless his
name; shew forth his salvation from
day to day.
3 Declare his glory among the heathen, his wonders among all people.
4 For the Lord is great, and greatly
to be praised: he is to be feared
above all gods.
5 For all the gods of the nations are
idols: but the Lord made the heavens.
6 Honour and majesty are before
him: strength and beauty are in his
sanctuary.
7 Give unto the Lord, O ye kindreds of the people, give unto the
Lord glory and strength.
8 Give unto the Lord the glory due
unto his name: bring an offering,
and come into his courts.
9 O worship the Lord in the beauty
of holiness: fear before him, all the
earth.
10 Say among the heathen that the
Lord reigneth: the world also shall
be established that it shall not be
moved: he shall judge the people
righteously.
11 Let the heavens rejoice, and let
the earth be glad; let the sea roar,
and the fulness thereof.
12 Let the field be joyful, and all
that is therein: then shall all the trees
of the wood rejoice
13 Before the Lord: for he cometh,
for he cometh to judge the earth: he
shall judge the world with righteousness, and the people with his
truth.

PSALM 97

THE LORD reigneth; let the earth
rejoice; let the multitude of
isles be glad thereof.
2 Clouds and darkness are round
about him: righteousness and judgment are the habitation of his
throne.
3 A fire goeth before him, and burneth up his enemies round about.
4 His lightnings enlightened the
world: the earth saw, and trembled.
5 The hills melted like wax at the
presence of the Lord, at the presence of the Lord of the whole
earth.
6 The heavens declare his righteousness, and all the people see his
glory.
7 Confounded be all they that serve
graven images, that boast themselves
of idols: worship him, all ye gods.
8 Zion heard, and was glad; and the
daughters of Judah rejoiced because
of thy judgments, O Lord.
9 For thou, Lord, art high above all
the earth: thou art exalted far above
all gods.
10 Ye that love the Lord, hate evil:
he preserveth the souls of his saints;
he delivereth them out of the hand
of the wicked.
11 Light is sown for the righteous,
and gladness for the upright in
heart.
12 Rejoice in the Lord, ye righteous; and give thanks at the remembrance of his holiness.

PSALM 98

A Psalm.

O SING unto the Lord a new song; for he hath done marvellous things: his right hand, and his holy arm, hath gotten him the victory.

2 The Lord hath made known his salvation: his righteousness hath he openly showed in the sight of the heathen.

3 He hath remembered his mercy and his truth toward the house of Israel: all the ends of the earth have seen the salvation of our God.

4 Make a joyful noise unto the Lord, all the earth: make a loud noise, and rejoice, and sing praise.

5 Sing unto the Lord with the harp; with the harp, and the voice of a psalm.

6 With trumpets and sound of cornet make a joyful noise before the Lord, the King.

7 Let the sea roar, and the fulness thereof; the world, and they that dwell therein.

8 Let the floods clap their hands: let the hills be joyful together

9 Before the Lord; for he cometh to judge the earth: with righteousness shall he judge the world, and the people with equity.

PSALM 99

THE LORD reigneth; let the people tremble: he sitteth between the cherubims; let the earth be moved.

2 The Lord is great in Zion; and he is high above all the people.

3 Let them praise thy great and terrible name; for it is holy.

4 The king's strength also loveth judgment; thou dost establish equity, thou executest judgment and righteousness in Jacob.

5 Exalt ye the Lord our God, and worship at his footstool; for he is holy.

6 Moses and Aaron among his priests, and Samuel among them that call upon his name; they called upon the Lord, and he answered them.

7 He spake unto them in the cloudy pillar: they kept his testimonies, and the ordinance that he gave them.

8 Thou answeredst them, O Lord our God: thou wast a God that forgavest them, though thou tookest vengeance of their inventions.

9 Exalt the Lord our God, and worship at his holy hill; for the Lord our God is holy.

PSALM 100

A Psalm of praise.

MAKE a joyful noise unto the Lord, all ye lands.

2 Serve the Lord with gladness: come before his presence with singing.

3 Know ye that the Lord he is God: it is he that hath made us, and not we ourselves; we are his people, and the sheep of his pasture.

4 Enter into his gates with thanksgiving, and into his courts with praise: be thankful unto him, and bless his name.

5 For the Lord is good; his mercy is everlasting; and his truth endureth to all generations.

PSALM 101

A Psalm of David.

I WILL sing of mercy and judgment: unto thee, O Lord, will I sing.

2 I will behave myself wisely in a perfect way. O when wilt thou come unto me? I will walk within my house with a perfect heart.

3 I will set no wicked thing before mine eyes: I hate the work of them that turn aside; it shall not cleave to me.

4 A froward heart shall depart from me: I will not know a wicked person.

5 Whoso privily slandereth his neighbour, him will I cut off: him that hath an high look and a proud heart will not I suffer.

6 Mine eyes shall be upon the faith-

ful of the land, that they may dwell
with me: he that walketh in a perfect way, he shall serve me.
7 He that worketh deceit shall not
dwell within my house: he that telleth lies shall not tarry in my sight.
8 I will early destroy all the wicked
of the land; that I may cut off all
wicked doers from the city of the
Lord.

PSALM 102

A Prayer of the afflicted, when he is overwhelmed, and poureth out his complaint before the Lord.

HEAR my prayer, O Lord, and let
my cry come unto thee.
2 Hide not thy face from me in the
day when I am in trouble; incline
thine ear unto me: in the day when
I call answer me speedily.
3 For my days are consumed like
smoke, and my bones are burned as
an hearth.
4 My heart is smitten, and withered
like grass; so that I forget to eat my
bread.
5 By reason of the voice of my
groaning my bones cleave to my
skin.
6 I am like a pelican of the wilderness: I am like an owl of the desert.
7 I watch, and am as a sparrow
alone upon the house top.
8 Mine enemies reproach me all the
day; and they that are mad against
me are sworn against me.
9 For I have eaten ashes like bread,
and mingled my drink with weeping,
10 Because of thine indignation
and thy wrath: for thou hast lifted
me up, and cast me down.
11 My days are like a shadow that
declineth; and I am withered like
grass.
12 But thou, O Lord, shalt endure
for ever; and thy remembrance unto
all generations.
13 Thou shalt arise, and have mercy
upon Zion: for the time to favour
her, yea, the set time, is come.
14 For thy servants take pleasure in
her stones, and favour the dust
thereof.
15 So the heathen shall fear the
name of the Lord, and all the kings
of the earth thy glory.
16 When the Lord shall build up
Zion, he shall appear in his glory.
17 He will regard the prayer of the
destitute, and not despise their
prayer.
18 This shall be written for the
generation to come: and the people
which shall be created shall praise
the Lord.
19 For he hath looked down from
the height of his sanctuary; from
heaven did the Lord behold the
earth;
20 To hear the groaning of the
prisoner; to loose those that are appointed to death;
21 To declare the name of the Lord
in Zion, and his praise in Jerusalem;
22 When the people are gathered
together, and the kingdoms, to serve
the Lord.
23 He weakened my strength in the
way; he shortened my days.
24 I said, O my God, take me not
away in the midst of my days: thy
years are throughout all generations.
25 Of old hast thou laid the foundation of the earth: and the heavens
are the work of thy hands.
26 They shall perish, but thou shalt
endure: yea, all of them shall wax
old like a garment; as a vesture shalt
thou change them, and they shall be
changed:
27 But thou art the same, and thy
years shall have no end.
28 The children of thy servants
shall continue, and their seed shall
be established before thee.

PSALM 103

A Psalm of David.

BLESS the Lord, O my soul: and
all that is within me, bless his
holy name.
2 Bless the Lord, O my soul, and
forget not all his benefits:

3 Who forgiveth all thine iniquities; who healeth all thy diseases;

4 Who redeemeth thy life from destruction; who crowneth thee with lovingkindness and tender mercies;

5 Who satisfieth thy mouth with good things; so that thy youth is renewed like the eagle's.

6 The Lord executeth righteousness and judgment for all that are oppressed.

7 He made known his ways unto Moses, his acts unto the children of Israel.

8 The Lord is merciful and gracious, slow to anger, and plenteous in mercy.

9 He will not always chide: neither will he keep his anger for ever.

10 He hath not dealt with us after our sins; nor rewarded us according to our iniquities.

11 For as the heaven is high above the earth, so great is his mercy toward them that fear him.

12 As far as the east is from the west, so far hath he removed our transgressions from us.

13 Like as a father pitieth his children, so the Lord pitieth them that fear him.

14 For he knoweth our frame; he remembereth that we are dust.

15 As for man, his days are as grass: as a flower of the field, so he flourisheth.

16 For the wind passeth over it, and it is gone; and the place thereof shall know it no more.

17 But the mercy of the Lord is from everlasting to everlasting upon them that fear him, and his righteousness unto children's children;

18 To such as keep his covenant, and to those that remember his commandments to do them.

19 The Lord hath prepared his throne in the heavens; and his kingdom ruleth over all.

20 Bless the Lord, ye his angels, that excel in strength, that do his commandments, hearkening unto the voice of his word.

21 Bless ye the Lord, all ye his hosts; ye ministers of his, that do his pleasure.

22 Bless the Lord, all his works in all places of his dominion: bless the Lord, O my soul.

PSALM 104

BLESS the Lord, O my soul. O Lord my God, thou art very great; thou art clothed with honour and majesty.

2 Who coverest thyself with light as with a garment: who stretchest out the heavens like a curtain:

3 Who layeth the beams of his chambers in the waters: who maketh the clouds his chariot: who walketh upon the wings of the wind:

4 Who maketh his angels spirits; his ministers a flaming fire:

5 Who laid the foundations of the earth, that it should not be removed for ever.

6 Thou coveredst it with the deep as with a garment: the waters stood above the mountains.

7 At thy rebuke they fled; at the voice of thy thunder they hasted away.

8 They go up by the mountains; they go down by the valleys unto the place which thou hast founded for them.

9 Thou hast set a bound that they may not pass over; that they turn not again to cover the earth.

10 He sendeth the springs into the valleys, which run among the hills.

11 They give drink to every beast of the field: the wild asses quench their thirst.

12 By them shall the fowls of the heaven have their habitation, which sing among the branches.

13 He watereth the hills from his chambers: the earth is satisfied with the fruit of thy works.

14 He causeth the grass to grow for the cattle, and herb for the service of man: that he may bring forth food out of the earth;

15 And wine that maketh glad the

heart of man, and oil to make his
face to shine, and bread which
strengtheneth man's heart.
16 The trees of the Lord are full of
sap; the cedars of Lebanon, which
he hath planted;
17 Where the birds make their
nests: as for the stork, the fir trees
are her house.
18 The high hills are a refuge for
the wild goats; and the rocks for the
conies.
19 He appointed the moon for seasons: the sun knoweth his going
down.
20 Thou makest darkness, and it is
night: wherein all the beasts of the
forest do creep forth.
21 The young lions roar after their
prey, and seek their meat from God.
22 The sun ariseth, they gather
themselves together, and lay them
down in their dens.
23 Man goeth forth unto his work
and to his labour until the evening.
24 O Lord, how manifold are thy
works! in wisdom hast thou made
them all: the earth is full of thy
riches.
25 So is this great and wide sea,
wherein are things creeping innumerable, both small and great beasts.
26 There go the ships: there is that
leviathan, whom thou hast made to
play therein.
27 These wait all upon thee; that
thou mayest give them their meat in
due season.
28 That thou givest them they
gather: thou openest thine hand,
they are filled with good.
29 Thou hidest thy face, they are
troubled: thou takest away their
breath, they die, and return to their
dust.
30 Thou sendest forth thy spirit,
they are created: and thou renewest
the face of the earth.
31 The glory of the Lord shall endure for ever: the Lord shall rejoice
in his works.
32 He looketh on the earth, and it
trembleth: he toucheth the hills, and
they smoke.
33 I will sing unto the Lord as long
as I live: I will sing praise to my God
while I have my being.
34 My meditation of him shall be
sweet: I will be glad in the Lord.
35 Let the sinners be consumed out
of the earth, and let the wicked be
no more. Bless thou the Lord, O my
soul. Praise ye the Lord.

PSALM 105

O GIVE thanks unto the Lord; call
upon his name: make known
his deeds among the people.
2 Sing unto him, sing psalms unto
him: talk ye of all his wondrous
works.
3 Glory ye in his holy name: let the
heart of them rejoice that seek the
Lord.
4 Seek the Lord, and his strength:
seek his face evermore.
5 Remember his marvellous works
that he hath done; his wonders, and
the judgments of his mouth;
6 O ye seed of Abraham his servant, ye children of Jacob his chosen.
7 He is the Lord our God: his judgments are in all the earth.
8 He hath remembered his
covenant for ever, the word which
he commanded to a thousand generations.
9 Which covenant he made with
Abraham, and his oath unto Isaac;
10 And confirmed the same unto
Jacob for a law, and to Israel for an
everlasting covenant:
11 Saying, Unto thee will I give the
land of Canaan, the lot of your inheritance:
12 When they were but a few men
in number; yea, very few, and
strangers in it.
13 When they went from one nation to another, from one kingdom
to another people;
14 He suffered no man to do them
wrong: yea, he reproved kings for
their sakes;
15 Saying, Touch not mine
anointed, and do my prophets no
harm.

16 Moreover he called for a famine upon the land: he brake the whole staff of bread.

17 He sent a man before them, even Joseph, who was sold for a servant:

18 Whose feet they hurt with fetters: he was laid in iron:

19 Until the time that his word came: the word of the Lord tried him.

20 The king sent and loosed him; even the ruler of the people, and let him go free.

21 He made him lord of his house, and ruler of all his substance:

22 To bind his princes at his pleasure; and teach his senators wisdom.

23 Israel also came into Egypt; and Jacob sojourned in the land of Ham.

24 And he increased his people greatly; and made them stronger than their enemies.

25 He turned their heart to hate his people, to deal subtly with his servants.

26 He sent Moses his servant; and Aaron whom he had chosen.

27 They showed his signs among them, and wonders in the land of Ham.

28 He sent darkness, and made it dark; and they rebelled not against his word.

29 He turned their waters into blood, and slew their fish.

30 Their land brought forth frogs in abundance, in the chambers of their kings.

31 He spake, and there came divers sorts of flies, and lice in all their coasts.

32 He gave them hail for rain, and flaming fire in their land.

33 He smote their vines also and their fig trees; and brake the trees of their coasts.

34 He spake, and the locusts came, and caterpillars, and that without number,

35 And did eat up all the herbs in their land, and devoured the fruit of their ground.

36 He smote also all the firstborn in their land, the chief of all their strength.

37 He brought them forth also with silver and gold: and there was not one feeble person among their tribes.

38 Egypt was glad when they departed: for the fear of them fell upon them.

39 He spread a cloud for a covering; and fire to give light in the night.

40 The people asked, and he brought quails, and satisfied them with the bread of heaven.

41 He opened the rock, and the waters gushed out; they ran in the dry places like a river.

42 For he remembered his holy promise, and Abraham his servant.

43 And he brought forth his people with joy, and his chosen with gladness:

44 And gave them the lands of the heathen: and they inherited the labour of the people;

45 That they might observe his statutes, and keep his laws. Praise ye the Lord.

PSALM 106

PRAISE ye the Lord. O give thanks unto the Lord; for he is good: for his mercy endureth for ever.

2 Who can utter the mighty acts of the Lord? who can show forth all his praise?

3 Blessed are they that keep judgment, and he that doeth righteousness at all times.

4 Remember me, O Lord, with the favour that thou bearest unto thy people: O visit me with thy salvation;

5 That I may see the good of thy chosen, that I may rejoice in the gladness of thy nation, that I may glory with thine inheritance.

6 We have sinned with our fathers, we have committed iniquity, we have done wickedly.

7 Our fathers understood not thy wonders in Egypt; they remembered

not the multitude of thy mercies;
but provoked him at the sea, even at
the Red sea.
8 Nevertheless he saved them for
his name's sake, that he might make
his mighty power to be known.
9 He rebuked the Red sea also, and
it was dried up: so he led them
through the depths, as through the
wilderness.
10 And he saved them from the
hand of him that hated them, and
redeemed them from the hand of
the enemy.
11 And the waters covered their enemies: there was not one of them
left.
12 Then believed they his words;
they sang his praise.
13 They soon forgat his works; they
waited not for his counsel:
14 But lusted exceedingly in the
wilderness, and tempted God in the
desert.
15 And he gave them their request;
but sent leanness into their soul.
16 They envied Moses also in the
camp, and Aaron the saint of the
Lord.
17 The earth opened and swallowed
up Dathan, and covered the company of Abiram.
18 And a fire was kindled in their
company; the flame burned up the
wicked.
19 They made a calf in Horeb, and
worshipped the molten image.
20 Thus they changed their glory
into the similitude of an ox that
eateth grass.
21 They forgat God their saviour,
which had done great things in
Egypt;
22 Wondrous works in the land of
Ham, and terrible things by the Red
sea.
23 Therefore he said that he would
destroy them, had not Moses his
chosen stood before him in the
breach, to turn away his wrath, lest
he should destroy them.
24 Yea, they despised the pleasant
land, they believed not his word:
25 But murmured in their tents,
and hearkened not unto the voice of
the Lord.
26 Therefore he lifted up his hand
against them, to overthrow them in
the wilderness:
27 To overthrow their seed also
among the nations, and to scatter
them in the lands.
28 They joined themselves also
unto Baal-peor, and ate the sacrifices of the dead.
29 Thus they provoked him to
anger with their inventions: and the
plague brake in upon them.
30 Then stood up Phinehas, and
executed judgment: and so the
plague was stayed.
31 And that was counted unto him
for righteousness unto all generations for evermore.
32 They angered him also at the
waters of strife, so that it went ill
with Moses for their sakes:
33 Because they provoked his spirit,
so that he spake unadvisedly with his
lips.
34 They did not destroy the nations, concerning whom the Lord
commanded them:
35 But were mingled among the
heathen, and learned their works.
36 And they served their idols:
which were a snare unto them.
37 Yea, they sacrificed their sons
and their daughters unto devils,
38 And shed innocent blood, even
the blood of their sons and of their
daughters, whom they sacrificed
unto the idols of Canaan: and the
land was polluted with blood.
39 Thus were they defiled with
their own works, and went a-whoring with their own inventions.
40 Therefore was the wrath of the
Lord kindled against his people, in-
somuch that he abhorred his own
inheritance.
41 And he gave them into the hand
of the heathen; and they that hated
them ruled over them.
42 Their enemies also oppressed
them, and they were brought into
subjection under their hand.
43 Many times did he deliver them;

but they provoked him with their counsel, and were brought low for their iniquity.

44 Nevertheless he regarded their affliction, when he heard their cry:

45 And he remembered for them his covenant, and repented according to the multitude of his mercies.

46 He made them also to be pitied of all those that carried them captives.

47 Save us, O Lord our God, and gather us from among the heathen, to give thanks unto thy holy name, and to triumph in thy praise.

48 Blessed be the Lord God of Israel from everlasting to everlasting: and let all the people say, Amen. Praise ye the Lord.

PSALM 107

O GIVE thanks unto the Lord, for he is good: for his mercy endureth for ever.

2 Let the redeemed of the Lord say so, whom he hath redeemed from the hand of the enemy;

3 And gathered them out of the lands, from the east, and from the west, from the north, and from the south.

4 They wandered in the wilderness in a solitary way; they found no city to dwell in.

5 Hungry and thirsty, their soul fainted in them.

6 Then they cried unto the Lord in their trouble, and he delivered them out of their distresses.

7 And he led them forth by the right way, that they might go to a city of habitation.

8 Oh that men would praise the Lord for his goodness, and for his wonderful works to the children of men!

9 For he satisfieth the longing soul, and filleth the hungry soul with goodness.

10 Such as sit in darkness and in the shadow of death, being bound in affliction and iron;

11 Because they rebelled against the words of God, and contemned the counsel of the most High:

12 Therefore he brought down their heart with labour; they fell down, and there was none to help.

13 Then they cried unto the Lord in their trouble, and he saved them out of their distresses.

14 He brought them out of darkness and the shadow of death, and brake their bands in sunder.

15 Oh that men would praise the Lord for his goodness, and for his wonderful works to the children of men!

16 For he hath broken the gates of brass, and cut the bars of iron in sunder.

17 Fools because of their transgression, and because of their iniquities, are afflicted.

18 Their soul abhorreth all manner of meat; and they draw near unto the gates of death.

19 Then they cry unto the Lord in their trouble, and he saveth them out of their distresses.

20 He sent his word, and healed them, and delivered them from their destructions.

21 Oh that men would praise the Lord for his goodness, and for his wonderful works to the children of men!

22 And let them sacrifice the sacrifices of thanksgiving, and declare his works with rejoicing.

23 They that go down to the sea in ships, that do business in great waters;

24 These see the works of the Lord, and his wonders in the deep.

25 For he commandeth, and raiseth the stormy wind, which lifteth up the waves thereof.

26 They mount up to the heaven, they go down again to the depths: their soul is melted because of trouble.

27 They reel to and fro, and stagger like a drunken man, and are at their wit's end.

28 Then they cry unto the Lord in their trouble, and he bringeth them out of their distresses.

29 He maketh the storm a calm, so that the waves thereof are still.

30 Then are they glad because they be quiet; so he bringeth them unto their desired haven.

31 Oh that men would praise the Lord for his goodness, and for his wonderful works to the children of men!

32 Let them exalt him also in the congregation of the people, and praise him in the assembly of the elders.

33 He turneth rivers into a wilderness, and the watersprings into dry ground;

34 A fruitful land into barrenness, for the wickedness of them that dwell therein.

35 He turneth the wilderness into a standing water, and dry ground into watersprings.

36 And there he maketh the hungry to dwell, that they may prepare a city for habitation;

37 And sow the fields, and plant vineyards, which may yield fruits of increase.

38 He blesseth them also, so that they are multiplied greatly; and suffereth not their cattle to decrease.

39 Again, they are minished and brought low through oppression, affliction, and sorrow.

40 He poureth contempt upon princes, and causeth them to wander in the wilderness, where there is no way.

41 Yet setteth he the poor on high from affliction, and maketh him families like a flock.

42 The righteous shall see it, and rejoice: and all iniquity shall stop her mouth.

43 Whoso is wise, and will observe these things, even they shall understand the lovingkindness of the Lord.

PSALM 108

A Song or Psalm of David.

O God, my heart is fixed; I will sing and give praise, even with my glory.

2 Awake, psaltery and harp: I myself will awake early.

3 I will praise thee, O Lord, among the people: and I will sing praises unto thee among the nations.

4 For thy mercy is great above the heavens: and thy truth reacheth unto the clouds.

5 Be thou exalted, O God, above the heavens: and thy glory above all the earth;

6 That thy beloved may be delivered: save with thy right hand, and answer me.

7 God hath spoken in his holiness; I will rejoice, I will divide Shechem, and mete out the valley of Succoth.

8 Gilead is mine; Manasseh is mine; Ephraim also is the strength of mine head; Judah is my lawgiver;

9 Moab is my washpot; over Edom will I cast out my shoe; over Philistia will I triumph.

10 Who will bring me into the strong city? who will lead me into Edom?

11 Wilt not thou, O God, who hast cast us off? and wilt not thou, O God, go forth with our hosts?

12 Give us help from trouble: for vain is the help of man.

13 Through God we shall do valiantly: for he it is that shall tread down our enemies.

PSALM 109

To the chief Musician, A Psalm of David.

Hold not thy peace, O God of my praise;

2 For the mouth of the wicked and the mouth of the deceitful are opened against me: they have spoken against me with a lying tongue.

3 They compassed me about also with words of hatred; and fought against me without a cause.

4 For my love they are my adversaries: but I give myself unto prayer.

5 And they have rewarded me evil for good, and hatred for my love.

6 Set thou a wicked man over him: and let Satan stand at his right hand.

7 When he shall be judged, let him

be condemned: and let his prayer become sin.
8 Let his days be few; and let another take his office.
9 Let his children be fatherless, and his wife a widow.
10 Let his children be continually vagabonds, and beg: let them seek their bread also out of their desolate places.
11 Let the extortioner catch all that he hath; and let the strangers spoil his labour.
12 Let there be none to extend mercy unto him: neither let there be any to favour his fatherless children.
13 Let his posterity be cut off; and in the generation following let their name be blotted out.
14 Let the iniquity of his fathers be remembered with the Lord; and let not the sin of his mother be blotted out.
15 Let them be before the Lord continually, that he may cut off the memory of them from the earth.
16 Because that he remembered not to show mercy, but persecuted the poor and needy man, that he might even slay the broken in heart.
17 As he loved cursing, so let it come unto him: as he delighted not in blessing, so let it be far from him.
18 As he clothed himself with cursing like as with his garment, so let it come into his bowels like water, and like oil into his bones.
19 Let it be unto him as the garment which covereth him, and for a girdle wherewith he is girded continually.
20 Let this be the reward of mine adversaries from the Lord, and of them that speak evil against my soul.
21 But do thou for me, O God the Lord, for thy name's sake: because thy mercy is good, deliver thou me.
22 For I am poor and needy, and my heart is wounded within me.
23 I am gone like the shadow when it declineth: I am tossed up and down as the locust.
24 My knees are weak through fasting; and my flesh faileth of fatness.
25 I became also a reproach unto them: when they looked upon me they shaked their heads.
26 Help me, O Lord my God: O save me according to thy mercy:
27 That they may know that this is thy hand; that thou, Lord, hast done it.
28 Let them curse, but bless thou: when they arise, let them be ashamed; but let thy servant rejoice.
29 Let mine adversaries be clothed with shame, and let them cover themselves with their own confusion, as with a mantle.
30 I will greatly praise the Lord with my mouth; yea, I will praise him among the multitude.
31 For he shall stand at the right hand of the poor, to save him from those that condemn his soul.

PSALM 110

A Psalm of David.

THE LORD said unto my Lord, Sit thou at my right hand, until I make thine enemies thy footstool.
2 The Lord shall send the rod of thy strength out of Zion: rule thou in the midst of thine enemies.
3 Thy people shall be willing in the day of thy power, in the beauties of holiness from the womb of the morning: thou hast the dew of thy youth.
4 The Lord hath sworn, and will not repent, Thou art a priest for ever after the order of Melchizedek.
5 The Lord at thy right hand shall strike through kings in the day of his wrath.
6 He shall judge among the heathen, he shall fill the places with the dead bodies; he shall wound the heads over many countries.
7 He shall drink of the brook in the way: therefore shall he lift up the head.

PSALM 111

PRAISE ye the Lord. I will praise the Lord with my whole heart, in the assembly of the upright, and in the congregation.

2 The works of the Lord are great,
sought out of all them that have
pleasure therein.
3 His work is honourable and glorious: and his righteousness endureth
for ever.
4 He hath made his wonderful
works to be remembered: the Lord
is gracious and full of compassion.
5 He hath given meat unto them
that fear him: he will ever be mindful of his covenant.
6 He hath shown his people the
power of his works, that he may
give them the heritage of the heathen.
7 The works of his hands are verity
and judgment; all his commandments are sure.
8 They stand fast for ever and ever,
and are done in truth and uprightness.
9 He sent redemption unto his people: he hath commanded his
covenant for ever: holy and reverend
is his name.
10 The fear of the Lord is the beginning of wisdom: a good understanding have all they that do his
commandments: his praise endureth
for ever.

PSALM 112

PRAISE ye the Lord. Blessed is the
man that feareth the Lord, that
delighteth greatly in his commandments.
2 His seed shall be mighty upon
earth: the generation of the upright
shall be blessed.
3 Wealth and riches shall be in his
house: and his righteousness endureth for ever.
4 Unto the upright there ariseth
light in the darkness: he is gracious,
and full of compassion, and righteous.
5 A good man showeth favour, and
lendeth: he will guide his affairs
with discretion.
6 Surely he shall not be moved for
ever: the righteous shall be in everlasting remembrance.
7 He shall not be afraid of evil tid-
ings: his heart is fixed, trusting in
the Lord.
8 His heart is established, he shall
not be afraid, until he see his desire
upon his enemies.
9 He hath dispersed, he hath given
to the poor; his righteousness endureth for ever; his horn shall be exalted with honour.
10 The wicked shall see it, and be
grieved; he shall gnash with his
teeth, and melt away: the desire of
the wicked shall perish.

PSALM 113

PRAISE ye the Lord. Praise, O ye
servants of the Lord, praise the
name of the Lord.
2 Blessed be the name of the Lord
from this time forth and for evermore.
3 From the rising of the sun unto
the going down of the same the
Lord's name is to be praised.
4 The Lord is high above all nations, and his glory above the heavens.
5 Who is like unto the Lord our
God, who dwelleth on high,
6 Who humbleth himself to behold
the things that are in heaven, and in
the earth!
7 He raiseth up the poor out of the
dust, and lifteth the needy out of
the dunghill;
8 That he may set him with
princes, even with the princes of his
people.
9 He maketh the barren woman to
keep house, and to be a joyful
mother of children. Praise ye the
Lord.

PSALM 114

WHEN Israel went out of Egypt,
the house of Jacob from a
people of strange language;
2 Judah was his sanctuary, and Israel
his dominion.
3 The sea saw it, and fled: Jordan
was driven back.
4 The mountains skipped like rams,
and the little hills like lambs.
5 What ailed thee, O thou sea, that

thou fleddest? thou Jordan, that
thou wast driven back?
6 Ye mountains, that ye skipped like
rams; and ye little hills, like lambs?
7 Tremble, thou earth, at the presence of the Lord, at the presence of
the God of Jacob;
8 Which turned the rock into a
standing water, the flint into a fountain of waters.

PSALM 115

NOT UNTO us, O Lord, not unto
us, but unto thy name give
glory, for thy mercy, and for thy
truth's sake.
2 Wherefore should the heathen
say, Where is now their God?
3 But our God is in the heavens: he
hath done whatsoever he hath
pleased.
4 Their idols are silver and gold, the
work of men's hands.
5 They have mouths, but they
speak not: eyes have they, but they
see not:
6 They have ears, but they hear not:
noses have they, but they smell not:
7 They have hands, but they handle
not: feet have they, but they walk
not: neither speak they through
their throat.
8 They that make them are like
unto them; so is every one that
trusteth in them.
9 O Israel, trust thou in the Lord:
he is their help and their shield.
10 O house of Aaron, trust in the
Lord: he is their help and their
shield.
11 Ye that fear the Lord, trust in the
Lord: he is their help and their
shield.
12 The Lord hath been mindful of
us: he will bless us; he will bless the
house of Israel; he will bless the
house of Aaron.
13 He will bless them that fear the
Lord, both small and great.
14 The Lord shall increase you
more and more, you and your children.
15 Ye are blessed of the Lord which
made heaven and earth.
16 The heaven, even the heavens,
are the Lord's: but the earth hath he
given to the children of men.
17 The dead praise not the Lord,
neither any that go down into silence.
18 But we will bless the Lord from
this time forth and for evermore.
Praise the Lord.

PSALM 116

I LOVE the Lord, because he hath
heard my voice and my supplications.
2 Because he hath inclined his ear
unto me, therefore will I call upon
him as long as I live.
3 The sorrows of death compassed
me, and the pains of hell gat hold
upon me: I found trouble and sorrow.
4 Then called I upon the name of
the Lord; O Lord, I beseech thee,
deliver my soul.
5 Gracious is the Lord, and righteous; yea, our God is merciful.
6 The Lord preserveth the simple: I
was brought low, and he helped me.
7 Return unto thy rest, O my soul;
for the Lord hath dealt bountifully
with thee.
8 For thou hast delivered my soul
from death, mine eyes from tears,
and my feet from falling.
9 I will walk before the Lord in the
land of the living.
10 I believed, therefore have I spoken: I was greatly afflicted:
11 I said in my haste, All men are
liars.
12 What shall I render unto the
Lord for all his benefits toward me?
13 I will take the cup of salvation,
and call upon the name of the Lord.
14 I will pay my vows unto the
Lord now in the presence of all his
people.
15 Precious in the sight of the Lord
is the death of his saints.
16 O Lord, truly I am thy servant; I
am thy servant, and the son of thine
handmaid: thou hast loosed my
bonds.

17 I will offer to thee the sacrifice of thanksgiving, and will call upon the name of the Lord.

18 I will pay my vows unto the Lord now in the presence of all his people,

19 In the courts of the Lord's house, in the midst of thee, O Jerusalem. Praise ye the Lord.

PSALM 117

O PRAISE the Lord, all ye nations: praise him all ye people.

2 For his merciful kindness is great toward us: and the truth of the Lord endureth for ever. Praise ye the Lord.

PSALM 118

O GIVE thanks unto the Lord; for he is good: because his mercy endureth for ever.

2 Let Israel now say, that his mercy endureth for ever.

3 Let the house of Aaron now say, that his mercy endureth for ever.

4 Let them now that fear the Lord say, that his mercy endureth for ever.

5 I called upon the Lord in distress: the Lord answered me, and set me in a large place.

6 The Lord is on my side; I will not fear: what can man do unto me?

7 The Lord taketh my part with them that help me: therefore shall I see my desire upon them that hate me.

8 It is better to trust in the Lord than to put confidence in man.

9 It is better to trust in the Lord than to put confidence in princes.

10 All nations compassed me about: but in the name of the Lord will I destroy them.

11 They compassed me about; yea, they compassed me about: but in the name of the Lord I will destroy them.

12 They compassed me about like bees; they are quenched as the fire of thorns: for in the name of the Lord I will destroy them.

13 Thou hast thrust sore at me that I might fall: but the Lord helped me.

14 The Lord is my strength and song, and is become my salvation.

15 The voice of rejoicing and salvation is in the tabernacles of the righteous: the right hand of the Lord doeth valiantly.

16 The right hand of the Lord is exalted: the right hand of the Lord doeth valiantly.

17 I shall not die, but live, and declare the works of the Lord.

18 The Lord hath chastened me sore: but he hath not given me over unto death.

19 Open to me the gates of righteousness: I will go into them, and I will praise the Lord:

20 This gate of the Lord, into which the righteous shall enter.

21 I will praise thee: for thou hast heard me, and art become my salvation.

22 The stone which the builders refused is become the head stone of the corner.

23 This is the Lord's doing; it is marvellous in our eyes.

24 This is the day which the Lord hath made; we will rejoice and be glad in it.

25 Save now, I beseech thee, O Lord: O Lord, I beseech thee, send now prosperity.

26 Blessed be he that cometh in the name of the Lord: we have blessed you out of the house of the Lord.

27 God is the Lord, which hath shown us light: bind the sacrifice with cords, even unto the horns of the altar.

28 Thou art my God, and I will praise thee: thou art my God, I will exalt thee.

29 O give thanks unto the Lord; for he is good: for his mercy endureth for ever.

PSALM 119

Aleph.

BLESSED are the undefiled in the way, who walk in the law of the Lord.

2 Blessed are they that keep his testimonies, and that seek him with the
whole heart.
3 They also do no iniquity: they
walk in his ways.
4 Thou hast commanded us to keep
thy precepts diligently.
5 O that my ways were directed to
keep thy statutes!
6 Then shall I not be ashamed,
when I have respect unto all thy
commandments.
7 I will praise thee with uprightness
of heart, when I shall have learned
thy righteous judgments.
8 I will keep thy statutes: O forsake
me not utterly.

Beth.

9 Wherewithal shall a young man
cleanse his way? by taking heed
thereto according to thy word.
10 With my whole heart have I
sought thee: O let me not wander
from thy commandments.
11 Thy word have I hid in mine
heart, that I might not sin against
thee.
12 Blessed art thou, O Lord: teach
me thy statutes.
13 With my lips have I declared all
the judgments of thy mouth.
14 I have rejoiced in the way of thy
testimonies, as much as in all riches.
15 I will meditate in thy precepts,
and have respect unto thy ways.
16 I will delight myself in thy
statutes: I will not forget thy word.

Gimel.

17 Deal bountifully with thy servant,
that I may live, and keep thy word.
18 Open thou mine eyes, that I may
behold wondrous things out of thy
law.
19 I am a stranger in the earth: hide
not thy commandments from me.
20 My soul breaketh for the longing that it hath unto thy judgments
at all times.
21 Thou hast rebuked the proud
that are cursed, which do err from
thy commandments.
22 Remove from me reproach and
contempt; for I have kept thy testimonies.
23 Princes also did sit and speak
against me: but thy servant did meditate in thy statutes.
24 Thy testimonies also are my delight and my counsellors.

Daleth.

25 My soul cleaveth unto the dust:
quicken thou me according to thy
word.
26 I have declared my ways, and
thou heardest me: teach me thy
statutes.
27 Make me to understand the way
of thy precepts: so shall I talk of thy
wondrous works.
28 My soul melteth for heaviness:
strengthen thou me according unto
thy word.
29 Remove from me the way of
lying: and grant me thy law graciously.
30 I have chosen the way of truth:
thy judgments have I laid before me.
31 I have stuck unto thy testimonies: O Lord, put me not to
shame.
32 I will run the way of thy commandments, when thou shalt enlarge my heart.

He.

33 Teach me, O Lord, the way of
thy statutes; and I shall keep it unto
the end.
34 Give me understanding, and I
shall keep thy law; yea, I shall observe it with my whole heart.
35 Make me to go in the path of
thy commandments; for therein do I
delight.
36 Incline my heart unto thy testimonies, and not to covetousness.
37 Turn away mine eyes from beholding vanity; and quicken thou
me in thy way.
38 Stablish thy word unto thy servant, who is devoted to thy fear.
39 Turn away my reproach which I
fear: for thy judgments are good.
40 Behold, I have longed after thy
precepts: quicken me in thy righteousness.

Vau.

41 Let thy mercies come also unto
me, O Lord, even thy salvation, according to thy word.
42 So shall I have wherewith to answer him that reproacheth me: for I
trust in thy word.
43 And take not the word of truth
utterly out of my mouth; for I have
hoped in thy judgments.
44 So shall I keep thy law continually for ever and ever.
45 And I will walk at liberty: for I
seek thy precepts.
46 I will speak of thy testimonies
also before kings, and will not be
ashamed.
47 And I will delight myself in thy
commandments, which I have
loved.
48 My hands also will I lift up unto
thy commandments, which I have
loved; and I will meditate in thy
statutes.
Zain.
49 Remember the word unto thy
servant, upon which thou hast
caused me to hope.
50 This is my comfort in my affliction: for thy word hath quickened
me.
51 The proud have had me greatly
in derision: yet have I not declined
from thy law.
52 I remembered thy judgments of
old, O Lord; and have comforted
myself.
53 Horror hath taken hold upon
me because of the wicked that forsake thy law.
54 Thy statutes have been my songs
in the house of my pilgrimage.
55 I have remembered thy name, O
Lord, in the night, and have kept thy
law.
56 This I had, because I kept thy
precepts.
Cheth.
57 Thou art my portion, O Lord: I
have said that I would keep thy
words.
58 I entreated thy favour with my
whole heart: be merciful unto me
according to thy word.
59 I thought on my ways, and
turned my feet unto thy testimonies.
60 I made haste, and delayed not to
keep thy commandments.
61 The bands of the wicked have
robbed me: but I have not forgotten
thy law.
62 At midnight I will rise to give
thanks unto thee because of thy
righteous judgments.
63 I am a companion of all them
that fear thee, and of them that keep
thy precepts.
64 The earth, O Lord, is full of thy
mercy: teach me thy statutes.
Teth.
65 Thou hast dealt well with thy
servant, O Lord, according unto thy
word.
66 Teach me good judgment and
knowledge: for I have believed thy
commandments.
67 Before I was afflicted I went
astray: but now have I kept thy
word.
68 Thou art good, and doest good;
teach me thy statutes.
69 The proud have forged a lie
against me: but I will keep thy precepts with my whole heart.
70 Their heart is as fat as grease; but
I delight in thy law.
71 It is good for me that I have
been afflicted; that I might learn thy
statutes.
72 The law of thy mouth is better
unto me than thousands of gold and
silver.
Jod.
73 Thy hands have made me and
fashioned me: give me understanding, that I may learn thy commandments.
74 They that fear thee will be glad
when they see me; because I have
hoped in thy word.
75 I know, O Lord, that thy judgments are right, and that thou in
faithfulness hast afflicted me.
76 Let, I pray thee, thy merciful
kindness be for my comfort, according to thy word unto thy servant.
77 Let thy tender mercies come

unto me, that I may live: for thy law is my delight.

78 Let the proud be ashamed; for they dealt perversely with me without a cause: but I will meditate in thy precepts.

79 Let those that fear thee turn unto me, and those that have known thy testimonies.

80 Let my heart be sound in thy statutes; that I be not ashamed.

Caph.

81 My soul fainteth for thy salvation: but I hope in thy word.

82 Mine eyes fail for thy word, saying, When wilt thou comfort me?

83 For I am become like a bottle in the smoke; yet do I not forget thy statutes.

84 How many are the days of thy servant? when wilt thou execute judgment on them that persecute me?

85 The proud have digged pits for me, which are not after thy law.

86 All thy commandments are faithful: they persecute me wrongfully; help thou me.

87 They had almost consumed me upon earth; but I forsook not thy precepts.

88 Quicken me after thy lovingkindness; so shall I keep the testimony of thy mouth.

Lamed.

89 For ever, O Lord, thy word is settled in heaven.

90 Thy faithfulness is unto all generations: thou hast established the earth, and it abideth.

91 They continue this day according to thine ordinances: for all are thy servants.

92 Unless thy law had been my delights, I should then have perished in mine affliction.

93 I will never forget thy precepts: for with them thou hast quickened me.

94 I am thine, save me; for I have sought thy precepts.

95 The wicked have waited for me to destroy me: but I will consider thy testimonies.

96 I have seen an end of all perfection: but thy commandment is exceeding broad.

Mem.

97 O how love I thy law! it is my meditation all the day.

98 Thou through thy commandments hast made me wiser than mine enemies: for they are ever with me.

99 I have more understanding than all my teachers: for thy testimonies are my meditation.

100 I understand more than the ancients, because I keep thy precepts.

101 I have refrained my feet from every evil way, that I might keep thy word.

102 I have not departed from thy judgments: for thou hast taught me.

103 How sweet are thy words unto my taste! yea, sweeter than honey to my mouth!

104 Through thy precepts I get understanding: therefore I hate every false way.

Nun.

105 Thy word is a lamp unto my feet, and a light unto my path.

106 I have sworn, and I will perform it, that I will keep thy righteous judgments.

107 I am afflicted very much: quicken me, O Lord, according unto thy word.

108 Accept, I beseech thee, the freewill offerings of my mouth, O Lord, and teach me thy judgments.

109 My soul is continually in my hand: yet do I not forget thy law.

110 The wicked have laid a snare for me: yet I erred not from thy precepts.

111 Thy testimonies have I taken as an heritage for ever: for they are the rejoicing of my heart.

112 I have inclined mine heart to perform thy statutes always, even unto the end.

Samech.

113 I hate vain thoughts: but thy law do I love.

114 Thou art my hiding place and my shield: I hope in thy word.

115 Depart from me, ye evildoers: for I will keep the commandments of my God.
116 Uphold me according unto thy word, that I may live: and let me not be ashamed of my hope.
117 Hold thou me up, and I shall be safe: and I will have respect unto thy statutes continually.
118 Thou hast trodden down all them that err from thy statutes: for their deceit is falsehood.
119 Thou puttest away all the wicked of the earth like dross: therefore I love thy testimonies.
120 My flesh trembleth for fear of thee; and I am afraid of thy judgments.

Ain.

121 I have done judgment and justice: leave me not to mine oppressors.
122 Be surety for thy servant for good: let not the proud oppress me.
123 Mine eyes fail for thy salvation, and for the word of thy righteousness.
124 Deal with thy servant according unto thy mercy, and teach me thy statutes.
125 I am thy servant; give me understanding, that I may know thy testimonies.
126 It is time for thee, Lord, to work: for they have made void thy law.
127 Therefore I love thy commandments above gold; yea, above fine gold.
128 Therefore I esteem all thy precepts concerning all things to be right; and I hate every false way.

Pe.

129 Thy testimonies are wonderful: therefore doth my soul keep them.
130 The entrance of thy words giveth light; it giveth understanding unto the simple.
131 I opened my mouth, and panted: for I longed for thy commandments.
132 Look thou upon me, and be merciful unto me, as thou usest to do unto those that love thy name.
133 Order my steps in thy word: and let not any iniquity have dominion over me.
134 Deliver me from the oppression of man: so will I keep thy precepts.
135 Make thy face to shine upon thy servant; and teach me thy statutes.
136 Rivers of waters run down mine eyes, because they keep not thy law.

Tzaddi.

137 Righteous art thou, O Lord, and upright are thy judgments.
138 Thy testimonies that thou hast commanded are righteous and very faithful.
139 My zeal hath consumed me, because mine enemies have forgotten thy words.
140 Thy word is very pure: therefore thy servant loveth it.
141 I am small and despised: yet do not I forget thy precepts.
142 Thy righteousness is an everlasting righteousness, and thy law is the truth.
143 Trouble and anguish have taken hold on me: yet thy commandments are my delights.
144 The righteousness of thy testimonies is everlasting: give me understanding, and I shall live.

Koph.

145 I cried with my whole heart; hear me, O Lord: I will keep thy statutes.
146 I cried unto thee; save me, and I shall keep thy testimonies.
147 I prevented the dawning of the morning, and cried: I hoped in thy word.
148 Mine eyes prevent the night watches, that I might meditate in thy word.
149 Hear my voice according unto thy lovingkindness: O Lord, quicken me according to thy judgment.
150 They draw nigh that follow after mischief: they are far from thy law.
151 Thou art near, O Lord; and all thy commandments are truth.

152 Concerning thy testimonies, I have known of old that thou hast founded them for ever.

Resh.

153 Consider mine affliction, and deliver me: for I do not forget thy law.

154 Plead my cause, and deliver me: quicken me according to thy word.

155 Salvation is far from the wicked: for they seek not thy statutes.

156 Great are thy tender mercies, O Lord: quicken me according to thy judgments.

157 Many are my persecutors and mine enemies; yet do I not decline from thy testimonies.

158 I beheld the transgressors, and was grieved; because they kept not thy word.

159 Consider how I love thy precepts: quicken me, O Lord, according to thy lovingkindness.

160 Thy word is true from the beginning: and every one of thy righteous judgments endureth for ever.

Schin.

161 Princes have persecuted me without a cause: but my heart standeth in awe of thy word.

162 I rejoice at thy word, as one that findeth great spoil.

163 I hate and abhor lying: but thy law do I love.

164 Seven times a day do I praise thee because of thy righteous judgments.

165 Great peace have they which love thy law: and nothing shall offend them.

166 Lord, I have hoped for thy salvation, and done thy commandments.

167 My soul hath kept thy testimonies; and I love them exceedingly.

168 I have kept thy precepts and thy testimonies: for all my ways are before thee.

Tau.

169 Let my cry come near before thee, O Lord: give me understanding according to thy word.

170 Let my supplication come before thee: deliver me according to thy word.

171 My lips shall utter praise, when thou hast taught me thy statutes.

172 My tongue shall speak of thy word: for all thy commandments are righteousness.

173 Let thine hand help me; for I have chosen thy precepts.

174 I have longed for thy salvation, O Lord; and thy law is my delight.

175 Let my soul live, and it shall praise thee; and let thy judgments help me.

176 I have gone astray like a lost sheep; seek thy servant; for I do not forget thy commandments.

PSALM 120

A Song of degrees.

IN MY distress I cried unto the Lord, and he heard me.

2 Deliver my soul, O Lord, from lying lips, and from a deceitful tongue.

3 What shall be given unto thee? or what shall be done unto thee, thou false tongue?

4 Sharp arrows of the mighty, with coals of juniper.

5 Woe is me, that I sojourn in Mesech, that I dwell in the tents of Kedar!

6 My soul hath long dwelt with him that hateth peace.

7 I am for peace: but when I speak, they are for war.

PSALM 121

A Song of degrees.

I WILL lift up mine eyes unto the hills, from whence cometh my help.

2 My help cometh from the Lord, which made heaven and earth.

3 He will not suffer thy foot to be moved: he that keepeth thee will not slumber.

4 Behold, he that keepeth Israel shall neither slumber nor sleep.
5 The Lord is thy keeper: the Lord is thy shade upon thy right hand.
6 The sun shall not smite thee by day, nor the moon by night.
7 The Lord shall preserve thee from all evil: he shall preserve thy soul.
8 The Lord shall preserve thy going out and thy coming in from this time forth, and even for evermore.

PSALM 122

A Song of degrees of David.

I WAS glad when they said unto me, Let us go into the house of the Lord.
2 Our feet shall stand within thy gates, O Jerusalem.
3 Jerusalem is builded as a city that is compact together:
4 Whither the tribes go up, the tribes of the Lord, unto the testimony of Israel, to give thanks unto the name of the Lord.
5 For there are set thrones of judgment, the thrones of the house of David.
6 Pray for the peace of Jerusalem: they shall prosper that love thee.
7 Peace be within thy walls, and prosperity within thy palaces.
8 For my brethren and companions' sakes, I will now say, Peace be within thee.
9 Because of the house of the Lord our God I will seek thy good.

PSALM 123

A Song of degrees.

UNTO thee lift I up mine eyes, O thou that dwellest in the heavens.
2 Behold, as the eyes of servants look unto the hand of their masters, and as the eyes of a maiden unto the hand of her mistress; so our eyes wait upon the Lord our God, until that he have mercy upon us.
3 Have mercy upon us, O Lord, have mercy upon us: for we are exceedingly filled with contempt.
4 Our soul is exceedingly filled with the scorning of those that are at ease, and with the contempt of the proud.

PSALM 124

A Song of degrees of David.

IF IT had not been the Lord who was on our side, now may Israel say;
2 If it had not been the Lord who was on our side, when men rose up against us:
3 Then they had swallowed us up quick, when their wrath was kindled against us:
4 Then the waters had overwhelmed us, the stream had gone over our soul:
5 Then the proud waters had gone over our soul.
6 Blessed be the Lord, who hath not given us as a prey to their teeth.
7 Our soul is escaped as a bird out of the snare of the fowlers: the snare is broken, and we are escaped.
8 Our help is in the name of the Lord, who made heaven and earth.

PSALM 125

A Song of degrees.

THEY that trust in the Lord shall be as mount Zion, which cannot be removed, but abideth for ever.
2 As the mountains are round about Jerusalem, so the Lord is round about his people from henceforth even for ever.
3 For the rod of the wicked shall not rest upon the lot of the righteous; lest the righteous put forth their hands unto iniquity.
4 Do good, O Lord, unto those that be good, and to them that are upright in their hearts.
5 As for such as turn aside unto their crooked ways, the Lord shall lead them forth with the workers of iniquity: but peace shall be upon Israel.

PSALM 126

A Song of degrees.

WHEN the Lord turned again
the captivity of Zion, we
were like them that dream.
2 Then was our mouth filled with
laughter, and our tongue with
singing: then said they among the
heathen, The Lord hath done great
things for them.
3 The Lord hath done great things
for us; whereof we are glad.
4 Turn again our captivity, O Lord,
as the streams in the south.
5 They that sow in tears shall reap
in joy.
6 He that goeth forth and weepeth,
bearing precious seed, shall doubtless come again with rejoicing,
bringing his sheaves with him.

PSALM 127

A Song of degrees for Solomon.

EXCEPT the Lord build the house,
they labour in vain that build it:
except the Lord keep the city, the
watchman waketh but in vain.
2 It is vain for you to rise up early,
to sit up late, to eat the bread of sorrows: for so he giveth his beloved
sleep.
3 Lo, children are an heritage of the
Lord and the fruit of the womb is
his reward.
4 As arrows are in the hand of a
mighty man; so are children of the
youth.
5 Happy is the man that hath his
quiver full of them: they shall not be
ashamed, but they shall speak with
the enemies in the gate.

PSALM 128

A Song of degrees.

BLESSED is every one that feareth
the Lord; that walketh in his
ways.
2 For thou shalt eat the labour of
thine hands: happy shalt thou be,
and it shall be well with thee.
3 Thy wife shall be as a fruitful vine
by the sides of thine house: thy children like olive plants round about
thy table.
4 Behold, that thus shall the man be
blessed that feareth the Lord.
5 The Lord shall bless thee out of
Zion: and thou shalt see the good of
Jerusalem all the days of thy life.
6 Yea, thou shalt see thy children's
children, and peace upon Israel.

PSALM 129

A Song of degrees.

MANY a time have they afflicted
me from my youth, may Israel
now say:
2 Many a time have they afflicted
me from my youth: yet they have
not prevailed against me.
3 The plowers plowed upon my
back: they made long their furrows.
4 The Lord is righteous: he hath
cut asunder the cords of the wicked.
5 Let them all be confounded and
turned back that hate Zion.
6 Let them be as the grass upon the
housetops, which withereth afore it
groweth up:
7 Wherewith the mower filleth not
his hand; nor he that bindeth
sheaves his bosom.
8 Neither do they which go by say,
The blessing of the Lord be upon
you: we bless you in the name of
the Lord.

PSALM 130

A Song of degrees.

OUT OF the depths have I cried
unto thee, O Lord.
2 Lord, hear my voice: let thine ears
be attentive to the voice of my supplications.
3 If thou, Lord, shouldest mark iniquities, O Lord, who shall stand?
4 But there is forgiveness with thee,
that thou mayest be feared.
5 I wait for the Lord, my soul doth
wait, and in his word do I hope.
6 My soul waiteth for the Lord
more than they that watch for the
morning: I say, more than they that
watch for the morning.
7 Let Israel hope in the Lord: for

with the Lord there is mercy, and
with him is plenteous redemption.
8 And he shall redeem Israel from
all his iniquities.

PSALM 131

A Song of degrees of David.

LORD, my heart is not haughty,
nor mine eyes lofty: neither do I
exercise myself in great matters, or
in things too high for me.
2 Surely I have behaved and quieted
myself, as a child that is weaned of
his mother: my soul is even as a
weaned child.
3 Let Israel hope in the Lord from
henceforth and for ever.

PSALM 132

A Song of degrees.

LORD, remember David, and all
his afflictions:
2 How he sware unto the Lord, and
vowed unto the mighty God of
Jacob;
3 Surely I will not come into the
tabernacle of my house, nor go up
into my bed;
4 I will not give sleep to mine eyes,
or slumber to mine eyelids,
5 Until I find out a place for the
Lord, an habitation for the mighty
God of Jacob.
6 Lo, we heard of it at Ephratah: we
found it in the fields of the wood.
7 We will go into his tabernacles:
we will worship at his footstool.
8 Arise, O Lord, into thy rest; thou,
and the ark of thy strength.
9 Let thy priests be clothed with
righteousness; and let thy saints
shout for joy.
10 For thy servant David's sake turn
not away the face of thine anointed.
11 The Lord hath sworn in truth
unto David; he will not turn from it;
Of the fruit of thy body will I set
upon thy throne.
12 If thy children will keep my
covenant and my testimony that I
shall teach them, their children shall
also sit upon thy throne for evermore.
13 For the Lord hath chosen Zion;
he hath desired it for his habitation.
14 This is my rest for ever: here will
I dwell; for I have desired it.
15 I will abundantly bless her provision: I will satisfy her poor with
bread.
16 I will also clothe her priests with
salvation: and her saints shall shout
aloud for joy.
17 There will I make the horn of
David to bud: I have ordained a
lamp for mine anointed.
18 His enemies will I clothe with
shame: but upon himself shall his
crown flourish.

PSALM 133

A Song of degrees of David.

BEHOLD, how good and how
pleasant it is for brethren to
dwell together in unity!
2 It is like the precious ointment
upon the head, that ran down upon
the beard, even Aaron's beard: that
went down to the skirts of his garments;
3 As the dew of Hermon, and as
the dew that descended upon the
mountains of Zion: for there the
Lord commanded the blessing, even
life for evermore.

PSALM 134

A Song of degrees.

BEHOLD, bless ye the Lord, all ye
servants of the Lord, which by
night stand in the house of the
Lord.
2 Lift up your hands in the sanctuary, and bless the Lord.
3 The Lord that made heaven and
earth bless thee out of Zion.

PSALM 135

PRAISE ye the Lord. Praise ye the
name of the Lord; praise him, O
ye servants of the Lord.
2 Ye that stand in the house of the
Lord, in the courts of the house of
our God,
3 Praise the Lord; for the Lord is

good: sing praises unto his name; for
it is pleasant.
4 For the Lord hath chosen Jacob
unto himself, and Israel for his peculiar treasure.
5 For I know that the Lord is great,
and that our Lord is above all gods.
6 Whatsoever the Lord pleased, that
did he in heaven, and in earth, in
the seas, and all deep places.
7 He causeth the vapours to ascend
from the ends of the earth; he
maketh lightnings for the rain; he
bringeth the wind out of his treasuries.
8 Who smote the firstborn of
Egypt, both of man and beast.
9 Who sent tokens and wonders
into the midst of thee, O Egypt,
upon Pharaoh, and upon all his servants.
10 Who smote great nations, and
slew mighty kings;
11 Sihon king of the Amorites, and
Og king of Bashan, and all the kingdoms of Canaan:
12 And gave their land for an heritage, an heritage unto Israel his
people.
13 Thy name, O Lord, endureth for
ever; and thy memorial, O Lord,
throughout all generations.
14 For the Lord will judge his people, and he will repent himself concerning his servants.
15 The idols of the heathen are silver and gold, the work of men's
hands.
16 They have mouths, but they
speak not; eyes have they, but they
see not;
17 They have ears, but they hear
not; neither is there any breath in
their mouths.
18 They that make them are like
unto them: so is every one that
trusteth in them.
19 Bless the Lord, O house of
Israel: bless the Lord, O house of
Aaron:
20 Bless the Lord, O house of Levi:
ye that fear the Lord, bless the Lord.
21 Blessed be the Lord out of Zion,
which dwelleth at Jerusalem. Praise
ye the Lord.

PSALM 136

O GIVE thanks unto the Lord; for
he is good: for his mercy endureth for ever.
2 O give thanks unto the God of
gods: for his mercy endureth for
ever.
3 O give thanks to the Lord of
lords: for his mercy endureth for
ever.
4 To him who alone doeth great
wonders: for his mercy endureth for
ever.
5 To him that by wisdom made the
heavens: for his mercy endureth for
ever.
6 To him that stretched out the
earth above the waters: for his mercy
endureth for ever.
7 To him that made great lights: for
his mercy endureth for ever:
8 The sun to rule by day: for his
mercy endureth for ever:
9 The moon and stars to rule by
night: for his mercy endureth for
ever.
10 To him that smote Egypt in their
firstborn: for his mercy endureth for
ever:
11 And brought out Israel from
among them: for his mercy endureth for ever:
12 With a strong hand, and with a
stretched out arm: for his mercy endureth for ever.
13 To him which divided the Red
sea into parts: for his mercy endureth for ever:
14 And made Israel to pass through
the midst of it: for his mercy endureth for ever:
15 But overthrew Pharaoh and his
host in the Red sea: for his mercy
endureth for ever.
16 To him which led his people
through the wilderness: for his
mercy endureth for ever.
17 To him which smote great kings:
for his mercy endureth for ever:
18 And slew famous kings: for his
mercy endureth for ever:

19 Sihon king of the Amorites: for his mercy endureth for ever:

20 And Og the king of Bashan: for his mercy endureth for ever:

21 And gave their land for an heritage: for his mercy endureth for ever:

22 Even an heritage unto Israel his servant: for his mercy endureth for ever.

23 Who remembered us in our low estate: for his mercy endureth for ever:

24 And hath redeemed us from our enemies: for his mercy endureth for ever.

25 Who giveth food to all flesh: for his mercy endureth for ever.

26 O give thanks unto the God of heaven: for his mercy endureth for ever.

PSALM 137

BY THE rivers of Babylon, there we sat down, yea, we wept, when we remembered Zion.

2 We hanged our harps upon the willows in the midst thereof.

3 For there they that carried us away captive required of us a song; and they that wasted us required of us mirth, saying, Sing us one of the songs of Zion.

4 How shall we sing the Lord's song in a strange land?

5 If I forget thee, O Jerusalem, let my right hand forget her cunning.

6 If I do not remember thee, let my tongue cleave to the roof of my mouth; if I prefer not Jerusalem above my chief joy.

7 Remember, O Lord, the children of Edom in the day of Jerusalem; who said, Rase it, rase it, even to the foundation thereof.

8 O daughter of Babylon, who art to be destroyed; happy shall he be, that rewardeth thee as thou hast served us.

9 Happy shall he be, that taketh and dasheth thy little ones against the stones.

PSALM 138

A Psalm of David.

I WILL praise thee with my whole heart: before the gods will I sing praise unto thee.

2 I will worship toward thy holy temple, and praise thy name for thy lovingkindness and for thy truth: for thou hast magnified thy word above all thy name.

3 In the day when I cried thou answeredst me, and strengthenedst me with strength in my soul.

4 All the kings of the earth shall praise thee, O Lord, when they hear the words of thy mouth.

5 Yea, they shall sing in the ways of the Lord: for great is the glory of the Lord.

6 Though the Lord be high, yet hath he respect unto the lowly: but the proud he knoweth afar off.

7 Though I walk in the midst of trouble, thou wilt revive me: thou shalt stretch forth thine hand against the wrath of mine enemies, and thy right hand shall save me.

8 The Lord will perfect that which concerneth me: thy mercy, O Lord, endureth for ever: forsake not the works of thine own hands.

PSALM 139

To the chief Musician, A Psalm of David.

O LORD, thou hast searched me, and known me.

2 Thou knowest my downsitting and mine uprising, thou understandest my thought afar off.

3 Thou compassest my path and my lying down, and art acquainted with all my ways.

4 For there is not a word in my tongue, but, lo, O Lord, thou knowest it altogether.

5 Thou hast beset me behind and before, and laid thine hand upon me.

6 Such knowledge is too wonderful for me; it is high, I cannot attain unto it.

7 Whither shall I go from thy spirit?

or whither shall I flee from thy presence?

8 If I ascend up into heaven, thou art there: if I make my bed in hell, behold, thou art there.

9 If I take the wings of the morning, and dwell in the uttermost parts of the sea;

10 Even there shall thy hand lead me, and thy right hand shall hold me.

11 If I say, Surely the darkness shall cover me; even the night shall be light about me.

12 Yea, the darkness hideth not from thee; but the night shineth as the day: the darkness and the light are both alike to thee.

13 For thou hast possessed my reins: thou hast covered me in my mother's womb.

14 I will praise thee; for I am fearfully and wonderfully made: marvellous are thy works; and that my soul knoweth right well.

15 My substance was not hid from thee, when I was made in secret, and curiously wrought in the lowest parts of the earth.

16 Thine eyes did see my substance, yet being unperfect; and in thy book all my members were written, which in continuance were fashioned, when as yet there was none of them.

17 How precious also are thy thoughts unto me, O God! how great is the sum of them!

18 If I should count them, they are more in number than the sand: when I awake, I am still with thee.

19 Surely thou wilt slay the wicked, O God: depart from me therefore, ye bloody men.

20 For they speak against thee wickedly, and thine enemies take thy name in vain.

21 Do not I hate them, O Lord, that hate thee? and am not I grieved with those that rise up against thee?

22 I hate them with perfect hatred: I count them mine enemies.

23 Search me, O God, and know my heart: try me, and know my thoughts:

24 And see if there be any wicked way in me, and lead me in the way everlasting.

PSALM 140

To the chief Musician, A Psalm of David.

DELIVER me, O Lord, from the evil man: preserve me from the violent man;

2 Which imagine mischiefs in their heart; continually are they gathered together for war.

3 They have sharpened their tongues like a serpent; adders' poison is under their lips. Selah.

4 Keep me, O Lord, from the hands of the wicked; preserve me from the violent man; who have purposed to overthrow my goings.

5 The proud have hid a snare for me, and cords; they have spread a net by the wayside; they have set gins for me. Selah.

6 I said unto the Lord, Thou art my God: hear the voice of my supplications, O Lord.

7 O God the Lord, the strength of my salvation, thou hast covered my head in the day of battle.

8 Grant not, O Lord, the desires of the wicked: further not his wicked device; lest they exalt themselves. Selah.

9 As for the head of those that compass me about, let the mischief of their own lips cover them.

10 Let burning coals fall upon them: let them be cast into the fire; into deep pits, that they rise not up again.

11 Let not an evil speaker be established in the earth: evil shall hunt the violent man to overthrow him.

12 I know that the Lord will maintain the cause of the afflicted, and the right of the poor.

13 Surely the righteous shall give thanks unto thy name: the upright shall dwell in thy presence.

PSALM 141

A Psalm of David.

LORD, I cry unto thee: make haste unto me; give ear unto my voice, when I cry unto thee.
2 Let my prayer be set forth before thee as incense; and the lifting up of my hands as the evening sacrifice.
3 Set a watch, O Lord, before my mouth; keep the door of my lips.
4 Incline not my heart to any evil thing, to practise wicked works with men that work iniquity: and let me not eat of their dainties.
5 Let the righteous smite me; it shall be a kindness: and let him reprove me; it shall be an excellent oil, which shall not break my head: for yet my prayer also shall be in their calamities.
6 When their judges are overthrown in stony places, they shall hear my words; for they are sweet.
7 Our bones are scattered at the grave's mouth, as when one cutteth and cleaveth wood upon the earth.
8 But mine eyes are unto thee, O God the Lord: in thee is my trust; leave not my soul destitute.
9 Keep me from the snares which they have laid for me, and the gins of the workers of iniquity.
10 Let the wicked fall into their own nets, whilst that I withal escape.

PSALM 142

Maschil of David;
A Prayer when he was in the cave.

I CRIED unto the Lord with my voice; with my voice unto the Lord did I make my supplication.
2 I poured out my complaint before him; I shewed before him my trouble.
3 When my spirit was overwhelmed within me, then thou knewest my path. In the way wherein I walked have they privily laid a snare for me.
4 I looked on my right hand, and beheld, but there was no man that would know me: refuge failed me; no man cared for my soul.
5 I cried unto thee, O Lord: I said, Thou art my refuge and my portion in the land of the living.
6 Attend unto my cry; for I am brought very low: deliver me from my persecutors; for they are stronger than I.
7 Bring my soul out of prison, that I may praise thy name: the righteous shall compass me about; for thou shalt deal bountifully with me.

PSALM 143

A Psalm of David.

HEAR my prayer, O Lord, give ear to my supplications: in thy faithfulness answer me, and in thy righteousness.
2 And enter not into judgment with thy servant: for in thy sight shall no man living be justified.
3 For the enemy hath persecuted my soul; he hath smitten my life down to the ground; he hath made me to dwell in darkness, as those that have been long dead.
4 Therefore is my spirit overwhelmed within me; my heart within me is desolate.
5 I remember the days of old; I meditate on all thy works; I muse on the work of thy hands.
6 I stretch forth my hands unto thee: my soul thirsteth after thee, as a thirsty land. Selah.
7 Hear me speedily, O Lord: my spirit faileth: hide not thy face from me, lest I be like unto them that go down into the pit.
8 Cause me to hear thy lovingkindness in the morning; for in thee do I trust: cause me to know the way wherein I should walk; for I lift up my soul unto thee.
9 Deliver me, O Lord, from mine enemies: I flee unto thee to hide me.
10 Teach me to do thy will; for thou art my God: thy spirit is good;

lead me into the land of uprightness.

11 Quicken me, O Lord, for thy name's sake: for thy righteousness' sake bring my soul out of trouble.

12 And of thy mercy cut off mine enemies, and destroy all them that afflict my soul: for I am thy servant.

PSALM 144

A Psalm of David.

BLESSED be the Lord my strength, which teacheth my hands to war, and my fingers to fight:

2 My goodness, and my fortress; my high tower, and my deliverer; my shield, and he in whom I trust; who subdueth my people under me.

3 Lord, what is man, that thou takest knowledge of him! or the son of man, that thou makest account of him!

4 Man is like to vanity: his days are as a shadow that passeth away.

5 Bow thy heavens, O Lord, and come down: touch the mountains, and they shall smoke.

6 Cast forth lightning, and scatter them: shoot out thine arrows, and destroy them.

7 Send thine hand from above; rid me, and deliver me out of great waters, from the hand of strange children;

8 Whose mouth speaketh vanity, and their right hand is a right hand of falsehood.

9 I will sing a new song unto thee, O God: upon a psaltery and an instrument of ten strings will I sing praises unto thee.

10 It is he that giveth salvation unto kings: who delivereth David his servant from the hurtful sword.

11 Rid me, and deliver me from the hand of strange children, whose mouth speaketh vanity, and their right hand is a right hand of falsehood:

12 That our sons may be as plants grown up in their youth; that our daughters may be as corner stones, polished after the similitude of a palace:

13 That our garners may be full, affording all manner of store: that our sheep may bring forth thousands and ten thousands in our streets:

14 That our oxen may be strong to labour; that there be no breaking in, nor going out; that there be no complaining in our streets.

15 Happy is that people, that is in such a case: yea, happy is that people, whose God is the Lord.

PSALM 145

David's Psalm of praise.

I WILL extol thee, my God, O king; and I will bless thy name for ever and ever.

2 Every day will I bless thee; and I will praise thy name for ever and ever.

3 Great is the Lord, and greatly to be praised; and his greatness is unsearchable.

4 One generation shall praise thy works to another, and shall declare thy mighty acts.

5 I will speak of the glorious honour of thy majesty, and of thy wondrous works.

6 And men shall speak of the might of thy terrible acts: and I will declare thy greatness.

7 They shall abundantly utter the memory of thy great goodness, and shall sing of thy righteousness.

8 The Lord is gracious, and full of compassion; slow to anger, and of great mercy.

9 The Lord is good to all: and his tender mercies are over all his works.

10 All thy works shall praise thee, O Lord; and thy saints shall bless thee.

11 They shall speak of the glory of thy kingdom, and talk of thy power;

12 To make known to the sons of men his mighty acts, and the glorious majesty of his kingdom.

13 Thy kingdom is an everlasting kingdom, and thy dominion endureth throughout all generations.

14 The Lord upholdeth all that fall, and raiseth up all those that be bowed down.

15 The eyes of all wait upon thee;
and thou givest them their meat in
due season.
16 Thou openest thine hand, and
satisfiest the desire of every living
thing.
17 The Lord is righteous in all his
ways, and holy in all his works.
18 The Lord is nigh unto all them
that call upon him, to all that call
upon him in truth.
19 He will fulfil the desire of them
that fear him: he also will hear their
cry, and will save them.
20 The Lord preserveth all them
that love him: but all the wicked
will he destroy.
21 My mouth shall speak the praise
of the Lord: and let all flesh bless his
holy name for ever and ever.

PSALM 146

PRAISE ye the Lord. Praise the
Lord, O my soul.
2 While I live will I praise the Lord:
I will sing praises unto my God
while I have any being.
3 Put not your trust in princes, nor
in the son of man, in whom there is
no help.
4 His breath goeth forth, he retur-
neth to his earth; in that very day his
thoughts perish.
5 Happy is he that hath the God of
Jacob for his help, whose hope is in
the Lord his God:
6 Which made heaven, and earth,
the sea, and all that therein is: which
keepeth truth for ever:
7 Which executeth judgment for
the oppressed: which giveth food to
the hungry. The Lord looseth the
prisoners:
8 The Lord openeth the eyes of the
blind: the Lord raiseth them that are
bowed down: the Lord loveth the
righteous:
9 The Lord preserveth the strangers; he relieveth the fatherless and
widow: but the way of the wicked
he turneth upside down.
10 The Lord shall reign for ever,
even thy God, O Zion, unto all
generations. Praise ye the Lord.

PSALM 147

PRAISE ye the Lord: for it is good
to sing praises unto our God; for
it is pleasant; and praise is comely.
2 The Lord doth build up
Jerusalem: he gathereth together the
outcasts of Israel.
3 He healeth the broken in heart,
and bindeth up their wounds.
4 He telleth the number of the
stars; he calleth them all by their
names.
5 Great is our Lord, and of great
power: his understanding is infinite.
6 The Lord lifteth up the meek: he
casteth the wicked down to the
ground.
7 Sing unto the Lord with thanksgiving; sing praise upon the harp
unto our God:
8 Who covereth the heaven with
clouds, who prepareth rain for the
earth, who maketh grass to grow
upon the mountains.
9 He giveth to the beast his food,
and to the young ravens which cry.
10 He delighteth not in the
strength of the horse: he taketh not
pleasure in the legs of a man.
11 The Lord taketh pleasure in
them that fear him, in those that
hope in his mercy.
12 Praise the Lord, O Jerusalem;
praise thy God, O Zion.
13 For he hath strengthened the
bars of thy gates; he hath blessed thy
children within thee.
14 He maketh peace in thy borders,
and filleth thee with the finest of
the wheat.
15 He sendeth forth his commandment upon earth: his word runneth
very swiftly.
16 He giveth snow like wool: he
scattereth the hoarfrost like ashes.
17 He casteth forth his ice like
morsels: who can stand before his
cold?
18 He sendeth out his word, and
melteth them: he causeth his wind
to blow, and the waters flow.
19 He sheweth his word unto
Jacob, his statutes and his judgments
unto Israel.

20 He hath not dealt so with any nation: and as for his judgments, they have not known them. Praise ye the Lord.

PSALM 148

PRAISE ye the Lord. Praise ye the Lord from the heavens: praise him in the heights.

2 Praise ye him, all his angels: praise ye him, all his hosts.

3 Praise ye him, sun and moon: praise him, all ye stars of light.

4 Praise him, ye heavens of heavens, and ye waters that be above the heavens.

5 Let them praise the name of the Lord: for he commanded, and they were created.

6 He hath also stablished them for ever and ever; he hath made a decree which shall not pass.

7 Praise the Lord from the earth, ye dragons, and all deeps:

8 Fire, and hail; snow, and vapour; stormy wind fulfilling his word:

9 Mountains, and all hills; fruitful trees, and all cedars:

10 Beasts, and all cattle; creeping things, and flying fowl:

11 Kings of the earth, and all people; princes, and all judges of the earth:

12 Both young men, and maidens; old men, and children:

13 Let them praise the name of the Lord: for his name alone is excellent; his glory is above the earth and heaven.

14 He also exalteth the horn of his people, the praise of all his saints; even of the children of Israel, a people near unto him. Praise ye the Lord.

PSALM 149

PRAISE ye the Lord. Sing unto the Lord a new song, and his praise in the congregation of saints.

2 Let Israel rejoice in him that made him: let the children of Zion be joyful in their King.

3 Let them praise his name in the dance: let them sing praises unto him with the timbrel and harp.

4 For the Lord taketh pleasure in his people: he will beautify the meek with salvation.

5 Let the saints be joyful in glory: let them sing aloud upon their beds.

6 Let the high praises of God be in their mouth, and a twoedged sword in their hand;

7 To execute vengeance upon the heathen, and punishments upon the people;

8 To bind their kings with chains, and their nobles with fetters of iron;

9 To execute upon them the judgment written: this honour have all his saints. Praise ye the Lord.

PSALM 150

PRAISE ye the Lord. Praise God in his sanctuary: praise him in the firmament of his power.

2 Praise him for his mighty acts; praise him according to his excellent greatness.

3 Praise him with the sound of the trumpet: praise him with the psaltery and harp.

4 Praise him with the timbrel and dance: praise him with stringed instruments and organs.

5 Praise him upon the loud cymbals: praise him upon the high sounding cymbals.

6 Let every thing that hath breath praise the Lord. Praise ye the Lord.

INDEX OF FIRST LINES

Ah Lord! how many be my foes!, 8
All, all my trust, Lord, I have put in thee., 41
All lands, the limbs of earthy round, 93
All they that fear the Lord, attain to bliss;, 169
Always returning to the promise, I remember, 165
Among the holy mountains high, 127
An undefiled course who leadeth, 175
A pack of liars, spitting adders, sometime, 167
Arouse—and let thy foes disperse, 95
At home, abroad most willingly I will, 169

Be gude till me, God, be gude till me;, 82
Blessed are all they that fear the Lord and walk in his ways., 194

Can this be justice, 83
Clap hands ye people, with applause rejoice;, 69
Clothed in state and girt with might, 140
Come let us heartily rejoice and sing, 142
Come, let us sound with melody the praises, 28

Deliver me, O Lord, 207

Eternal God, (for whom who ever dare, 3
Even before kings by thee as gods commended, 204
Except the Lord had been with us—, 191

Fountain of pity now with pity flow:, 80
Fret not thyself, if thou do see, 52
From afar, O God, the nations, 116
From depth of sin, and from a deep despair, 195

Give ear to my suit, Lord, fromward hide not thy face., 79
Give this child judgment, and more children, 106
God is my light, my health, mine aid, 37
God is our strength and our refuge: therefore will we not tremble, 69
Good God unlock thy magazines, 75
Great God of hosts, revenge our wrong, 141

Hear (Lord my strength) the cries I make to thee;, 38
Hear me, O hear me, when I call, 9
Hear my prayer, O Lord, hear my request, 210
Hear, O my God, my voice accept, 90
He blessed is who with wise temper can, 59

Help, Lord, for godly men have took their flight, 20
High praises, 40
How long (O Lord) shall I forgotten be?, 21
How lovely is thy dwelling, 123

I called out to the one and he heard me say, 189
If I could tell it all, 16
If the work be not direct, 193
I love the Lord; for he an ear, 173
In God, my trust is placed still;, 19
In God our strength, let us rejoice;, 119
Inside my heart I hear, 51
In this my cause, O Lord, preside, 24
I said, I will watch my mouth, 56
I saw a picture of the earth afloat, 144
It helps to make a lot of noise, 147
It's so good, the turn of a season, 197
I will unto the Lord, 45

Judge thou my cause, and right me, 64

Let us with a gladsome mind, 200
Like as the hart desires the brook, 63
Lord hear my prayer, and let my cry pass, 148
Lord, I thy present help implore, 208
Lord, judge me and my case, 36
Lord my God to thee I fly, 13
Lord, on thee my trust is grounded:, 104
Lord, our fathers' true relation, 65
Lord weigh my words, and take consideration, 10
Lord, wha sal bide i' that howff o' thine?, 23

Make the great God thy fort, and dwell, 138
Mount Sion-like, forever fixed are those, 192
My God, my God, why hast thou me forsaken?, 30
My heart indites an argument of worth, 67
My heart, O Lord, was-na haughty; nor my een, they hae-na been heigh:, 196
My Lord is the judge, 120
My soul, with all thy powers thy maker praise;, 150
My voice to thee, O God, I rear, 210

New song? Nearly. Better, 225
Not to ourselves the praise we take, 171

O fame most joyful! O joy most lovely delightful!, 190
Oft and ever from my youth, 194

O God, be-na whush; be-na quaiet;, 122
O God, I call to thee for help, 78
O God, my king, I will adore, 214
O God, the cup, 86
O God, thy gracious ear apply, 87
O God, till be skowth to me;, 103
O God, ye are God o' my ain;, 89
O happy are they that have forgiveness got, 43
O Lord, as I thee have both prayed and pray, 55
O Lord in me there lieth nought, 204
O Lord, since in my mouth thy mighty name, 10
O Lord, thou art our home, to whom we fly, 137
O Lord, thy supplicant receive, 125
O Lord, upon whose will dependeth my welfare., 128
O lovely thing, 139
O mighty God, preserve thou me, for on thee do I rest., 23
O my God, my cause espousing, 48
Only to Judah God his will doth signify;, 112
O praise the Lord, and bless his name, 198
O! praise the Lord, and let his fame be told, 216
O sing Jehovah, he hath wonders wrought, 145
O to the Lord restore your thanks, 154
O ye people, hear and ponder, 71

Praised be the Lord of might, 212
Praise him that aye, 174

Quo' the Lord till that Lord o' mine, 168

Remember Lord what David's troubles be, 196

Save me from such as me assail:, 84
Show us thy mercy, Lord, and grace divine;, 95
Sing and let the song be new, 143
Sing to the Lord, for what can better be, 217
Sion's true, glorious God! on thee, 92
Sitting by the streams that glide, 202

Thank goodness just one god always returning., 174
The city of your love, 147
The earth is God's, and what the globe of earth containeth, 33
Thee, God, O thee, we sing, we celebrate:, 111
Thee will I love, O Lord, with all my heart's delight, 25
The foolish wicked men can say, 21
The fool says to himself, What God?, 77
The God of love my shepherd is, 32

The haves shall have and have more, 29
The Lord give ear to thee in thy distress, 29
The Lord is great, and great his fame, 70
The loving-kindness of the Lord, 129
The man, in life wherever placed, 7
The mighty God, the ever living Lord, 73
The past is riddled with old stories, 114
There is no new thing in God's sight., 45
Though, Lord, to Israel thy graces plenteous be:, 109
Thou shepherd that dost Israel keep, 117
Thy land to favor graciously, 124
Thy name, O Lord, how great is found before our sight!, 15
To God I cried. He heard my cries, 113
To him with trumpets and with flutes, 226
To sing and play my heart is bent, 166
To thee from thy temple I lift up mine eyes, 191
To thee, O Lord, I lift my soul, 33
Troublous seas my soul surround:, 100
Tyrant, why swellst thou thus, 76

Up, O my soul, and bless the Lord. O God, 152
Up to those bright, and gladsome hills, 190

What if nations rage and fret?, 146
When God returned us graciously, 192
When the seed of Jacob fled, 170
While, long, I did with patient constancy, 57
Why always angry, God? Why smoke against us and inhale, 110
Why do the Gentiles tumult, and the nations, 7
Why standest thou so far, 17
With grateful hearts Jehovah's praise resound, 159

Ye children of the Lord, that wait, 170
Ye men of birth and high renown, 38
Yet shall my soul in silence still, 88
You blessed spirits that bestow, 219
You that Jehovah's servants are, 197

INDEX OF POETS

Bacon, Francis (1561–1626), 20, 137, 192
Burns, Robert (1759–1796), 7
Campion, Thomas (1567–1619), 28
Carew, Thomas (ca. 1598–ca. 1639), 75, 138, 170, 202
Coleridge, Samuel Taylor (1772–1834), 69
Coverdale, Miles (1488–1569), 21, 191, 194
Davies, John (1569–1626), 10, 29, 64, 69, 95, 142, 150, 226
Donne, John (1573–1631), 3
Finch, Anne (1661–1720), 216
Hall, John (1529–1566), 33, 45, 78, 207
Hall, Joseph (1574–1656), 8
Herbert, George (1593–1633), 32
Herbert, Mary Sidney (1562–1621), 65, 67, 73, 76, 80, 84, 88, 93, 100, 104, 111, 112, 123, 139, 140, 143, 145, 146, 166, 169, 174, 175, 190, 194, 197, 204, 212, 217
Milton, John (1608–1674), 7, 13, 117, 124, 127, 200
Quarles, Francis (1592–1644), 23
Rosenberg, David (1943–), 51, 83, 120, 147, 197
Sandys, George (1578–1644), 113, 141, 159
Sidney, Philip (1554–1586), 9, 17, 21, 25, 30, 33, 41, 52, 57, 59
Smart, Christopher (1722–1771), 24, 48, 63, 71, 87, 90, 95, 116, 125, 129, 154, 171, 191, 193, 198, 208, 214
Stanley, Thomas (1625–1678), 219
Surrey, Henry Howard of (1516–1547), 15, 79, 109, 128
Vaughan, Henry (1622–1695), 92, 152, 190
Waddell, P. Hately (1817–1891), 23, 82, 89, 103, 122, 168, 196
Wieder, Laurance (1946–), 16, 29, 45, 56, 77, 86, 106, 110, 114, 144, 147, 165, 167, 174, 189, 225
Wither, George (1588–1667), 19, 70, 119, 169, 173, 192, 196, 210
Wyatt, Thomas (1503–1542), 10, 43, 55, 148, 195, 210

Composed in Adobe Bembo and Adobe Trajan

by TBH Typecast, Inc.

Printed on Cornwall Book